The Dieter's Gourmet Cookbook

Delicious Low-fat, Low-cholesterol
Cooking and Baking Recipes
Using No Sugar or Salt!

Francine Prince

Cornerstone Library  *New York*

Reprinted 1980

THE DIETER'S GOURMET COOKBOOK BY
FRANCINE PRINCE

PUBLISHED BY CORNERSTONE
LIBRARY, INC.,
A SIMON & SCHUSTER SUBSIDIARY OF
GULF & WESTERN CORPORATION

SIMON & SCHUSTER BUILDING
ROCKEFELLER CENTER
1230 AVENUE OF THE AMERICAS
NEW YORK, NEW YORK 10020

"CORNERSTONE LIBRARY" AND THE
CUBE DESIGN
ARE REGISTERED TRADEMARKS OF
CORNERSTONE LIBRARY, INC.,
A SIMON & SCHUSTER SUBSIDIARY
OF GULF & WESTERN CORPORATION.

ISBN: 346-12398-4 (PAPER)
671-96115-2 (HARDCOVER EDITION)

CONTENTS

*THIS BOOK IS DEDICATED TO MY DEAR HUSBAND,
WHOSE COURAGE INSPIRED THE INCENTIVE AND DRIVE
TO CREATE MY NEW CUISINE.*

How to Use This Book

My new cuisine is for food lovers no matter what kind of diet they're on: reducing, maintenance, low-fat, low-saturated fat, low-sodium, low-carbohydrate or low-cholesterol. And it's a gastronomic extravaganza for nondieters who are turning from the lethal egg-butter-cream-sugar-and-salt-laden meals of the past to repasts that are as light as they are healthful.

My cuisine is the new language of the kitchen, based on a vocabulary of ingredients devoid of, or low in, not just one, but all of the nutriments indicted by medical science as potentially harmful to you—including saturated fats, cholesterol, sugar and salt. (A complete list of forbidden foods begins on page 3.) With a vocabulary of sane and sensible ingredients, I've written the recipes in this book. They comprise my new haute cuisine of health.

Following each recipe, you'll find this line:

CAL	F	P:S	SOD	CAR	CHO

CAL stands for food energy in calories; F for fat in grams; P:S for the ratio of polyunsaturated fats to saturated fats; SOD for sodium in milligrams; CAR for carbohydrates in grams; and CHO for cholesterol in milligrams. (There are 454 grams in a pound; and a milligram is one thousandth of a gram.) Figures under each heading represent quantities per serving. They have been calculated mainly from data on the composition of foods made available by the Agricultural Research Service of the United States Department of Agriculture. Figures have been rounded out, and where a quantity is less than 1, it is regarded as zero.

Here is the maximum daily intake recommended by the American Medical Association and/or most doctors for restricted and maintenance diets in each of the six categories:

CAL	F	P:S	SOD	CAR	CHO
Restricted Diets					
1200	47	>1:1	500	120	160-185
Maintenance Diets					
>1200*	60-70	1:1	2000	>120**	300

> means greater than.
*To calculate your maintenance calories, see below under "If you're on a weight maintenance diet."
**Divide your maintenance calories (see preceding asterisked item) by 10 to obtain maximum carbohydrate intake.

To stay under all, or any, of the limits of these diets, just select a daily menu in which the sum of the relevant figures per serving never exceeds the corresponding figures in the foregoing chart.

If you're on a reducing diet, you'll find it child's play to hold your caloric intake to less than 1,200 calories a day, or whatever figure your doctor prescribes. Breakfast and luncheon dishes range mainly between 100 and 150 calories, the most extravagant of my dinner entrees just edge over 400 calories, and the majority of my desserts hover around 100 calories. Salt hangs on to water—a pint's a pound—and with no added salt, you can knock off as much as five pounds in one week.

If you're on a weight-maintenance diet, use this rule of thumb to calculate your daily caloric intake: Multiply your weight by 12 and 15. Example: You weigh 130 pounds, so 130 × 12 = 1,560, and 130 × 15 = 1,950. To maintain your weight, ingest only between 1,560 and 1,950 calories per day. You'll have no difficulty at all staying within maintenance caloric range on my new cuisine, because there's no reason for you to stray from it, it's so varied, interesting and delicious.

If you're on a fat-restricted diet,

you'll find my cuisine excessively stingy with fats, but it offers sufficient amounts of fats to satisfy your body's vital needs. The Prudent Diet recommended by the American Medical Association contains no more than 35 percent of its calories in fat. On a 1,200 calories a day reducing diet, that means no more than 47 grams of fat; and on a maintenance diet, 60 to 70 grams. Whatever figure your doctor sets for you, you can meet it and still feast on steak pizzaiola and pineapple chiffon pie.

If you're on a saturated-fat restricted diet, you'll want to know that the ratio of polyunsaturated fat to saturated fat is much higher than the 1:1 recommended for most Americans by the American Medical Association. Almost all of my dishes have a ratio in excess of 1:1, most ratios are around 4.5:1, and some even top 5:1. (If fats contain every possible hydrogen atom they can cling to, they're called saturated fats. Fats with many empty spots in their structure unfilled by hydrogen atoms are called polyunsaturated fats. If there's only one space left to be filled with hydrogen, the fat is monounsaturated. If saturated fats are "bad," and polyunsaturated fats are "good," monounsaturated fats are "neutral." The intake of excessive saturated fats over long periods of time can lead to a host of health problems including obesity, high blood pressure, coronary heart disease, diabetes and some cancers.)

If you're on a salt-restricted diet, you're keeping your salt intake down to lower your blood pressure, reduce swelling of water-logged tissues, and prevent salt from playing hob with your fat metabolism, a condition which could lead to one or more of the saturated-fat-induced diseases, the prime example of which is heart attack. One of the chemical components of salt is sodium (chlorine is the other), and the salt in your diet is measured in terms of milligrams of sodium. My new cuisine is utterly miserly when it comes to sodium—not a grain of salt is ever added—and yet you'll never miss it. And you can still eat that most saline of condiments—pickles, my style!

If you're on a carbohydrate-restricted diet, it's comforting to know that not an atom of sugar—that is, sucrose or white sugar—ever finds its way into my creations. Even if you're not on this kind of diet, you'll find the medical indictment against excessive use of sugar shocking. Highly refined, stripped of its vitamins, minerals and fiber, sugar is nothing more than a mass of empty calories. It can swell you into obesity, skyrocket the levels of saturated fats and cholesterol in your blood, and overload the pancreas, the gland manufacturing insulin which controls carbohydrate metabolism. Hyperglycemia and hypoglycemia are just the top of the iceberg of diseases to which it contributes. My new cuisine offers you a confectionary shop of sweets—sugar-free. And you can eat your fill of other carbohydrates, too—including a rich variety of crisp, crackling, crunchy breads.

If you're on a cholesterol-restricted diet, with my cuisine you'll find no difficulty staying within 160-185 milligrams a day, the practical "safety zone" established by one group of medical researchers, or of even lowering that limit. And yet your weekly menu can include steak, veal, pork, lamb—even shrimps! (Cholesterol is not, as most people think, a fat. It's a waxy alcohol which in the body turns into tough tiny crystalline spears which embed themselves into the walls of the circulatory system, trapping fat particles and clogging the arteries. Blood flowing to the heart is reduced to a trickle or shut off entirely, and heart attack occurs. That's why the American Medical Association recommends a daily cholesterol ceiling of 300 milligrams—half of what the average American now consumes.)

The trouble with other dietary cuisines is that the best of them—reducing diets that are not gourmet, but not untasty—are loaded with sugar, salt, saturated fat and cholesterol, all insidious time bombs; and the worst of them—the austere no-no restrictive diets—are so drab, monotonous, and just so ugh-ly that few people can live with them over an extended period of time. My new cuisine is as safe as it is livable with.

With it, you can stay on a specific restrictive diet, or on a prudent diet that minimizes/eliminates all harmful ingredients, without a sense of deprivation, depression, or a feeling that you're somehow inferior to everybody else. You'll eat better, and enjoy your food more, than most people—and not even realize you're dieting. The truth is, my new cuisine is not a "diet" in the limiting sense at all. It's a new way of expanding the joys of the table—healthfully.

Ingredients: The Forbidden and the Favored

The selection of ingredients for my new cuisine is based on a simple principle. Ingredients which, when used in large quantities over long periods of time, can be harmful are forbidden. Ingredients which are certain to be healthful are favored. Favored ingredients replace forbidden ones as shown in the following listing. Use it as a guide when you spin off on my recipes or create new ones of your own.

Forbidden. Butter, vegetable shortening, lard, margarine made partially with animal fats, and the following vegetable oils: coconut, palm, olive and peanut. All these fats and oils are high in saturated fats and have low polyunsaturated:saturated fat ratios.

Favored. Corn oil. Other high polyunsaturated vegetables oils can be used as well, but I prefer corn oil with its excellent polyunsaturated:saturated fat ratio of 4.5:1, because it's far and away the best tasting.

Forbidden. Mayonnaise.

Favored. My low-calorie, no-cholesterol, no-sugar-or-salt mayonnaise, which has a high polyunsaturated:saturated fat ratio (Page 106).

Forbidden. Whole milk and cream.

Favored. Non-fat dry milk, buttermilk made from skim milk, and low-fat yogurt—for the elimination or virtual elimination of milk fats, which are highly saturated, and of cholesterol.

Forbidden. Whole eggs, because each egg yolk contains 250 milligrams of cholesterol, plus saturated fats.

Favored. Egg whites which contain no cholesterol or fats of any kind. (I use a *half* egg yolk in a handful of recipes for flavor and to hold ingredients together. It adds just a few milligrams of cholesterol per portion.)

Forbidden. Whole milk cheeses.

Favored. Low-fat cheeses. Dry curd (uncreamed) cottage cheese has less than .5 percent milkfat and no cholesterol. Gjetost is a pure skim-milk dessert cheese. Other part skim-milk cheeses which I use sparingly include: Jarlsberg, Esrom, Tilsit Havarti, Swedish Farmer's Cheese, Nockelost, St. Paulin, Chiberta, Samsoe, Danbo, Swiss Lorraine, King Christian, Lorraine Cheddar, Fjordland, and Valembert.

Forbidden. Sucrose—refined white sugar. Also brown sugar, turbinado sugar, and "raw" sugar which are all sucrose thinly disguised, as well as maple syrup which is a concentrated sucrose solution.

Favored. Fresh and cooked fruits, dried fruits no sugar added, fresh fruit juices and canned or bottled fruit juices no sugar added, sweet vegetables such as carrots, tomatoes and onions, and a small amount of honey. I also use sweet spices and herbs including allspice, anise, basil, cinnamon, cardamom, coriander, ginger, nutmeg and mace, as well as flavoring extracts such as vanilla and almond. Date powder, too, makes a fine sweetener.

Forbidden. Non-caloric sugar substitutes, such as saccharin, which are under suspicion as carcinogens. I also avoid the caloric substitutes, xylitol, mannitol and sorbitol, because they have a tendency to induce diarrhea; and this jury of one is still out on fructose.

Favored. See the preceding item.

Forbidden. Salt, and that includes sea salt which is salt plus a garnish of trace elements; kosher salt which is coarse grained salt; and dried seaweed preparations—kelp and dulse, for example—which are valuable sources of trace minerals, particularly iodine, but which are sky-high in sodium. I also turn my back on chemical salt substitutes because my cuisine simply doesn't need them.

Favored. Tangy spices, and fresh and dried herbs and vegetables, as well as aromatic seeds. These include: bay leaf, caraway seed, celery (but not celery salt or celery flakes), chives, cloves, cumin, curry powder (no salt or pepper added), dill, fennel, garlic and garlic powder (but not garlic salt), marjoram, mint, mustard (but not prepared mustard), onions and onion powder, oregano, mild paprika, parsley, poppy seed, rosemary, sage, sesame seed, tarragon and thyme. On rare occasions, I make use of a small amount of a powdered vegetable concentrate, no salt added.

Forbidden. Pepper, black or white, because it's alleged to be associated with high blood pressure.

Favored. Cayenne pepper which, some herbologists believe, has a salutory effect on the circulatory system, and which tastes properly pepperish to boot.

Forbidden. Commercial soy sauces, tabasco, Worcestershire sauce and ketchup. Their high sodium content alone disqualifies them.

Favored. I rely on blendings of herbs and spices, not to duplicate the flavors of those condiments, which can't be done, but to create an intriguing new spectrum of pungencies. I do use minuscule to small amounts of a sodium-free soy sauce.

Forbidden. Baking powder or soda because of their high sodium content.

Favored. Low-sodium baking powder which substitutes potassium for sodium.

Forbidden. Bleached flour, not only because it's been nutritionally damaged in the processing, but because the texture is poor.

Favored. For my breads I insist on unbleached wheat flour, and I use wholewheat, rye, gluten and buckwheat as well. Stone grinding preserves the taste, texture and the nutritional value of the grains. For my other baked goods, I also use old-fashioned rolled oats, unprocessed bran, cracked wheat and wheat germ.

Forbidden. Pasta products made with eggs and salt.

Favored. Whole wheat spaghetti and macaroni made without eggs and salt.

Forbidden. Commercial brown rice, not because of any nutritional defect, but because it cooks to a starchy, gooey eyesore.

Favored. A short-grained brown rice flecked with green, which can be found in health food stores. When brown rice is not compatible with the other ingredients of a recipe, I use white rice, cooking it in such a way that each kernel is plump and fluffy and quite separate from every other kernel.

Forbidden. Almost all nuts because they're high in saturated fats. Beware especially of cashews and Brazil nuts.

Favored. Walnuts and almonds which have whoppingly high polyunsaturated:saturated fat ratios.

Forbidden. Fatty cuts of meats, including the fattest of them all, bacon and tongue. Meat fat is high in saturated fats. Keep away as well from organ meats—brains, kidneys, liver, sweetbreads—which are phenomenally high in cholesterol.

Favored. Lean cuts of meats, which—and here's a bonus—are the least expensive. They're tougher than prime meats, but you can tenderize them by marinating, braising or, when applicable, by pounding, as for a veal scallopine. Prime meats, though, can be lean. Use your eye to judge whether a cut is sufficiently fat-free to earn a place on your table. To obtain a bacony flavor, I use smoked yeast in extremely small quantities.

Forbidden. Salted or smoked fish (smoking is actually a mild salting process).

Favored. Fresh fish, with the following leaner fish (listed in order of ascending fatness) preferred: tilefish, cod, scrod, sea bass, sole, flounder, red snapper, striped bass, halibut, whiting, and tuna. Tilefish is virtually fatless.

Forbidden. Duck. A quarter of a pound contains more than twice the daily acceptable cholesterol intake.

Favored. Chicken and turkey which are among the least fatty and lowest in cholesterol of all fowl. Fryers are less fatty than roasters; and young turkeys are leaner than mature ones.

Forbidden. Frozen foods. For some reason—and I confess I don't understand the technology behind it—ounce for ounce, frozen foods are more caloric and contain more sodium than their fresh counterparts.

Favored. Fresh foods without chemical additives. Aside from their possible deleterious effects on your body, additive-laden foods are objectionable because they don't taste as good or cook as well as untampered-with foods. This is particularly true of mushrooms.

Forbidden. Canned or jarred foods containing one or more of the following ingredients: added salt, sugar, saturated fats or cholesterol.

Favored. Canned or jarred foods packed in water or in their own juices, such as tomatoes, tomato paste, tomato puree, red pimentos and waterchestnuts (which I use to add crunchiness to some of my dishes), as well as pineapples, apple and pomegranate juice, and tuna fish, sardines and salmon.

Forbidden. Flavored gelatin which is extremely high in sugar.

Favored. Unflavored gelatin or agar-agar. Agar-agar makes a spreadable, custardy mixture; gelatin, a stiffer chiffon-like one.

Forbidden. Corn starch, only because it imparts its own flavor and sometimes leaves a chalky taste.

Favored. Arrowroot flour. It's as effective a thickening agent as corn starch, and has more nutritional value, cooks more quickly, and never alters the taste of the ingredients with which it is combined.

Forbidden. Coffee because it contains caffeine which has been accused of responsibility for a range of ailments from coffee nerves and insommnia to heart, liver and kidney disorders. Chocolate and cocoa are banned for the same reason (a large chocolate bar contributes as much caffeine as a half cup of coffee), and also because they're high in saturated fats.

Favored. Cafix, a coffee taste-alike made from a blend of cereals, contains no caffeine or other harmful ingredients. Carob, which is ground from the pod of the carob tree, has a pleasant chocolaty flavor, is low in saturated fat, easily digested, and rich in natural sweeteners. Manufacturers are always trying to gild the lily, and they've come up with a carob powder to which sugar has been added. Avoid it, and ask for the real thing.

Not preferred. Tap water, except to boil eggs.

Favored. Spring water (not distilled water, which is devoid of all minerals, and is utterly tasteless). Try it, it will do wonders for the flavor of your foods.

Where to Shop for the Ingredients You Need

I've found that, by and large, fruit and vegetable markets, butcher shops and fish markets offer a wider variety of fresher, tastier and higher quality provender than supermarkets. The food, moreover, is generally unpackaged, and you can touch-, smell- and eye-test it before purchase. (How often have you been unpleasantly surprised when you opened a supermarket package?) Prices tend to be a bit higher than supermarkets', but not always, and the careful shopper can come away with some amazing bargains. And you don't have to fret on a checkout line!

Health food stores are egregiously expensive. Nowadays, supermarkets stock many of the items that were once health food store exclusives, and often at better prices. On the other hand, some items can actually be purchased cheaper in health food stores. Four-ounce packages of granular yeast, for example, provide great savings over the supermarkets' pre-measured smaller packages. (Don't worry about the remaining yeast in the four-ounce package keeping once you've opened the package. Just follow label instructions for sealing, and the yeast will keep up to a month.)

Some of my *Favored* ingredients are obtainable only in health food stores. Here's a list of those ingredients: Cold-pressed corn oil. Non-fat dry milk, low in sodium (Fearn's non-instant is the tastiest). Date powder. Vegetable concentrate, no salt added (my preference is Barth's Instant Nutra-Soup Protein Enriched). Sodium-free soy sauce (Dr. Bronner's All-One Seasoning gets my vote). Low-sodium baking powder. Gluten and buckwheat flours. Pasta made without eggs or salt. Unprocessed bran. Short-grained brown rice (organic). Smoked yeast. Tomato paste and tomato puree, no salt added. Pomegranate juice. Cafix, the coffee taste-alike I prefer. Carob powder, no sugar added, and agar-agar.

The Story Behind My New Cuisine

"I have to tell you, Mr. Prince, that you've had a heart attack. Not a major one, but nevertheless, the evidence definitely shows up on your cardiogram. I suggest you take it easy, take nitroglycerin when you feel the angina pain across your chest, and cut down on your salt intake."

My husband and I were in the doctor's office when we received that shocking verdict, and we were numb for days after hearing it. Why him, not me? It shouldn't have happened to him. But it did.

After the numbness wore off, the depression set in. Harold was taking the nitro when needed. It gave him headaches and didn't do much good. We had never used much salt in cooking, but now with no salt at all, the food became so tasteless, it added to Harold's depression. It also added to mine, because I refused to make separate meals. We had always eaten the same foods, and I wouldn't change now. If Harold had to go through tasteless meals, I'd go through them with him. But the meals were as miserable as they made us feel.

"Don't be so conscious of food," relatives and friends would advise. "It's not that important. After all, you only eat to live. Besides, you'll get used to it."

Not us. We couldn't get used to it. Particularly Harold. As a young man Harold had been very heavy. He had reduced early in life and kept it off by controlling the amount of food he consumed. But he loves food—not the bulk of it, but the taste of it when it's good. Before his heart attack, one of his greatest pleasures had been to dine in the fine restaurants of New York. Every meal out had been an adventure to him, and I had tried to make the meals at home almost as enticing. Harold had learned to limit the quantity of food on his plate, but he had grown used to savoring every bit of that food.

A month after his heart attack, some of his strength returned, but his low spirits and the angina remained. His heart specialist had no remedy for his low spirits, but he prescribed an additional medication for the angina. He also advised Harold to take a stress test to determine just how much blood was flowing through his arteries. He took the test. It showed that there was heavy blockage in all three of the major arteries supplying blood to the heart. The heart specialist warned Harold that if he walked one block vigorously, he could drop dead. "The only way to save your life," the heart specialist told him, "is to undergo by-pass surgery as soon as I can schedule it. There's no time to lose."

That would mean time away from work for the operation, and for months afterwards during recuperation. Harold is a free-lance writer and editor. He is not a salaried employee. If he couldn't work on current assignments, and spend some of his time lining up new assignments, he'd have no income at all. Besides, the operation was expensive. When all the costs were added up, it could go as high as $12,000. The financial toll of surgery would be crushing.

There was an even more important drawback to the operation. It was dangerous. Harold had read that one out of every ten patients who underwent by-pass surgery died. He told me he'd have better odds for survival as a combat soldier in Vietnam. Harold had also read that while a successful operation frequently relieved the pain of angina, it seemed to have no effect on prolonging the life of the patient.

The heart specialist was not able to schedule an immediate operation. That gave Harold time to think. After two weeks of soul searching, which he did without consulting me, he came to a decision. There would be no surgery. "What then?" I asked him. "I'll try to reverse the blockage through diet," he told me. Having in the early '60s ghosted the first popular book on the nutritional aspects of heart disease, he knew that some reversals due to a change in diet had been reported in the medical literature, although most doctors viewed the reports with lifted eyebrows.

What I wanted to know was: What would this new diet be like? He told me it would be based on the Prudent Diet prescribed by the American Heart Association. It's an excellent diet, Harold said, but for his purpose it had loopholes. He'd tighten them. His son would help. Barry, a Californian, had given up a promising career as a film maker to study nutrition. In a few years he would found the first organic bakery in San Francisco. The diet Harold and his son worked out eliminated all added salt and sugar. It permitted only a small amount of cholesterol and saturated fat. That meant no butter or margarine, no cream or whole milk, no synthetic shortenings, and only a rare egg yolk.

But—and this was a big but for me—how could such a diet be made palatable? Not enjoyable, just palatable? Have you ever tasted any commercial food made without salt? Or any made without sugar? Or any made without either butter, margarine, synthetic shortenings, or egg yolks? They're inedible. Imagine what food made without all those ingredients would taste like! Harold insisted that he could learn to cope with it. But could he?

I knew I couldn't. For the next few months, I cooked his kind of food for him, and what had once been our regular kind of food for myself. Sharing food with someone you love is an intimate act and one of life's greatest joys. When we sat down at the table together, we felt that we were apart. It was dreadful. Besides, from the look on Harold's face when he swallowed his food, I could see that he wouldn't be able to stay on his severe version of the Prudent Diet much longer. Yet his life could depend on his sticking with it. Something had to be done, and it was up to me to do it.

It would have been fairly easy to do if I could have simply broiled a steak or hamburger every night, but Harold had thrust a restrictive weekly menu on me. It consisted of:

- meat twice a week—very lean
- chicken twice a week—very lean
- fish (which Harold had never developed a taste for) twice a week
- and at other times—vegetables, grains, rice, low-fat salt-free pasta, and salads.

And to top it all—sugarless desserts.

I faced a difficult task, but I was prepared for it. I love cooking and baking. But not for myself. I love to cook for someone close to me. To prepare delicious food for Harold, and for my son when he lived at home, I had studied cooking for many years. My new task was to take the dishes Harold and I had loved so much over the years and see if I could somehow reproduce them without using the ingredients Harold had forbidden. I started with simple dishes such as roast chicken, stews, roasts, fish and vegetables.

When the recipe called for salt, I used herbs. I replaced butter and margarine with low-saturated oils. Cream and whole milk gave way to no-fat milk and low-fat yogurt. Fruit juices, chopped dried fruits, and occasionally honey, made sugar unnecessary. After a few experimental months, I was sure I was on the right track. I could tell by the gusto with which Harold devoured his meals. I could also tell by my own taste buds. We were eating the same dishes at mealtime once again, and we were both much happier.

Then I drew upon our dining adventures in the great restaurants of the world during our several trips abroad in the '70s. I set out to recreate the memorable flavors we had experienced then. The very basis of haute cuisine is cream, butter, eggs, sugar and salt—and I was trying to reproduce haute cuisine dishes without any of those ingredients. It was a tall order. But dinner guests, who knew nothing of our extreme change in diet, congratulated me on my food. When I told them of the restrictions with which it had been prepared, they couldn't believe it. It had taken about a year, but I had begun to succeed.

[illegible] too. He started to get some relief from the chest pains and was able to walk a little farther each day without pain. He was continuing to take the medication his heart specialist had prescribed for him, but its side effects were disturbing. It was making him dull, and he was unable to perform at top of his writing skills. Now he was sufficiently encouraged to drop the medication.

He continued to improve. And that encouraged me. There wasn't a day that my mind was not on another new recipe—another new flavor—another new surprise! It lifted his spirits, which is so important to anybody fighting his way back to health (or just wanting to stay healthy). And the diet seemed to work.

After three years on it, Harold visited his son in California. My husband, whom a doctor told would die if he walked a block briskly, actually climbed up and down a mountain. He brought home snapshots to prove it. No angina! No breathlessness! Good, pink complexion—excellent appetite—stable weight—all good things had returned! But most of all, that terrible fear we had both been living with had disappeared. Fear and depression—gone!

Perhaps, we *had* reversed the arterial blockage. It seemed so to us. And for my own health's sake, I was glad I was on the diet along with Harold. Besides, the food was delicious. So good, in fact, that I started giving private lessons on how to cook without sugar, salt, and very little saturated fat and cholesterol.

Surprisingly, most of my students were young people who wanted to cut their weight, or keep to their ideal weight, or who were watching sugar or salt or some other ingredient in their diet, or who simply desired to live the kind of life that would forestall all of the diseases associated with dangerous eating habits. "I don't want to look like my mother and suffer like her," one young woman told me with a shudder. It was then that I realized I had invented a cuisine for people of all ages on any kind of a restricted diet, and for people eager to do all they can to live in good health always.

Every recipe has been tested in my own kitchen, which is very much like yours, and in the kitchens of my students and friends. If you're not an expert cook, all you have to do is follow my instructions, which I've made so explicit and so detailed that you're bound to come up with a rave dish the first time. If you're an experienced cook, you can appreciate the painstaking care that went into every recipe—the careful calculation of the right quantities of ingredients and the just-so techniques for blending them. You'll never have to repeat that age-old recipe follower's lament, "But will it turn out as good the next time?" Every recipe will produce the same mouth-watering results every time.

Good cooking! And good health!

Stocks

Stocks are the foundation of great gourmet cooking. They are clear, concentrated broths made by gently simmering meats and bones—or fish parts—with water, vegetables, herbs and spices. They are used to impart flavor to sauces, soups, vegetables, stews, braised meats, and poached chicken or fish. They can instantly convert a plain side dish such as boiled rice into a gastronomic event. And they're made with carefree ease, simmering along with a minimum of attention from you.

I recommend the use of five stocks.

Chicken stock is the easiest to make. It's really a rich chicken soup, its flavor augmented by many chicken bones and longer cooking time. Its uses seem endless. It's a base for a variety of soups and sauces, a flavoring for rice, barley and kasha, and it does wonders when you're poaching either fish or poultry.

Beef stock is used for meat sauces, braised meats and vegetables, and to add a hearty flavor to soups.

Brown beef stock imparts a dark brown color as rich as its flavor to sauces and braised meats.

Fish stock is employed for fish sauces and fish soups. Used in poaching, it adds appeal to the simplest fish and enriches the most flavorsome.

Veal stock provides a fine delicate flavor for sauces, soups, and braised veal. It is sometimes substituted for chicken stock.

Read over my recipes for stocks, see how simple they are to prepare, and make one. (Chicken stock is the easiest for a starter.) Then try one of my recipes calling for the stock you've made, and taste for yourself what wonders a stock can accomplish, particularly in this new cuisine. Stocks keep well in the freezer, so be sure to have them on hand always. (For my "instant frozen stocks," see Page 150).

Note: If you run out of stock, or if you haven't enough stock, use the commercial vegetable concentrate described on Pages 4 and 6.

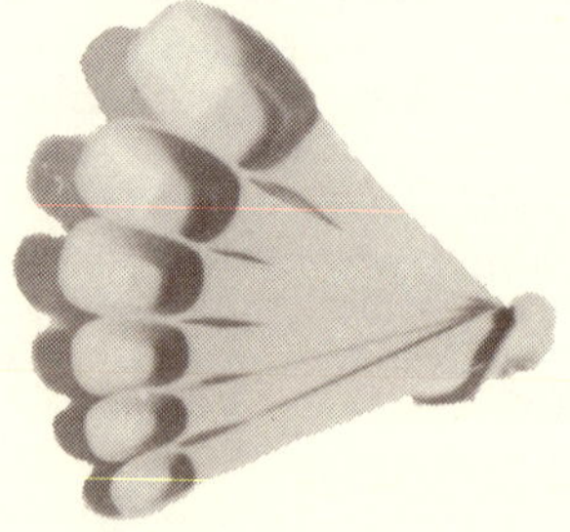

Chicken Stock

4 *pounds chicken giblets, backs and wings, or stewing chicken, cut, plus its giblets*
1 *large carrot, peeled and cut into four pieces*
4 *large cloves garlic, minced*
1 *large onion, cut into quarters*
2 *large shallots, minced*
1 *leek, white part only, washed, trimmed and coarsely chopped*
1 *small parsnip, scraped and cut in half*
1 *small white turnip, peeled and diced*
4 *large fresh mushrooms, trimmed, washed and coarsely chopped*
1 *large rib celery, cut into four pieces*
2-2½ *quarts water, enough to cover*
¾ *cup dry Vermouth or white wine*
6 *dashes cayenne pepper*
Large bouquet garni which includes dill sprigs as well as parsley

Remove all skin from chicken and casings from necks. Trim off fat and discard. Wash well.

Place all ingredients in large kettle or waterless cooker, no wider than 9″ in diameter. Bring to simmering point and simmer, uncovered, for 10 minutes, removing scum that rises to top. Cover partially, and continue simmering for 2½-3 hours, removing scum periodically. Uncover partially and let cool in pot.

Transfer to chinois, placing bowl underneath, and press ingredients to remove all stock. Reserve chicken pieces for light lunch or hors d'oeuvres. Transfer stock to freeze-proof containers. Cover loosely with waxed paper, and cool at room temperature. Cover tightly, and refrigerate overnight. Then cut away and discard hardened fat from top of stock. Refrigerate some of the stock for use within a few days, covering tightly, and freeze the balance.

Yield: About 2 quarts

CAL	F	P:S	SOD	CAR	CHO
Per cup					
41	0	0	17	3	0

Fish Stock

2½-3 pounds bones and heads of any white-fleshed fish, chopped into 3" pieces
2 large cloves garlic, minced
1 large onion, coarsely chopped
1 large rib celery, cut into four pieces
2 large shallots, minced
3 tablespoons corn oil
1 carrot, peeled and diced
5 large fresh mushrooms, washed, trimmed, and coarsely chopped
¼ teaspoon dried marjoram leaves, crushed
½ teaspoon dried tarragon leaves, crushed
3 whole cloves
⅓ cup dry Vermouth or white wine
½ teaspoon Vegetable Concentrate (Page 6)
5½-6 cups water, enough to cover
Bouquet garni

Wash bones and heads under cold running water. Pat dry with paper toweling. Heat oil until hot in stainless steel pot or waterless cooker. (Diameter of pot should not exceed 9".) Sauté bones, heads, vegetables, and garlic for 3 minutes. Add wine and cook for 5 minutes. Add balance of ingredients except herbs and bring to simmering point. Cook, uncovered, for 5 minutes, removing scum that rises to top. Add herbs, partially cover, and continue to simmer for another 25 minutes, periodically removing scum that rises to top. Uncover and let stock cool in pot.

Pour into chinois, placing bowl underneath, and press to remove all stock. Transfer stock to freeze-proof containers. Let cool, uncovered, at room temperature. Cover tightly, and refrigerate overnight. Cut away and discard thin film of hardened fat which may rise to top. Refrigerate some of the stock for immediate use and freeze the balance.

Yield: About 1 quart

CAL	F	P:S	SOD	CAR	CHO
Per cup					
20	0	0	28	3	0

Veal Stock

1½ pounds veal bones, cracked
1½ pounds veal knuckle, cracked
2 tablespoons corn oil
2 carrots, peeled and diced
1 small rib celery, diced
4 large fresh mushrooms, washed, dried, trimmed and thickly sliced
1 large onion, minced
3 large cloves garlic, minced
1 large shallot, minced
¼ cup yellow turnip, peeled and diced
1 tablespoon tomato paste, no salt added (Page 6)
½ teaspoon smoked yeast (Page 6)
½ teaspoon dried tarragon leaves, crushed
½ cup dry Vermouth or white wine
2½ quarts water, enough to cover
Bouquet garni

Heat oil in 3-quart heavy-bottomed kettle until hot. Add bones, onion, garlic, celery, and shallot. Sauté over medium high heat until lightly browned. Add water and bring to simmering point. Simmer, uncovered, for 10 minutes, removing scum that rises to top. Add balance of ingredients. Partially cover and simmer for about 2½ hours. Let cool in kettle.

Remove bones with slotted spoon. Pour stock and other ingredients into chinois, placing bowl underneath, and press to remove all stock. Transfer stock to freeze-proof containers. Cover loosely with waxed paper, and cool at room temperature. Cover tightly, and refrigerate overnight. Cut away and discard hardened fat from top of stock. Cover tightly and refrigerate some of the stock for use within a few days and freeze the balance.

Yield: About 2 quarts

CAL	F	P:S	SOD	CAR	CHO
Per cup					
40	0	0	65	3	0

Beef Stock

4 *pounds beef shin, each shin cut in half*
3 *pounds beef bones, cracked*
2 *carrots, peeled and thickly sliced*
1 *large onion, cut into quarters*
3 *cloves garlic, minced*
1 *large shallot, minced*
6 *whole cloves*
6 *large fresh mushrooms, washed, trimmed and coarsely chopped*
½ *cup yellow turnip, peeled and diced*
2 *ribs celery, cut into four pieces*
2-2½ *quarts water, enough to cover*
½ *teaspoon Dr. Bronner's seasoning (Page 6)*
Bouquet garni

Trim away fat from meat and bones. Wash under cold running water. Place in large kettle or waterless cooker no wider than 9″ in diameter. Add water to cover. Bring to boil. Turn flame down. Cover partially and simmer for 5 minutes. Drain contents of pot in colander.

Rinse kettle. Rinse meat and bones briefly under cold running water and return to kettle. Add fresh water to cover. Add balance of ingredients. Bring to simmering point. Cover partially, and simmer for 3 hours, periodically removing scum that rises to top.

Remove meat and bones from kettle with slotted spoon. Discard bones and reserve meat for leftovers. Pour stock and other ingredients into chinois, placing bowl underneath, and press to remove all stock. Transfer stock to freeze-proof containers. Cover loosely with waxed paper, and cool at room temperature. Cover tighly, and refrigerate overnight. Then cut away and discard hardened fat from top of stock. Refrigerate some of the stock for use within a few days, covering tightly, and freeze the balance.

Yield: About 2 quarts.

CAL	F	P:S	SOD	CAR	CHO
Per cup					
45	0	0	49	3	0

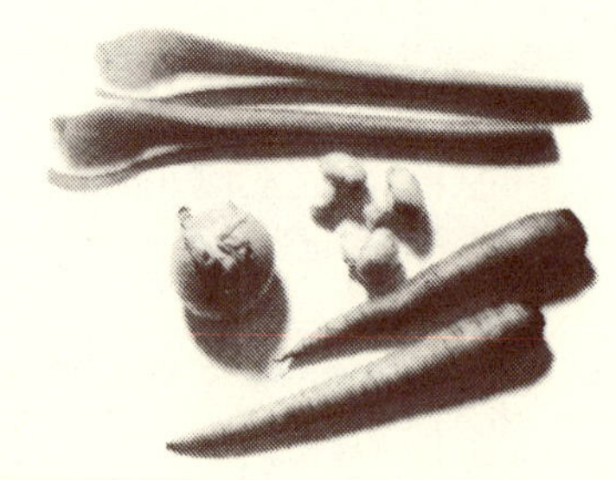

Brown Beef Stock

2 *pounds lean beef such as top round, shin, or shoulder, cut into large chunks*
1½-2 *pounds veal knuckle, cracked*
1 *pound veal bones, cracked*
2 *ribs celery, sliced into large pieces*
2 *leeks, white part only, well washed, and coarsely chopped*
1 *large carrot, peeled and thickly sliced*
2 *large onions, cut into quarters*
6 fresh mushrooms, washed and thickly sliced
¾ *cup yellow turnip, peeled and diced*
4 *large cloves garlic, coarsely chopped*
8 *whole cloves*
⅓ *cup robust red wine (a French country wine or a California jug wine will do nicely)*
2 *tablespoons coriander seeds, toasted and crushed (Page 99)*
5 *dashes cayenne pepper*
Large bouquet garni
3 *quarts water, enough to cover*

Trim and discard fat from bones and meat. Wash under cold running water. Pat dry. Arrange bones, meat, knuckle, vegetables and garlic in metal roasting pan large enough to hold all ingredients in one layer. Roast, uncovered, in 450 degree preheated oven for 45 minutes, turning frequently so that all ingredients are well browned. Remove from oven and pour off fat.

Transfer all ingredients to a large kettle not wider than 9″ in diameter. Place roasting pan on top of stove over high heat. Add wine and cook for 2 minutes, scraping pan to loosen browned particles. Pour into kettle with browned ingredients. Add water. Bring to simmering point. Cook, uncovered, for 20 minutes, removing scum that rises to top. Add herbs, cayenne, and bouquet garni. Cover partially and continue simmering for 5 hours.

Remove meat and bones with slotted spoon. Save meat for leftovers. Pour stock into chinois, placing bowl underneath, and drain, pressing to remove all stock. Then pour through washed cotton cheesecloth.

Pour into freeze-proof containers and cool at room temperature. Cover tightly and refrigerate overnight. When cold, cut away hardened fat. Then cover tightly and store in freezer, reserving some for refrigerator if planning to use within a few days.

Yield: About 2 quarts

CAL	F	P:S	SOD	CAR	CHO
Per cup					
63	0	0	98	3	0

Vegetables, Grains, and Pasta

Duxelles

The French know the value of duxelles. They use it in the preparation of sauces, omelettes, stuffings, and vegetables for added flavor and texture. It's an excellent filling for crepes, and spread on thinly sliced bread, it makes a delicious canapé. I keep it in my freezer at all times. Duxelles, by the by, is pronounced dew-zelles.

½ *pound fresh mushrooms, washed, dried, and trimmed*
3 *tablespoons corn oil*
1 *large clove garlic, finely minced*
2 *large shallots, finely minced*
½ *teaspoon dried tarragon leaves, crushed*
3 *dashes cayenne pepper*
1 *teaspoon freshly chopped parsley*

Heat oil in large iron skillet until hot. Add garlic and shallots and cook, turning constantly for one minute. Add mushrooms, spreading smoothly over skillet. Cook for 2 minutes. Turn over with large spoon, and smooth out in skillet. Continue turning over and smoothing out in skillet until all liquid is evaporated (about 8-10 minutes). Sprinkle with tarragon, cayenne, and chopped parsley. Stir to blend.

Yield: 1 cup

CAL	F	P:S	SOD	CAR	CHO
Per tablespoon					
26	3	4.5:1	2	1	0

Braised Belgian Endive

When it's time for a change, and your purse is jingling with extra change—why not serve Belgian endive? This luxury vegetable will add sophistication to any main course.

- 4 *whole Belgian endives*
- ⅓ *cup chicken or veal stock (Pages 10 or 11)*
- 1 *tablespoon corn oil*
- ⅛ *teaspoon smoked yeast (Page 6)*
- 4 *dashes cayenne pepper*
- 1 *tablespoon fresh lemon juice*
- 2 *dashes Dr. Bronner's seasoning (Page 6)*
- 1 *teaspoon honey*
- 1 *tablespoon freshly chopped chives or finely minced scallion*

Choose fresh endives. They should be white with pale green outer leaves. Wash and pat dry. Cut lengthwise. Heat oil in teflon skillet until very warm. Sauté endives briefly on both sides, cut side down first (2 minutes). Sprinkle with lemon juice, Dr. Bronner's seasoning, smoked yeast, and cayenne. Add stock and honey. Bring to simmering point. Reduce heat, partially cover, and simmer gently for 30-35 minutes, basting frequently, until tender. Serve piping hot sprinkled with chopped chives or scallion.

Yield: Serves 4
Variations:

1. Sprinkle with low-fat cheese and place under broiler for 3 minutes.
2. Instead of chives or scallion, sprinkle lightly with nutmeg before serving.

CAL	F	P:S	SOD	CAR	CHO
59	4	4.5:1	18	5	0
Sprinkled with cheese					
60	4+	4.4:1	19	5+	0

Asparagus with Toasted Coriander

Cooked to perfection, then adorned with a showering of lemon juice, shallots, and toasted coriander, this heavenly vegetable makes one of the most elegant of side dishes. Use it to add glamor to any of your main courses.

- 1¼ *pounds fresh asparagus, washed*
- 1 *cup chicken stock (Page 10)*
- 2 *tablespoons corn oil*
- 2 *shallots, minced*
- ½ *teaspoon fresh lemon juice*
- 1 *teaspoon honey*
- ¼ *teaspoon dried thyme leaves, crushed*
- 1 *tablespoon toasted coriander seeds, finely crushed (Page 99)*
- 2 *dashes Dr. Bronner's seasoning (Page 6)*
- 2 *dashes cayenne pepper*

Remove tough ends of asparagus (about 2″ from the bottom). From cut end, peel back tough layer of skin, revealing soft flesh underneath. Cut each asparagus into 3 pieces.

Bring stock to boil in saucepan wide enough to hold asparagus laying down. Add asparagus. Reduce heat, and simmer, partially covered, for 8 minutes. The time will vary with the thickness of the asparagus. Transfer to colander. Rinse under cold running water. Drain well.

Heat oil in teflon skillet until hot. Add shallots and sauté for 2 minutes. Add asparagus and toss gently to coat. Sprinkle with lemon juice and thyme. Dribble honey into skillet. Add Dr. Bronner's seasoning and cayenne. Cook one minute.

Transfer to heated serving plate, sprinkle with coriander, and serve.

Yield: Serves 4

CAL	F	P:S	SOD	CAR	CHO
115	7	4.5:1	10	14	0

French Green Beans

This superbly refreshing green vegetable is cooked simply in vegetable stock, then brought to a peak of perfection by tossing with lemon juice, herbs, and spices.

1 *pound fresh green beans, washed*
1 *cup chicken stock (Page 10)*
Enough water to barely cover green beans
2 *tablespoons corn oil*
1 *large onion, thinly sliced*
1 *large clove garlic, minced*
1 *large shallot, minced*
1 *tablespoon fresh lemon juice*
¼ *teaspoon ground nutmeg*
4 *dashes smoked yeast (Page 6)*
¼ *teaspoon dried tarragon leaves, crushed*
1 *tablespoon freshly chopped parsley*

Cut off ends of beans. Slice lengthwise. Bring stock to boil in heavy-bottomed saucepan. Add green beans, and enough water to barely cover. Bring to boil. Lower heat to simmering point. Partially cover, and cook for 15-20 minutes. Green beans should be firm yet tender. Drain in colander, reserving stock for another dish.

Heat oil in large teflon skillet until hot. Add onions, garlic, and shallot, and sauté until wilted. Add green beans and toss. Sprinkle with tarragon, nutmeg, smoked yeast, and cayenne. Cook for 3 minutes, or until beans are heated through. Sprinkle with lemon juice and parsley. Toss well, and serve.

Yield: Serves 4
Note: If you prefer your green beans *au naturel,* as many people do, serve them directly from the colander, sprinkled with freshly chopped parsley.

CAL	F	P:S	SOD	CAR	CHO
121	7	4.5:1	16	11	0
Au naturel					
32	0	—	7	7	0

Green Bean Purée

Best prepared with a food processor, this smoothly textured accompaniment to almost any dish can also be used in small amounts to thicken a gravy interestingly without adding many calories.

1½ *pounds green beans, cut into ½" slices*
4 *large fresh mushrooms, washed, trimmed, and coarsely chopped*
1½ *cups chicken stock (Page 10)*
Enough water to barely cover green beans
½ *teaspoon dried tarragon leaves, crushed*
¼ *teaspoon dried dill weed, crushed*
3 *dashes cayenne pepper*

Bring stock to boil in heavy-bottomed saucepan. Add green beans, mushrooms, herbs, and cayenne, and enough water to barely cover. Bring to boil. Turn flame down, partially cover, and simmer for 25 minutes. Uncover, and let cool in liquid for 15 minutes. Drain in colander, and reserve liquid for another dish. (This broth will be particularly delicious to add to soups and sauces.)

Transfer to food processor and purée until smooth. Reheat over very low flame, and serve.

Yield: Serves 4
Variation: If you like the consistency of this purée, you may want to try carrots or fresh peas made the same way. Just substitute either vegetable, and follow recipe.
Note: If you don't have a food processor, you can use a food mill with a fine blade, and purée twice.

CAL	F	P:S	SOD	CAR	CHO
69	0	—	22	12	0
Carrots					
79	0	—	77	15	0
Peas					
73	0	—	13	13	0

Stir-fried Zucchini

Here's a favorite Italian vegetable undercooked in the classic Chinese manner. Stir-frying is quick cooking, which means the vegetable retains its crunchy texture and its garden-fresh savor. To my mind, this is the best way to prepare zucchini.

4 *medium-sized zucchini, well scrubbed, trimmed, cut in half, then cut into long slender ½" strips*
2 *tablespoons corn oil*
2 *large cloves garlic, minced*
1 *teaspoon fresh lemon juice*
½ *teaspoon dried tarragon leaves, crushed*
¼ *teaspoon dried thyme leaves, crushed*
4 *dashes smoked yeast (Page 6)*
1 *teaspoon Dr. Bronner's seasoning (Page 6)*
4 *dashes cayenne pepper*

Heat oil in large iron skillet until hot. Add garlic and sauté one minute. Add zucchini and sauté for 3 minutes, turning with spatula. Sprinkle with lemon juice, turning well to coat. Sprinkle with cayenne, smoked yeast, and herbs, and continue to sauté, turning frequently for 3-4 minutes. Add Dr. Bronner's seasoning and cook one minute. Serve immediately.

Yield: Serves 4
Notes:

1. Any dried herb of your choice may be successfully substituted for tarragon.

2. If your skillet is not large enough to accommodate all of the zucchini at once, cook in two batches, dividing ingredients in half. When cooked, combine in one skillet, and turn with spatula to blend seasonings.

CAL	F	P:S	SOD	CAR	CHO
139	7	4.5:1	13	12	0

Zucchini-Tomato Casserole

Here's a dish for the summer months when both vegetables are plentiful and inexpensive. Prepare it in the cool of the morning, then just pop it into the oven and relax at the end of a long hot day.

1 *pound zucchini, scrubbed and cubed*
1 *pound fresh tomatoes, cored, skinned, seeded, and drained*
2 *tablespoons corn oil, plus ½ teaspoon for oiling casserole*
1 *small onion, minced*
2 *large cloves garlic, minced*
2 *shallots, minced*
½ *green pepper, parboiled one minute, then sliced into strips*
1 *tablespoon tomato paste, no salt added (Page 6)*
½ *teaspoon each dried basil and oregano leaves, crushed*
1 *teaspoon unbleached flour*
⅓ *cup chicken stock (Page 10)*
½ *cup sharp low-fat cheese, grated (Page 3)*
1 *bay leaf*
½ *teaspoon smoked yeast (Page 6)*
4 *dashes cayenne pepper*
Freshly chopped parsley

Heat oil in large iron skillet until hot. Sauté onion, garlic, and shallots until wilted. Add green pepper and sauté for one minute. Sprinkle with flour and cook one minute, stirring well. Add balance of ingredients, with exception of cheese and parsley, and bring to simmering point.

Pour into lightly oiled oven-proof casserole dish, cover loosely with aluminum foil, and bake in preheated 350 degree oven for 20 minutes. Remove from oven and sprinkle with grated cheese. Place under broiler for 2-3 minutes, or until cheese is lightly browned. Sprinkle with parsley and serve.

Yield: Serves 4

CAL	F	P:S	SOD	CAR	CHO
175	9	4.5:1	17	17	0

Honeyed White Onions

Pearly onions are a delicious accompaniment to poultry or meat. Gilded with honey, they give off a translucent sheen that's utterly enticing.

1½ *pounds small white onions, peeled*
1 *cup water*
1 *cup chicken or veal stock (Page 10 or 11)*
2 *tablespoons corn oil*
1 *shallot, minced*
1 *clove garlic, minced*
1 *tablespoon honey*
¼ *teaspoon combined dried marjoram and tarragon leaves, crushed*
1 *teaspoon fresh lemon juice*
⅛ *teaspoon ground ginger*
2 *dashes cayenne pepper*

Bring water and stock to boil in heavy-bottomed saucepan. Add onions and cook, partially covered, for 15 minutes, or until almost tender when tested through their center with sharp knife. Drain, reserving liquid for another dish.

In teflon skillet, heat oil until hot. Add shallot and garlic, and cook 3 minutes or until wilted but not brown.

Arrange onions in lightly oiled shallow baking dish. Sprinkle with lemon juice, cayenne, ginger, dried herbs, and sautéed ingredients. Dribble honey over onions, and bake in preheated 350 degree oven, uncovered, for 20 minutes, turning twice. Serve immediately.

Yield: Serves 4

CAL	F	P:S	SOD	CAR	CHO
150	7	4.5:1	22	8	0

Honeyed Carrots

For a touch of color, serve this orange-hued slightly sweet-and-sour vegetable alongside sliced chicken, turkey, or roast fresh ham. It does wonders for simply prepared food.

6 *large fresh carrots, peeled and trimmed*
1 *tablespoon corn oil*
1 *large shallot, minced*
1 *cup chicken stock (Page 10)*
Enough water to barely cover carrots
1 *tablespoon apple cider vinegar*
2 *dashes cayenne pepper*
4 *dashes smoked yeast (Page 6)*
¼ *teaspoon ground ginger*
¼ *teaspoon dried tarragon leaves, crushed*
1 *tablespoon freshly chopped parsley*
1 *tablespoon honey*

Cut each carrot in half. Lay cut side on board. Then slice lengthwise into ½″ strips. Place carrots in medium-sized heavy-bottomed saucepan. Add stock and enough water to barely cover. Bring to boil. Turn heat down, and simmer, partially covered, for 12-15 minutes. Carrots should be tender but still firm. Drain, reserving stock for another dish.

Rinse and dry saucepan. Add oil and heat until hot. Add shallot and cook one minute. Add vinegar and cook for one minute. Add carrots. Turn to coat. Sprinkle with tarragon, cayenne, ginger, and smoked yeast. Shake around pan. Add honey, and cook over very low flame until heated through. Turn into serving dish and sprinkle with freshly chopped parsley.

Yield: Serves 4

CAL	F	P:S	SOD	CAR	CHO
89	4	4.5:1	73	11	0

Broccoli Magic

Broccoli is such an adaptable vegetable. It can be eaten cold as an hors d'oeuvre, tossed in oil and herbs as a hot side dish, or embellished with cheese for your main course. It can also be puréed with other vegetables to produce an entirely different flavor and texture (Page 19).

1 *package fresh broccoli*
2 *tablespoons corn oil*
2 *large cloves garlic, minced*
2 *large shallots, minced*
½ *teaspoon each dried tarragon and oregano leaves, crushed*
2 *teaspoons freshly chopped parsley*
½ *teaspoon smoked yeast (Page 6)*
4 *dashes cayenne pepper*

Both the stalks and flowerettes are used in this recipe. To promote tenderness and reduce the bitterness that usually accompanies broccoli, the skin must first be removed.

Cut apart each section of broccoli about 1″ down from flowerettes, and again 1″ up from bottom of the stalk. Standing the stalks upright, cut away the thick skin all around, making a smooth cylinder. Then cut into small cubes and set aside.

Grasping the ends of the flowerettes, gently peel off the thick skin upwards so that the meaty soft mass underneath is exposed. Place peeled flowerettes in colander and wash under cold running water.

Fill a large kettle with water and bring to rolling boil. Drop cubed stalks into water and boil, partially covered, for 4 minutes. Drop the flowerettes into the same boiling water, and when it again comes to a boil, cook for 5 minutes. Color should remain bright green. Do not overcook!

Drain in colander and rinse immediately under cold water to stop the cooking action. Broccoli can now be set aside, and the final preparation resumed hours later.

Heat oil in large teflon skillet until hot. Add garlic and shallots and sauté until wilted. Add broccoli, herbs, smoked yeast, and cayenne, shaking pot around gently, taking care not to break flowerettes. Serve immediately.

Yield: Serves 4
Variation: Place cooked broccoli in lightly oiled casserole. Top with ¼ cup bread crumbs that have been mixed with ¼ cup tangy low-fat cheese, and place under broiler until cheese is melted and lightly brown. (Pages 147 and 3.) Serve as a luncheon main course.

CAL	F	P:S	SOD	CAR	CHO
79	7	4.5:1	10	5	0
Luncheon main course					
133	8	4.5:1	10	18	0

Broccoli-Vegetable Purées

Smooth purées are a delightful contrast to chewy meats and poultry. They can be made from most leftover vegetables, but are particularly interesting when made with broccoli. Here's how to prepare a few of them.

2 *cups cooked broccoli (Page 18)*
1 *large carrot, peeled and diced*
1 *large potato, peeled and diced*
3 *dashes smoked yeast (Page 6)*
1 *tablespoon freshly chopped parsley*

Cook carrot and potato together until tender (about 15 minutes). Drain. Combine with broccoli and put through food mill or food processor while still warm. Add smoked yeast and chopped parsley and blend. Serve hot as a side dish.

Variations:

1. Add one level tablespoon non-fat plain yogurt before puréeing. Reheat, taking care not to boil.

2. Combine one cup cooked broccoli, one cup cooked turnip (Page 20), and 2 large carrots, peeled, diced, and cooked in boiling water for 15 minutes. Place in food mill or food processer and proceed as for recipe above.

Yield: Serves 4

CAL	F	P:S	SOD	CAR	CHO
104	7	4.5:1	24	12	0
With yogurt					
107	8	4.1:1	25	12	0
With vegetables					
100	7	4.5:1	30	9	0

Herbed Cauliflower

Start with snow-white, fresh cauliflower, cook to a crunchy consistency, accent with spices and herbs, and—behold!—this bland vegetable is transformed into a delicacy. And you don't need hollandaise!

1 *small white head cauliflower*
2 *tablespoons corn oil*
2 *large shallots, minced*
1 *large clove garlic, minced*
1 *tablespoon wine vinegar*
2 *dashes cayenne pepper*
⅛ *teaspoon ground ginger*
½ *teaspoon dried tarragon leaves, crushed*
2 *teaspoons freshly chopped dill*
3 *dashes smoked yeast (Page 6)*

Peel off outer green leaves. Soak cauliflower, head down, in water to cover for 15 minutes. Separate into flowerettes. Peel back skin from stems as you would for broccoli (Page 18).

Bring large pot of water to rolling boil. Drop flowerettes into water and cook, partially covered, for 12-15 minutes, or until tender but firm. Drain in colander.

In a large teflon skillet, heat oil until hot. Add garlic and shallots and sauté until wilted. Add vinegar and cook one minute. Add cauliflower. Stir gently with wooden spoon. Sprinkle with cayenne, tarragon, ginger, and smoked yeast and stir, being careful not to break flowerettes. Heat through, and serve immediately, sprinkled with freshly chopped dill.

Yield: Serves 4, one leftover
Variations:

1. *Gratinéed cauliflower.* Prepare according to recipe. Transfer drained cauliflower to oven-proof baking dish. Sprinkle with ½ cup grated low-fat cheese. Place under broiler for 3-5 minutes, or until cheese is lightly browned. Serve as a luncheon main course.

2. *Cauliflower with dill sauce.* Prepare according to recipe. Transfer to heated serving dish. Pour dill sauce (Page 51) over cauliflower, and serve.

CAL	F	P:S	SOD	CAR	CHO
94	7	4.5:1	9	5	0
Gratinéed					
99	8	4.0:1	9	6	1
With dill sauce					
152	13	4.5:1	27	7	0

Sautéed Yellow Turnip

Turnip is a much neglected vegetable—and that's a shame. Farmers in time of drought have been known to live solely on turnip for a year or so and still feel great—it's that nutritious. Its natural tangy flavor and potato-like texture make it a winner in the taste department, too.

- 1 *yellow turnip, about 1½ pounds, peeled and cut into 1" cubes*
- 2 *tablespoons corn oil*
- 2 *large cloves garlic, minced*
- 2 *shallots, minced*
- ¼ *teaspoon each dried thyme, oregano, and basil leaves, crushed*
- ½ *teaspoon smoked yeast (Page 6)*
- 2 *tablespoons combined freshly chopped parsley and dill*
- 4 *dashes cayenne pepper*

Fill a 2-3 quart heavy-bottomed saucepan with water. Bring to rolling boil. Add turnip. Bring to boil again. Turn heat down, partially cover, and simmer for 45-50 minutes. Turnip should be tender yet firm. Drain well.

Wipe out saucepan. Add oil and heat until hot. Add garlic and shallot, and sauté until wilted (3-4 minutes). Return cooked turnip to saucepan turning to coat. Sprinkle with smoked yeast, dried herbs, and cayenne and toss by shaking pan. Sprinkle with freshly chopped parsley and dill, and serve.

Yield: Serves 4
Variation: *Puréed turnip.* Herbed turnip may be put through food mill or food processer with one tablespoon plain low-fat yogurt. Reheat, taking care not to boil

CAL	F	P:S	SOD	CAR	CHO
111	7	4.5:1	26	11	0
Pureéd turnip					
119	9	3.7:1	36	12	7

Creamed Spinach

Here's how to transform this basically bitter green into a succulent dish with an intriguing edge of sweetness. Frozen spinach is *verboten*. Somehow—maybe because it's frequently defrosted and refrosted in shipping—it comes into your kitchen with a super bitterness that can't be erased. Wait until fresh spinach is available for this treat.

2 *pounds fresh spinach*
1 *teaspoon corn oil*
1 *small onion, minced*
1 *shallot, minced*
4 *dashes cayenne pepper*
1/8 *teaspoon ground nutmeg*
2 1/2 *teaspoons unbleached flour*
1/4 *cup non-fat milk, warmed*
1/4 *cup chicken stock (Page 10)*
1 *teaspoon honey*

Break off and discard tough stems of spinach. Wash very well in cold water. Pat dry with paper toweling. Chop coarsely.

In a heavy-bottomed saucepan, heat oil until hot. Add onion and shallot and sauté until wilted (2 minutes). Add stock, spinach, cayenne, honey, and nutmeg. Cover and cook over medium heat for 5-7 minutes. Sprinkle with flour, stirring well. Add warmed milk and blend until smooth and thickened. Serve immediately.

Yield: Serves 4

CAL	F	P:S	SOD	CAR	CHO
108	4	4.5:1	47	13	0

Vera's Red Cabbage

My dear friend, Vera Kay, developed this fragrant middle-European dish from an old family recipe. Its delicate tanginess and smooth texture make it vastly superior to any commercially prepared red cabbage. Try it with my sweet-and-sauerbraten (Page 79) for a touch of old Vienna.

1 *red cabbage, about 2 pounds, cut into thin strips*
2 *tablespoons corn oil*
2 *large cloves garlic, minced*
1 *shallot, minced*
1 *small onion, minced*
1 *crisp apple such as Washington State, cored, peeled and cubed*
8 *whole cloves*
1/4 *teaspoon ground allspice*
1 *teaspoon caraway seeds*
2 *tablespoons apple cider vinegar*
1 *teaspoon wine vinegar*
1 *tablespoon honey*
1/2 *cup apple juice, no sugar added*
1/2 *cup water*
Juice of one lemon and grated rind of 1/2 lemon
4 *dashes cayenne pepper*

Heat oil in heavy covered small iron casserole or waterless cooker until hot. Add garlic, shallot, and onion, and sauté until wilted (about 3 minutes). Add cabbage. Turn and stir to coat well with sautéed ingredients. Add balance of ingredients and bring to boil. Reduce heat, cover, and simmer for 45 minutes, stirring frequently. Turn heat off and let cabbage sit in pot, covered, for one hour. When ready to serve, reheat over low flame, and serve in individual dishes.

Yield: Serves 4; one portion left over
Variation: We like our red cabbage unthickened. Restaurants usually thicken it slightly. If you want to try it that way, dissolve two teaspoons arrowroot flour in equal amount of water, and add a little at a time to the finished cabbage, stirring well. Add enough of the flour mixture to give just a hint of thickening.
Note: This dish improves with age.

Store in glass jar overnight, and serve reheated.

CAL	F	P:S	SOD	CAR	CHO
120	5	4.5:1	10	17	0
Thickened					
124	5	4.5:1	10	20	0

Baked Acorn Squash

Acorn squash, my scientific friends advise me, has been around for millions of years. But I've just discovered it. And what a discovery! It tastes like a sophisticated sweet potato, and it marries perfectly with sweet and tart seasonings. A miraculous alternative to the more familiar root vegetables.

2 *medium-sized acorn squash*
2 *tablespoons corn oil*
2 *tablespoons honey*
¼ *teaspoon ground ginger*
½ *teaspoon ground cinnamon*
½ *teaspoon poppy seeds or 1 teaspoon anise seeds, crushed*

Cut each squash in half. Remove seeds. Cut off no more than ½" from narrow end, being careful not to penetrate pulp, so that you can stand halved squash upright. (Some squash will stand upright without this procedure.) Stand squash in shallow baking dish.

Combine balance of ingredients. Spoon equally over each half of squash. Add ¼" boiling water to the bottom of the dish. Cover with aluminum foil. Bake in preheated 375 degree oven for 45-50 minutes or until tender when pierced with sharp knife. Serve.

Yield: Serves 4

CAL	F	P:S	SOD	CAR	CHO
120	7	4.5:1	1	2	0

Parsleyed Potatoes

Dressed up with generous showerings of herbs of your choice, and sprinkled with bright freshly chopped parsley, this subtle lovely potato is a perfect accompaniment to most any dish.

4 *medium-sized potatoes, preferably Idaho or russet, peeled, and each cut into six pieces*
1 *tablespoon corn oil*
1 *large clove garlic, minced*
1 *shallot, minced*
¼ *teaspoon each dried thyme and tarragon leaves, crushed*
1 *tablespoon freshly chopped parsley*
4 *dashes cayenne pepper*
¼ *teaspoon smoked yeast (Page 6)*

Place potatoes in large saucepan. Fill with water to cover. Bring to boil. Reduce heat to simmering point. Partially cover and cook for 15 minutes or until tender. Pour into colander and drain. Rinse under cold water until cooled.

Heat oil until hot in a teflon skillet. Add garlic and shallot and sauté for one minute. Add potatoes. Sprinkle with cayenne, yeast, and dried herbs. Toss gently until heated through. Serve immediately, sprinkled with freshly chopped parsley.

Yield: Serves 4

Notes:

1. You can interchange herbs to match your main course.

2. Small red-skinned potatoes are an excellent substitute for baking potatoes described in recipe. Boil whole in jackets for 15-20 minutes, or until tender. Pour into colander and cool under cold running water. Peel and follow recipe.

CAL	F	P:S	SOD	CAR	CHO
161	4	4.5:1	8	25	0

Spiced Potatoes in a Crock

When my husband and I dined at the three-star restaurant, Barrier, in Tours, the maitre d' challenged us to identify a vegetable dish. It was exquisite, but it was like nothing we ever tasted before. It turned out to be the common cucumber transformed into something marvelous. I've always wanted to do the same kind of thing with the even more common potato—and here it is. Serve it to your guests and challenge them to guess what it is.

4 *baking potatoes, preferably Idaho (about 1½ pounds)*
1 *tablespoon corn oil*
1 *large shallot, finely minced*
2 *cloves garlic, finely minced*
¼ *teaspoon dry mustard dissolved in 1 teaspoon water*
½ *teaspoon smoked yeast (Page 6)*
4 *dashes mild paprika*
1 *dash cayenne pepper*
¼ *teaspoon each dried rosemary and thyme leaves, crushed*
½ *teaspoon apple cider vinegar*
4 *dashes Dr. Bronner's seasoning (Page 6)*
1 *tablespoon duxelles (Page 13)*
3 *tablespoons non-fat milk*
2 *tablespoons plain low-fat yogurt*
2 *tablespoons freshly chopped parsley and dill*

Peel potatoes. Cut into 1″ cubes. Place in heavy-bottomed saucepan and fill with water to cover. Bring to boil. Reduce heat to simmering point, and continue to cook, partially covered, for 12-15 minutes or until tender. Pour into colander and drain for 3 minutes.

Dry saucepan and add oil. Heat until very warm. Sauté garlic and shallot until wilted. Add vinegar and cook one minute. Turn off heat and add dried herbs and stir well.

Mash potatoes with fork. Do not whip, since firm texture must be retained. Add spices, duxelles, Dr. Bronner's seasoning, smoked yeast, mustard, and parsley and dill. Blend with fork. Add sautéed mixture and blend again. Add milk, a tablespoon at a time, blending with fork. Fold in yogurt until all is absorbed.

Lightly oil 4 oven-proof crocks. Spoon in equal amounts of mixture. Place on baking sheet, and bake in preheated 425 degree oven for 20 minutes. The mixture will puff up when done. Serve immediately in crocks.

Yield: Serves 4

CAL	F	P:S	SOD	CAR	CHO
181	8	3.4:1	59	29	0

Stuffed Idaho Potatoes

The shell of an Idaho always retains its shape, making it ideal for stuffing, and the potato itself maintains its firm, dry, texture always. You'll want to serve this potato-lover's delight often with braised meats, roasts, or broilings.

2 *Idaho potatoes*
1 *tablespoon corn oil*
½ *small onion, minced*
1 *clove garlic, minced*
1 *large shallot, minced*
½ *teaspoon wine vinegar*
¼ *teaspoon smoked yeast (Page 6)*
½ *teaspoon dried tarragon, oregano, or basil leaves, crushed*
2 *teaspoons freshly chopped parsley and dill*
3 *dashes cayenne pepper*
About 3 tablespoons non-fat milk
¼ *cup finely grated low-fat cheese (Page 3)*
Several dashes mild paprika

Scrub potatoes. Dry well. Bake for

one hour in preheated 400 degree oven, or until baked through.

In a small skillet, heat oil until very hot. Add onion, garlic and shallot and sauté until lightly browned. Add vinegar and cook one minute. Stir and set aside.

Cut each potato in half lengthwise. Scoop out potato, being careful not to break shell. Set shells aside. Transfer potatoes to bowl and mash. Add smoked yeast, herbs, and cayenne. Blend well. Add sautéed mixture and enough milk to produce a firm consistency when blended.

Stuff potato shells with mixture, pressing lightly. Place stuffed shells, skin down, on a baking dish. Sprinkle with cheese. Then sprinkle lightly with paprika. Bake in preheated 425 degree oven for 10 minutes. Then place under broiler for 2-3 minutes, or until lightly browned.

Yield: Serves 4

CAL	F	P:S	SOD	CAR	CHO
119	7	3.9:1	31	21	8

Rich Home-Fried Potatoes

Start with neatly cut potatoes, add a generous showering of herbs and spices, sauté until golden brown, and you'll produce crisp, greaseless home fries, the likes of which you've never tasted before. Adds a new zest to your chops, steaks, and roasts.

- 2 *large baking potatoes, preferably Idaho, peeled*
- 3 *tablespoons corn oil*
- 3 *cloves garlic, minced*
- 1 *large shallot, minced*
- 1 *rib celery, minced*
- 1 *large onion, cut in half and thinly sliced*
- ¼ *teaspoon mild paprika*
- ½ *teaspoon dried thyme leaves, crushed*
- ⅛ *teaspoon dried oregano leaves, crushed*
- 4 *dashes cayenne pepper*
- ¼ *teaspoon smoked yeast (Page 6)*
- *Freshly chopped parsley and dill or freshly chopped basil*

Wash peeled potatoes. Slice carefully into ¼″ thick rounds. Fill a large saucepan with water and bring to rolling boil. Add potatoes and boil for 13 minutes. Drain in colander. Place under slow-running cold water for several minutes until cooled. Transfer to bowl. Cover and refrigerate for at least 2 hours.

Heat 1 tablespoon oil in large iron skillet until hot. Sauté garlic, shallot, celery, and onion until lightly browned. Remove from skillet and set aside.

Lay cooled potatoes on paper toweling. Pat dry, taking care not to break slices. Heat one tablespoon oil in same skillet until hot. Lay as many potatoes in skillet as will fit in a single layer. Combine dried herbs, cayenne, smoked yeast, and paprika, blending well. Sprinkle one-third of spicy mixture over potatoes, and top with spread of sautéed ingredients. Cover with balance of sliced potatoes in a single layer. Sprinkle with another third of spicy mixture. Press gently with spatula and sauté, without turning, until browned. Add balance of oil directly to skillet. Turn with large spatula. Add balance of spicy mixture. Press gently with spatula, and sauté until brown. Continue to turn and brown until all potatoes are well browned (about 30 minutes).

Serve immediately sprinkled with freshly chopped herbs.

Yield: Serves 4

CAL	F	P:S	SOD	CAR	CHO
163	10	4.5:1	32	16	0

Potato Pancakes

"Potato pancakes! They're so fattening. I can't eat them!" Oh yes, you can. You can eat them as a side dish, as a luncheon treat, or—rolled up and secured with toothpicks—as an hors d'oeuvre. The calorie count per dinner-serving is not much more than that of a glass of orange juice.

- 4 *medium-sized baking potatoes (Idahos are preferred)*
- 1 *large onion, grated*
- 1 *large clove garlic, minced*
- 1 *shallot, grated*
- 2 *egg whites and ½ yolk from extra-large eggs*
- 3 *tablespoons unbleached flour*
- ¼ *teaspoon smoked yeast (Page 6)*
- ¼ *teaspoon dried thyme leaves, crushed*
- ½ *teaspoon low-sodium baking powder (Pages 4 and 6)*
- 3 *dashes cayenne pepper*
- *Oil for coating teflon skillet (about 1 teaspoon)*

Peel potatoes and pat dry. Medium-grate immediately into bowl. Pour off any excess water. Grate onion and shallot into potatoes. Add garlic, thyme, eggs, cayenne, baking powder, smoked yeast, and flour. Stir to blend.

Brush teflon skillet lightly with oil and heat until very hot. Drop a full tablespoon of mixture into skillet and spread to form pancake. Make three pancakes at the same time. Brown well. Turn and brown on other side. Brush heated skillet with oil before each batch of pancakes are made. It adds little to calories and lots to crispness and flavor.

Yield: 12 pancakes, serves four
Note: I've tried this recipe with a thermostatically controlled teflon (which is excellent for crepes) and it doesn't work. You must have a continual high heat to produce crispness.

CAL	F	P:S	SOD	CAR	CHO
140	2	2.6:1	35	30	31

Holiday Whipped Yams

If you're getting a bit tired of the same old Thanksgiving sweet-potatoes-and-marshmallows, try this exciting alternative. You'll love the new flavor. And you won't have to worry about all those calories. Use this dish as a complement to turkey, chicken, beef or veal on any day you declare a holiday.

- 4 *yams, about 1½ pounds*
- 2 *tablespoons corn oil, plus ½ teaspoon to oil crocks*
- 1 *shallot, minced*
- 1 *teaspoon ground ginger*
- 1 *teaspoon ground mace*
- 2 *tablespoons fresh orange juice*
- 1 *teaspoon orange zest (see instructions in recipe)*
- 3-4 *dashes ground cinnamon*
- 3 *dashes cayenne pepper*
- 3 *egg whites*

Bake yams in 350 degree oven for one hour, or until thoroughly tender when given a gentle squeeze. Remove from skins and mash in small bowl while still warm. Add oil, shallot, ginger, mace, orange juice, orange zest, and cayenne. Blend. (To make orange zest, peel off outer colored skin of orange with potato peeler. Be sure not to include bitter pulpy rind. Chop into small pieces.)

Beat egg whites until almost stiff. Do this by continuing to beat for a few moments after soft peaks form. Fold into mashed yam mixture (page 128).

Spoon into 4 individual crocks which have been lightly oiled. Sprinkle with cinnamon. Place in 400 degree preheated oven until lightly puffed on top (about 15 minutes). Serve immediately.

Yield: Serves 6
Variation: For a particularly festive occasion, try baking the yam mixture in orange shells. You'll need one orange per person. Cut off oranges 1″ from top. Scoop out pulp and reserve for fruit salad. Fill shells with yam mixture. Place on lightly oiled baking sheet. Bake in preheated 400 degree oven for 15 minutes or until heated through.
Note: A yam is not a sweet potato, although most people think it is. You can make this dish with yellow sweet potatoes, but they're not as sweet as yams, so you may want to add honey. Yams and sweet potatoes have roughly the same calorie, sodium and carbohydrate counts, and honey has 62 calories and 1.5 mg. sodium per tablespoon.

CAL	F	P:S	SOD	CAR	CHO
176	3	4.5:1	53	32	0

Extraordinary Kasha

My mother prepared kasha when I was a youngster, and I hated it. Not until years and years later, after I had taught myself to cook this delicious grain successfully, did I realize why my mother's kasha was inedible. She overcooked it. The result was a gooey mess that had all the worst characteristics of an instant hot breakfast cereal. If you follow instructions on a box of kasha, you'll get the same horrendous dish. The key to retaining the bright nutlike taste of the groats is to keep the cooking time down low. Then, bathed in your homemade stock and coddled by herbs and spices, kasha ascends to culinary heights.

- 1 *cup kasha (there are several varieties of kasha; use the variety designated "whole")*
- 2 *cups stock, veal, beef, or chicken, to match your main course (Pages 11, 12, or 10). (If serving fish, use chicken stock)*
- 1 *shallot, minced*
- 2 *tablespoons freshly chopped parsley and dill*
- ½ *teaspoon dried tarragon, oregano, or basil leaves, crushed*
- 4 *dashes smoked yeast (Page 6)*
- 3 *dashes cayenne pepper*

Bring stock to boil in heavy-bottomed saucepan. Add kasha and bring to boil again. Reduce heat to simmering point. Stir well. Simmer, uncovered, for 8 minutes, not a minute longer, adding a soupçon more stock if necessary. All liquid should be absorbed and each kernel should remain separate. Add balance of ingredients, tossing well. Serve immediately.

Yield: Serves 4
Variation: Add the following to cooked mixture, toss, and serve:

½ *small onion, minced*
¼ *pound fresh mushrooms, sliced and sautéed*

Note: This full-grained kasha dish and its variation are suitable for stuffing chicken and turkey. For a kasha with a paté-like texture suitable for stuffing veal, see page 81.

CAL	F	P:S	SOD	CAR	CHO
With chicken stock					
44	0	—	2	8	0
With veal stock					
49	0	—	14	8	0
With beef stock					
48	0	—	23	8	0
Variation, add					
7	0	—	3	0	0

Baked Barley Casserole

Here's an innovative, nutritious alternate to rice and potatoes. It's an excellent main dish for your meatless, fishless, poultryless days—and it's marvelous with one of my green salads. Smaller portions make an impeccable side dish, too.

CAL	F	P:S	SOD	CAR	CHO
153	8	4.5:1	22	6	0
With veal stock					
153	8	4.5:1	32	6	0
With chicken stock/apple juice					
156	8	4.5:1	29	7	0
With veal stock/apple juice					
156	8	4.5:1	25	7	0

¾ *cup pearl barley, washed and drained*
2 *tablespoons corn oil, plus ½ teaspoon to oil casserole*
1 *large clove garlic, minced*
1 *small onion, minced*
½ *green pepper, minced*
1 *shallot, minced*
1 *teaspoon wine vinegar*
½ *teaspoon dried thyme leaves, crushed*
2 *tablespoons freshly chopped dill and parsley*
2¼-2½ *cups chicken or veal stock (Pages 10 or 11)*
½ *carrot, peeled and grated*
½ *teaspoon caraway seeds, lightly crushed*
2 *dashes cayenne pepper*
3 *dashes Dr. Bronner's seasoning (Page 6)*
1″ *sliver orange peel*

Heat oil in iron skillet until hot. Add garlic, shallot, onion, and pepper, and sauté until lightly browned. Add vinegar, and cook for 2 minutes. Add barley and stir to coat well with sautéed mixture. Add 2¼ cups stock, thyme, carrot, cayenne, Dr. Bronner's seasoning, and caraway seeds, and bring to simmering point. Drop in orange peel. Pour into lightly oiled 2- or 3-quart ovenproof casserole, and bake, covered, in preheated 375 degree oven for 45 minutes, stirring twice. Liquid should be absorbed and barley tender. If you prefer a very moist barley, add ¼ cup hot stock at this point, and stir.

Sprinkle with fresh herbs, and serve.

Yield: Serves 4, one leftover
Variation: For stock, substitute a mixture of half chicken or veal stock and half apple juice (no sugar added). Add 3 whole cloves to casserole.

Macaroni Stuffed Peppers

I served this beautiful entree for lunch. My guests loved it, and clamored for the recipe. When they read it, they were astonished that so rich-tasting a delight could be utterly devoid of butter, salt, black pepper and egg yolks. You won't believe its satisfying heartiness until you make it yourself.

1 *cup whole wheat elbow macaroni, no salt or eggs added (Page 6)*
2 *tablespoons corn oil plus ½ teaspoon to coat baking dish*
3 *large cloves garlic, finely minced*
1 *shallot, finely minced*
1 *large onion, finely minced*
2 *large green peppers, stuffing size, parboiled for one minute and cooled under cold running water*
½ *10-ounce can tomato purée, no salt added (Page 6)*
4 *tablespoons tomato juice, no salt added*
¼ *cup dry Vermouth or white wine*
½ *cup bread crumbs (Page 147)*
½ *cup chicken stock (Page 10)*
1 *egg white, lightly beaten with fork*
3 *dashes cayenne pepper*
¼ *teaspoon dried mint leaves, crushed*
½ *teaspoon each dried oregano and rosemary leaves, crushed*
½ *cup sharp low-fat cheese, grated (Page 3)*
Chopped fresh parsley and dill

Bring large pot of water to rolling boil. Drop macaroni into water and cook, partially covered, for 10 minutes. Drain and set aside.

Cut parboiled green peppers in half, removing seeds and pulp. Set aside.

Heat oil in teflon skillet until hot. Sauté onion, garlic, and shallot until wilted (about 3 minutes). Add wine and cook for one minute. Add tomato purée, cayenne, dried herbs, and stock, and simmer, partially covered, for 10 minutes.

Transfer cooked macaroni to large bowl. Add bread crumbs and egg, blending well. Then add cooked mixture, stirring well.

Shape 4 pieces of aluminum foil into boats to hold each half of green pepper in such a way that foil will catch any overflow of macaroni as it's added. Fill each half of pepper with mixture, pressing gently. Place on lightly oiled baking dish. Cover loosely with aluminum foil.

Place filled dish into a larger baking pan to which 1″ of boiling water has been added. Bake in preheated 350 degree oven for 20 minutes. Remove from oven, uncover, and sprinkle with grated cheese. Dribble a tablespoon of tomato juice over the top of each pepper and return to oven. Bake, uncovered, for 20 minutes until pepper is cooked through when tested with sharp knife. Serve sprinkled with chopped fresh parsley and dill.

Yield: Serves 4
Note: If you're planning to freeze some of the peppers, remove from oven 10 minutes before the end of cooking time so that when reheated, they will retain their firmness.

CAL	F	P:S	SOD	CAR	CHO
225	9	2.4:1	30	24	7

Spaghetti with Tomato and Mushroom Sauce

If you've never had whole wheat spaghetti made without eggs or sugar or salt, you'll be surprised at its delicious taste and texture. Top it with my ever so slightly spicy tomato and mushroom sauce, and enjoy the earthy yet heavenly taste of the pasta of a small roadside inn in Italy.

¾ *pound whole wheat spaghetti, without eggs or salt (Page 6)*
3 *cups fresh ripe tomatoes, cored, skinned and drained (about 1½ pounds), or 3 cups canned tomatoes, no salt added*
2 *shallots, minced*
3 *large cloves garlic, minced*
1 *large onion, minced*
1 *large green pepper, minced*
1 *rib celery, minced*
2 *tablespoons corn oil*
¼ *cup dry Vermouth or white wine*
2 *tablespoons tomato paste, no salt added (Page 6)*
¾ *cup chicken stock (Page 10)*
½ *teaspoon each dried oregano, thyme, and basil leaves, crushed*
½ *teaspoon smoked yeast (Page 6)*
4 *dashes cayenne pepper*
½ *pound fresh mushrooms, washed, dried, trimmed and sliced*
Bouquet garni made up of 3 sprigs parsley, ½ teaspoon fennel, and 1 bay leaf tied together in small piece of washed cotton cheesecloth
Freshly chopped parsley

Heat oil until very warm in iron skillet. Sauté onion, garlic, celery, and shallots until wilted (about 3 minutes). Add green pepper and sauté 2 minutes. Add wine. Bring to boil. Turn flame down and cook, uncovered, for 2 minutes. Add tomatoes, tomato paste, stock, dried herbs, smoked yeast, cayenne and bouquet garni. Cover and simmer for 25 minutes. Add mushrooms. Stir well. Bring to simmering point. Cover and simmer for 35 minutes.

Fifteen minutes before sauce is done, bring large potful of water to a rolling boil. Ease spaghetti gently into boiling water without breaking pieces, and boil for 12-15 minutes. You will find that the whole wheat spaghetti will remain *al dente* (firm to the bite) which is the way spaghetti should be cooked. Drain well in colander. Transfer to hot serving dish, and top with hot sauce. Sprinkle with chopped parsley and serve.

Yield: Serves 6
Variations:

1. Serve with a sprinkling of grated low-fat cheese (Page 3).

2. If you like your spaghetti with meat balls, try my recipe (Page 97).

CAL	F	P:S	SOD	CAR	CHO
263	3	4.5:1	29	59	0
Sprinkled with cheese					
267	3+	4.4:1	29	59+	0

Risotto (Rice, Peas, and Mushrooms)

This is an Italian-inspired side dish that you'll want to repeat often because it's compatible with just about every meat, poultry or fish course. Try it once and you'll be hooked.

1 *cup white rice, washed and drained*
2 *tablespoons corn oil*
2 *cloves garlic, minced*
2 *shallots, minced*
½ *pound fresh peas, shelled*
½ *pound fresh mushrooms, washed, dried, trimmed and sliced*
2 *teaspoons apple cider vinegar*
¼ *teaspoon each dried oregano and marjoram leaves, crushed*
1 *cup water*
1 *cup chicken, veal, or beef stock to match your main course (Pages 10, 11, or 12). (If serving fish, use chicken stock)*
3 *dashes cayenne pepper*
Freshly chopped parsley

In this recipe, rice, peas, and mushrooms are cooked separately, then assembled.

Boil peas briskly in water to cover

for 15 minutes or until tender. Drain and set aside.

Bring stock and water to boil. Add rice, and cook, partially covered, for 15 minutes. All liquid should be absorbed.

Heat ¾ tablespoon of oil in large teflon skillet until hot. Add half of the mushrooms and sauté until lightly browned, turning often (about 3-4 minutes). Transfer with slotted spoon to bowl. Add ¾ tablespoon oil to skillet, and sauté balance of mushrooms. Transfer to bowl.

Heat balance of oil in same skillet until hot. Add garlic and shallots and sauté until lightly browned. Add vinegar and cook for one minute. Add cooked rice, peas, mushrooms, and dried herbs, and toss gently until heated through. Transfer to heated serving dish, and serve immediately, sprinkled with freshly chopped parsley.

Yield: Serves 4, one portion left over
Notes:

1. Mushrooms must be cooked in small batches so that they don't touch each other. This produces a tasty non-watery mushroom which fully retains its character when mixed with other ingredients.

2. One cup brown rice may be substituted for white rice in this recipe. The short-grain organic variety is preferable to the starchy variety, which ordinarily comes boxed in supermarkets. Soak rice for one hour in 2 cups liquid. Bring to boil, cover, and simmer for 25 minutes.

CAL	F	P:S	SOD	CAR	CHO
With chicken stock					
177	9	4.5:1	16	28	0
With veal stock					
181	9	4.5:1	28	28	0
With beef stock					
180	9	4.5:1	37	28	0

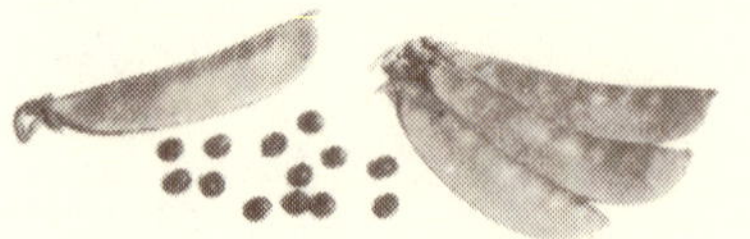

Chinese Restaurant Spiced Rice

There isn't a Chinese ingredient other than rice in this surprising dish. But the well married herbs and spices, and the exceptional cooking procedure make it taste as if it came from your favorite Chinese restaurant. Rice aficionados, don't pass this one by.

1 *cup uncooked rice, washed and drained*
2 *tablespoons corn oil*
1 *onion, finely minced*
2 *large cloves garlic, finely minced*
1 *large scallion, finely minced*
1 *medium-sized green pepper, parboiled, and cut into slivers*
1 *cup water*
1 *cup chicken stock (Page 10)*
¼ *teaspoon each dried marjoram and tarragon leaves, crushed*
2 *tablespoons freshly chopped parsley and dill*
3 *dashes cayenne pepper*
4 *dashes Dr. Bronner's seasoning (Page 6)*
½ *teaspoon ground ginger*

Bring water and stock to boil in heavy-bottomed saucepan. Add rice. Bring to boil again. Reduce heat and cook, partially covered, for 12-15 minutes, or until all water is absorbed and rice is tender but firm.

Heat oil in iron skillet until hot. Add onion, garlic, scallion, and pepper and sauté until lightly browned, turning frequently (5-7 minutes). Add rice to skillet and turn to coat with sautéed mixture. Sprinkle with herbs, spices, and Dr. Bronner's seasoning. Stir. Cover tightly and place in preheated 450 degree oven for 5 minutes. Serve immediately.

Yield: Serves 4, one portion left over

CAL	F	P:S	SOD	CAR	CHO
212	3	4.5:1	10	28	0

Orange-Pineapple Rice

Try this exciting innovative dish, and you'll never go back to just plain rice again. Utterly superb when served with steamed or baked fish.

1 *cup rice, washed and drained*
2 *tablespoons corn oil, plus ½ teaspoon to oil casserole*
1 *shallot, minced*
2 *cloves garlic, minced*
1 *rib celery with leaves, finely chopped*
5 *large fresh mushrooms, washed, dried, trimmed, and sliced*
¼ *teaspoon each dried sage and thyme leaves, crushed*
½ *cup each orange and pineapple juice, no sugar added*
1 *cup water*
3 *dashes cayenne pepper*

Heat oil in large teflon skillet until hot. Sauté onion, garlic, shallot, and celery, until wilted. Push vegetables to the side of skillet, and add mushrooms. Sauté 2 minutes, stirring constantly. Mix together all ingredients in skillet. Add rice and turn and stir to coat. Cook one minute. Add combined juices, water, herbs, and cayenne. Bring to boil. Pour into 2-quart lightly oiled casserole. Cover and bake in preheated 400 degree oven for 30-35 minutes or until all liquid is absorbed and rice is tender.

Yield: Serves 4, one leftover
Note: This dish will stay hot for 30 minutes if left covered on top of warm stove.

CAL	F	P:S	SOD	CAR	CHO
223	3	4.5:1	32	30	0

Soups

Creamy Asparagus Soup

What can be lovelier than a meal enriched with the luxurious flavor of asparagus? Here that flavor is captured in an emerald-green soup, and enhanced with touches of herbs and spices.

1½ *pounds fresh asparagus*
2 *cups chicken stock (Page 10)*
1½ *cups water*
1 *thin slice orange*
3 *tablespoons regular cream of wheat*
1 *tablespoon corn oil*
1 *small onion, minced*
1 *shallot, minced*
1 *clove garlic, minced*
½ *teaspoon smoked yeast (Page 6)*
1 *teaspoon dried tarragon leaves, crushed*
3 *tablespoons low-fat plain yogurt*
½ *cup non-fat milk*

In a quart-size saucepan, bring stock and water to boil. Sprinkle cream of wheat into hot liquid, stirring constantly. Lower flame and cook, uncovered, for seven minutes.

Meanwhile cut away tough bottom sections of asparagus stalks. Holding each stalk cut end up, peel downwards towards tips to remove skin. Cut each peeled stalk into 1″ pieces. Reserve tips. Drop balance of cut asparagus into boiling liquid. Add orange slice, tarragon, cayenne, and smoked yeast. Bring to simmering point. Turn flame down, and simmer, partially covered, for 10 minutes. Add reserved asparagus tips. Cover and simmer another 7 minutes. Turn off heat. Uncover, remove orange slice, and let soup cool in pot.

Heat oil in small skillet until hot.

Add onion, garlic, and shallot, and sauté until wilted. Set aside.

When soup has cooled down, remove 4 teaspoons asparagus, picking out as many tips as you can. Set aside for garnish. Pour balance of soup, together with sautéed mixture into blender. Blend for one minute.

Return to saucepan. Add milk and stir. Whisk in yogurt. Finally, add reserved tips. Reheat over very low flame, taking care not to boil.

Yield: 4 ample portions

CAL	F	P:S	SOD	CAR	CHO
113	4	3.8:1	29	12	1

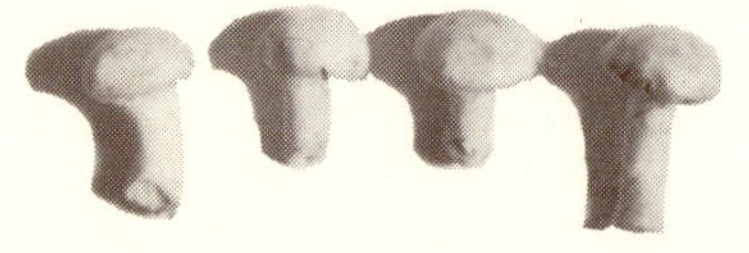

Creamy Mushroom Soup

Tender fresh mushrooms, lightly sautéed with vegetables, then gently simmered in rich stock, are the basis of this delicately creamy soup. Make a lunch of it with my crispy French Bread (Page 135) and a slice of low-fat cheese (Page 3), or serve it as a light first course at your evening meal.

- 2 *tablespoons corn oil*
- ¾ *pound fresh mushrooms, washed, dried, trimmed, and coarsely chopped*
- 2 *cups chicken stock (Page 10)*
- 1 *cup water*
- ¾ *cup extra strength non-fat milk prepared from powder by using ⅓ less water than called for by instructions*
- 1 *small onion, minced*
- ½ *rib celery, minced*
- 2 *cloves garlic, minced*
- 1 *shallot, minced*
- ½ *teaspoon dried tarragon leaves, crushed*
- 1 *tablespoon dry sherry*
- 2 *tablespoons freshly chopped dill and parsley*
- 2 *dashes cayenne pepper*
- ½ *teaspoon honey*
- 3 *dashes smoked yeast (Page 6)*
- 2 *tablespoons regular cream of wheat*
- ½″ *sliver orange peel*

Heat 1½ tablespoons oil until hot in teflon skillet. Sauté mushrooms until lightly browned, turning frequently with spoon. Take out 2 tablespoons mushrooms and reserve for garnish. Transfer balance of mushrooms to medium-sized heavy-bottomed saucepan.

Heat balance of oil in skillet. Add onion, shallot, celery, and garlic. Sauté until lightly browned. Add sherry and cook for one minute. Pour into saucepan with mushrooms. Add stock and water. Stir to blend. Add tarragon, one tablespoon chopped parsley and dill, smoked yeast and cayenne. Heat to simmering point. Slowly sprinkle cream of wheat into soup, stirring constantly. Add honey and orange peel. Cover partially, and simmer for 25 minutes.

Remove orange peel. Pour into blender and blend until smooth. Pour back into saucepan. Add milk and heat to simmering point, stirring constantly. Serve hot, sprinkled with reserved mushrooms and balance of chopped parsley and dill.

Yield: Serves 4, with one leftover

CAL	F	P:S	SOD	CAR	CHO
100	6	4.5:1	40	6	0

Clear Vegetable Consommé

Here's a fresh and sprightly broth, as nutritious as it is delicious. The secret is simple: bright fresh vegetables and herbs simmered gently to extract their natural sunny flavors.

3 *carrots, peeled and thinly sliced*
3 *ribs celery, diced*
2 *large onions, each onion cut into eighths*
3 *large cloves garlic, coarsely chopped*
2 *large shallots, coarsely chopped*
½ *cup yellow turnip, peeled and diced*
¼ *pound fresh mushrooms, trimmed and coarsely chopped*
1 *small parsnip, peeled and thinly sliced*
2 *whole leeks, well washed, and coarsely chopped*
½ *cup green cabbage, sliced*
1 *pound green beans, cut into ½" slices*
4 *fresh tomatoes, cored, and coarsely chopped*
3 *whole cloves*
¼ *teaspoon Dr. Bronner's seasoning (Page 6)*
1 *quart water*

Place all ingredients except Dr. Bronner's seasoning in stainless steel pot or waterless cooker. Bring to boil. Remove scum that rises to top. Add Dr. Bronner's seasoning. Turn flame down and simmer, partially covered, for 30 minutes. Let cool, covered, in pot.

Pour into chinois, placing bowl underneath, and press to remove all consommé. Reserve vegetables for leftover purée. Transfer consommé to freeze-proof containers. Cover tightly, and refrigerate sufficient quantity for immediate needs, and freeze balance.

Yield: Serves 4
Note: After soup is drained from vegetables, pour vegetables into blender, and purée, adding small amount of consommé. Serve as a change-of-pace side dish.

CAL	F	P:S	SOD	CAR	CHO
74	0	—	98	14	0
Purée					
92	0	—	100	35	0

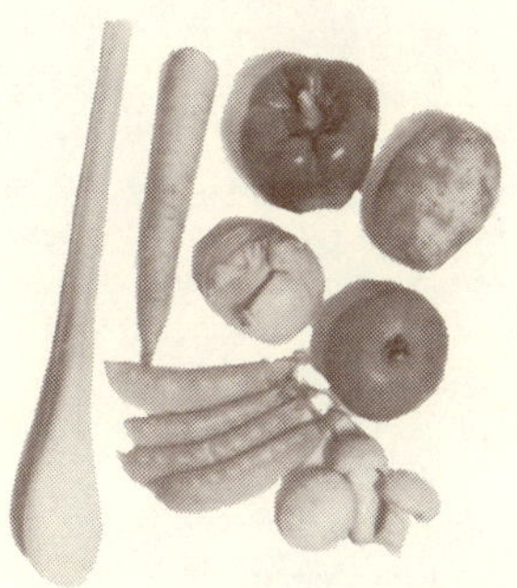

Twelve-Vegetable Beef Soup

A dozen kinds of fresh vegetables plus lean beef give this soup a rich, hearty flavor unlike anything you've ever tasted. With a food processer, you can whip it up in a jiffy. But if you prefer to mince and chop by hand, double the recipe, freeze the leftover soup, and—presto!—you have an instant dish the next time around. Serve with my crisp French Herb Bread (Page 136).

½ *pound lean beef, such as top or bottom round, cut into 2" cubes*
1 *large beef or veal bone*
5 *cups water*
¼ *cup Great Northern beans, soaked overnight and drained*
2 *tablespoons medium barley*
2 *carrots, peeled and finely diced*
1 *rib celery, finely diced*
½ *cup fresh shelled peas*
2 *yellow onions, cut into eighths*
2 *large pieces dried mushrooms, or 6 fresh mushrooms, washed, trimmed, and sliced*
1 *small potato, peeled and diced*
1 *cup green beans, cut into ½" slices (¼ pound)*
½ *cup yellow turnip, peeled and diced*
1 *small green pepper, diced*
2 *fresh tomatoes, peeled, cored, and chopped*
3 *large cloves garlic, minced*
1 *large shallot, minced*
2 *tablespoons tomato paste, no salt added (Page 6)*
½ *teaspoon smoked yeast (Page 6)*
6 *dashes cayenne pepper*
½ *teaspoon each dried thyme and rosemary leaves, crushed*
4 *whole cloves*
3 *tablespoons brown beef stock (Page 13)*
1 *tablespoon wine vinegar*
Bouquet garni

Trim away any fat from meat. Place meat, bone, water, and bouquet garni in large kettle. Add drained beans. Bring to boil. Cover and simmer for one hour, removing scum that rises to top.

Add all vegetables (except peas), garlic, herbs, stock, tomato paste, smoked yeast, cloves, barley, cayenne, and vinegar. Bring to boil. Turn heat down, partially cover, and simmer for another hour. Add peas and continue to simmer for another 30 minutes.

Let soup cool in pot for at least one hour. Remove bone and bouquet garni. Remove meat, cutting into small pieces, and return to pot. Reheat, and serve.

Yield: Serves 6
Note: Here are some substitutions you can make:

Fresh lima beans for dried beans, split peas for fresh peas, and white turnip for yellow turnip.

CAL	F	P:S	SOD	CAR	CHO
183	2	1:1	57	14	27
With fresh lima beans					
150	2	1:1	57	19	27
With split peas					
239	2	1:1	51	23	27
With white turnip					
No appreciable difference					

Cucumber-Tomato Soup

This extremely tasty rose-hued soup is equally as delicious served hot or cold. Appetite-stimulating, and certainly not filling, it's a perfect first course.

2 *medium-sized cucumbers, peeled and diced*
3 *large fresh tomatoes, skinned, coarsely chopped*
1 *tablespoon corn oil*
⅓ *cup combination chopped leeks (white part only), garlic and shallots, minced*
1 *tablespoon wine vinegar*
2½ *cups chicken stock (Page 10)*
1 *cup water*
1 *teaspoon freshly chopped dill or ½ teaspoon dried dill weed*
4 *dashes cayenne pepper*
¼-½ *cup low-fat plain yogurt*
2 *teaspoons arrowroot flour dissolved in 1 tablespoon cold water (optional)*

Drop tomatoes in boiling water for one minute. Remove skin, and core. (Skin will peel right off.)

Heat oil in stainless steel pot or

waterless cooker until very warm. Sauté shallots, leeks, and garlic until just wilted but not brown. Add vinegar and cook for 2 minutes. Add cucumbers, tomatoes, stock, water and cayenne. Bring to boil. Turn flame down and simmer, partially covered, for 25 minutes. Cool.

Pour into blender and purée for one minute. Then pour through fine sieve. Rinse out pot in which soup was cooked. Pour puréed soup back into pot. Add yogurt and whisk well. Reheat over low flame (do not boil), and serve.

If you prefer a thicker soup, before adding yogurt, reheat soup to simmering point, and add dissolved arrowroot flour mixture, a little at a time, whisking until you've achieved desired thickness. Then add ¼ cup yogurt, whisking well.

Yield: Serves 4
Note: This soup is also delicious served cold.

CAL	F	P:S	SOD	CAR	CHO
90	5	3.2:1	28	9	1
Thickened					
102	5	3.2:1	28	11	1

Fresh Tomato Soup

Dedicated food buffs will applaud this version of America's most popular soup. Its gourmet flavor derives from *fresh* tomatoes, gently simmered in rich stock, herbed with basil, and creamed with just a hint of yogurt. A perfect light first course.

4 *large tomatoes, washed, cored, and quartered*
1 *tablespoon corn oil*
1 *leek, white part only, washed and coarsely chopped*
2 *large cloves garlic, minced*
½ *rib celery, coarsely chopped*
1 *shallot, minced*
1 *small onion, coarsely chopped*
½ *carrot, peeled and diced*
½ *teaspoon each dried basil and tarragon leaves, crushed*
1 *tablespoon freshly chopped basil or dill*
2 *cups chicken stock (Page 10)*
2 *cups water*
1 *tablespoon tomato paste, no salt added (Page 6)*
4 *dashes cayenne pepper*
1½ *tablespoons plain low-fat yogurt*
Bouquet garni

Heat oil until hot in heavy-bottomed saucepan. Add onion, shallot, garlic, celery, and leek. Sauté until wilted. Add stock, water, tomatoes, tomato paste, dried herbs, carrot, cayenne, and bouquet garni. Bring to simmering point. Partially cover, and simmer for 20 minutes.

Remove bouquet garni and pour into blender. Blend for one minute. Pour through fine sieve directly into saucepan. Whisk in yogurt. Reheat to just below simmering point. Do not boil. Serve hot sprinkled with freshly chopped basil or dill.

Yield: Serves 4
Note: This soup is also delicious served cold. Just pour into jar, refrigerate, and sprinkle with basil or dill when ready to serve.

CAL	F	P:S	SOD	CAR	CHO
110	4	4.2:1	29	16	0

Tomato-Watercress Soup

Take advantage of tomatoes when in season, and enjoy this light, compatible combination of watercress and tomatoes often. It's equally delicious served piping hot or icy cold.

1 *leek, white part only, well washed, and minced*
1 *small onion, minced*
2 *large cloves garlic, minced*
1 *small shallot, minced*
1 *tablespoon corn oil*
1 *teaspoon wine vinegar*
3 *ripe fresh tomatoes, cored and chopped*
1 *tablespoon tomato paste, no salt added (Page 6)*
½ *bunch fresh watercress, leaves only, washed and chopped, 2 tablespoons reserved for garnish*
3½ *cups chicken stock (Page 10)*
½ cup water
4 *dashes cayenne pepper*
Bouquet garni, including ¼ teaspoon fennel seeds, ½ teaspoon thyme leaves, ¼ teaspoon basil leaves, tied together in washed white cotton cheesecloth

Heat oil in large heavy-bottomed saucepan. Sauté onion, garlic, leek, and shallot until wilted but not brown. Add vinegar, and cook two minutes longer. Add chicken stock, water, tomato paste, tomatoes, chopped watercress, cayenne, and bouquet garni. Bring to simmering point, partially cover, and simmer for 20 minutes. Let cool, covered, in saucepan. Remove bouquet garni.

Pour into blender and purée for one minute. Then pour through fine sieve. Serve reheated or chilled sprinkled with chopped watercress.

Yield: Serves 6
Variation: If serving cold, try whisking in ¼ cup low-fat plain yogurt before serving. It thickens soup and makes it creamier.

CAL	F	P:S	SOD	CAR	CHO
129	4	4.5:1	22	14	0
With yogurt					
132	4	4.4:1	26	14+	0

Gazpacho

Fresh vegetables, puréed to perfection and gently spiced, are the basis of my version of the traditional dish from Spanish Andalusia. It's a perfect prelude to a main fish course. Or make a whole luncheon of it accompanied by my crackling French Bread (Page 135).

1 *cup tomato juice, no salt added*
2 *onions, minced*
2 *large cloves garlic, minced*
2 *green peppers, minced*
1 *shallot, minced*
1 *cucumber, peeled and chopped*
¼ *teaspoon smoked yeast (Page 6)*
½ *teaspoon paprika*
8 *dashes cayenne pepper*
½ *teaspoon oregano leaves, crushed*
3 *dashes Dr. Bronner's seasoning (Page 6)*
2 *tablespoons wine vinegar*
1 *tablespoon corn oil*
2 *tablespoons freshly chopped parsley and dill*

Combine ¼ cup tomato juice, onions, garlic, green peppers, shallot, and cucumber in blender. Blend until puréed, adding more juice if mixture is too thick to blend. Add oil, one tablespoon chopped parsley and dill, vinegar, smoked yeast, oregano, paprika, cayenne, and Dr. Bronner's seasoning. Blend again on high speed for 30 seconds. Add balance of tomato juice. Pour into glass jar and refrigerate for 2-3 hours before serving. Sprinkle with balance of freshly chopped parsley and dill, and serve.

Yield: Serves 4
Note: If you're using a food processer, coarsely chop vegetables and follow balance of recipe.
Variation: You may substitute any of the following for oregano: tarragon, basil, or curry powder no salt or pepper added.

CAL	F	P:S	SOD	CAR	CHO
70	4	4.5:1	15	10	0

Chinese Sweet and Pungent Soup

This is a happy marriage of contrasting flavors and textures, which is what Chinese cooking is all about. This lovely-to-look-at soup is simple to make, authentic tasting, and makes a satisfying light repast.

1 *eye of center cut pork chop (1 ounce) cut into thin slivers*
2 *cloves garlic, minced*
1½ *teaspoons fresh ginger, peeled and cut into thin slivers*
2 *teaspoons corn oil*
¾ *cup Chinese cabbage, shredded*
3 *cups chicken stock (Page 10)*
1 *cup water*
1 *tablespoon wine vinegar*
1 *tablespoon white vinegar*
1 *teaspoon honey*
1 *cake bean curd, 2"-3" square, diced*
3 *dashes cayenne pepper*
1 *teaspoon Dr. Bronner's seasoning (Page 6)*
1 *scallion, cut into ½" pieces*
4 *large fresh mushrooms, washed, trimmed and coarsely chopped*
2 *teaspoons dry sherry*

Heat oil in heavy-bottomed saucepan until hot. Add garlic and ginger. Sauté one minute. Add stock, water, and pork. Bring to boil. Turn flame down, and simmer, uncovered, for 10 minutes, removing scum that rises to top. Add mushrooms, bean curd, cabbage, cayenne, and scallion, and simmer for another 5 minutes. Turn heat down very low. Add honey, vinegars, and sherry. Stir well. Bring to just under simmering point. Stir in Dr. Bronner's seasoning. Serve immediately.

Yield: Serves 4

CAL	F	P:S	SOD	CAR	CHO
189	6	4.3:1	28	4	5

French Onion Soup

When a hungry Louis XV returned from a hunting trip to find no provisions in his lodge other than onions, champagne, and butter, he mixed them together, so the story goes, and invented French onion soup. Here's my tangy, slimming version of this regal delight.

4 *large onions, thinly sliced*
1 *large shallot, minced*
1 *large clove garlic, minced*
2 *tablespoons corn oil*
3 *cups beef stock (Page 12)*
1 *cup water*
4 *dashes cayenne pepper*
½ *teaspoon smoked yeast (Page 6)*
¼ *teaspoon dried thyme leaves, crushed*
2 *tablespoons unbleached flour*
4 *thick slices My French Bread (Page 135)*
4 *tablespoons sharp low-fat cheese, grated (Page 3)*
2 *teaspoons wine vinegar*

Heat oil until hot in heavy-bottomed 2-quart saucepan. Add onions, garlic, and shallot and sauté until golden brown, turning constantly (about 10-12 minutes). Sprinkle with flour and continue cooking another 5 minutes, or until mixture is golden brown. Gradually add stock and water, stirring well.

Add thyme, cayenne, and smoked yeast. Bring to boil. Turn flame down and simmer, covered, for 20 minutes. Add vinegar and stir.

Lightly toast bread slices. Pour soup into individual serving dishes, and float one slice of bread on top of each serving. Sprinkle with cheese, and serve.

Yield: Serves 4

CAL	F	P:S	SOD	CAR	CHO
214	8	4.8:1	59	20	3

Vichyssoise

Although most people think this soup is *so* French, it was actually originated by the chef at the Ritz-Carlton in New York. So I've made my version strictly Manhattan haute cuisine. It's as zingy as Madison Avenue, as svelte as Park, and as rich as Fifth.

2 *leeks, white part only, well washed and thinly sliced*
1 *medium onion, minced*
2 *large cloves garlic, minced*
1 *tablespoon corn oil*
2 *medium-sized potatoes, peeled and thinly sliced*
2 *ribs celery, minced*
1 *tablespoon finely minced carrot*
3 *sprigs parsley*
½ *teaspoon powdered thyme*
¼ *teaspoon smoked yeast (Page 6)*
6 *dashes cayenne pepper*
2 *cups chicken stock (Page 10)*
1 *cup water*
3 *tablespoons dry Vermouth or white wine*
2 *teaspoons wine vinegar*
1 *tablespoon low-fat plain yogurt*
1 *cup non-fat milk*
1 *tablespoon freshly chopped dill and parsley*
2 *tablespoons freshly chopped chives or scallion*

Heat oil in heavy-bottomed saucepan until very warm. Add leeks, onion, garlic and celery. Sauté until wilted. Add Vermouth or wine, and cook over high heat for 2 minutes. Add stock, water, potatoes, carrot, parsley sprigs, thyme, smoked yeast, and cayenne pepper. Bring to simmering point. Partially cover and simmer for 20 minutes. Add vinegar and stir. Let cool in pot, partially covered.

Put through food mill. Add milk, chopped parsley and dill, and blend. Whisk in yogurt.

Serve hot or cold sprinkled with chopped chives or chopped scallion.

Yield: Serves 4, one leftover
Variations:

1. Do not use food mill, and serve hot with vegetables intact.

2. If you prefer a smoother textured soup, use a blender instead of food mill. Blend one minute, then pour through fine sieve.

CAL	F	P:S	SOD	CAR	CHO
156	3	3.9:1	79	23	1

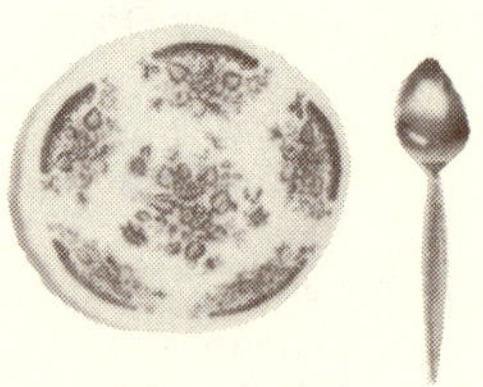

Meatless Lentil Soup

A steaming bowl of this thick flavorsome soup is just the thing when you come in from the icy outdoors. Enjoy it as a first or main course. You can also reduce the liquid and serve it as a deliciously different vegetable side-dish.

1½ cups lentils, washed
3 cloves garlic, minced
1 onion, minced
1 leek, white part only, washed, and minced
½ rib celery, finely minced
1 small carrot, peeled and diced
1 tablespoon corn oil
3 cups chicken stock (Page 10)
2 cups water, or enough to cover lentils
2 teaspoons apple cider vinegar
4 dashes cayenne pepper
½ teaspoon each dried thyme and tarragon leaves, crushed
2 teaspoons tomato paste, no salt added (Page 6)
2 tablespoons arrowroot flour dissolved in 2 tablespoons water (optional)
Bouquet garni

Soak lentils in water to cover until all water is absorbed (about 3 hours). Heat oil in stainless steel pot or waterless cooker until hot. Add onion, garlic, leek, and celery. Sauté until wilted but not brown. Add vinegar and cook over high heat for one minute. Add balance of ingredients, except flour, and bring to boil. Turn heat down and simmer, partially covered, for 1½ hours.

If you want to thicken soup, dribble dissolved flour into simmering soup, stirring constantly, until it reaches desired consistency. Serve hot.

Yield: Serves 6
Variation: To convert into an interesting side dish, reduce the liquid by cooking, uncovered, over medium-high heat, stirring constantly, until quite thick.

CAL	F	P:S	SOD	CAR	CHO
145	2	4.5:1	28	20	0
Thickened					
153	2	4.5:1	28	22	0

Split Pea Soup

Even in days of zooming inflation, dried peas won't put a strain on your budget. And they're so rich in protein and taste so meaty, that they make an admirable alternative to expensive meats. Here are two versions of a lusty, satisfying split pea soup, one with just a suggestion of meat, and the other meatless. You choose.

3 veal bones, cracked and well washed under running water
1¼ cups split peas, washed
2 small carrots, peeled and diced
1 tablespoon corn oil
1 large onion, minced
3 large cloves garlic, minced
1 large shallot, minced
2 cups chicken or veal stock (Pages 10 or 11)
1 cup water
3 dashes cayenne pepper
¼ teaspoon each dried marjoram, thyme, and basil leaves, crushed
½ teaspoon smoked yeast (Page 6)
Large bouquet garni

Place bones in 3-quart kettle. Add water to cover. Bring to boil and cook for 10 minutes. Pour into colander and drain. Wash bones under cold running water.

Rinse out kettle and dry. Add oil, and heat until very warm. Add onion, garlic, and shallot, and sauté until wilted. Add balance of ingredients. Bring to simmering point. Turn heat off and cover. Let stand for one hour.

Reheat to simmering point, and cook, partially covered, for 45 minutes. Let soup cool in pot. Remove bones. Pour into blender and purée for one minute. Reheat and serve.

Yield: Serves 4, one leftover
Variation: *Split Pea Soup Without Bones.* Basic ingredients are the same except for the following increased amounts:

2 *shallots (instead of 1)*
1 *teaspoon smoked yeast (instead of ½)*
½ *teaspoon each thyme and basil leaves (instead of ¼)*

CAL	F	P:S	SOD	CAR	CHO
170	3	4.5:1	35	18	0

Without bones
No appreciable difference

Mushroom and Barley Soup

You won't believe the hearty flavor of this thick, bracing soup until you try it. Crisp firm cloves of garlic make all the difference. Be certain the garlic is minced rather than crushed, and you'll never taste the garlic as such. Serve steaming hot either as a first course (small portion, please) or as a one-dish meal accompanied by my crisp French Bread (Page 135).

1 *tablespoon corn oil*
1 *small onion, minced*
1 *scallion, minced, or ½ leek, white section only, well washed, and minced*
3 *cloves garlic, minced*
1 *small rib celery, minced*
1 *large shallot, minced*
1 *small carrot, peeled and diced*
½ *ounce imported dried dark mushrooms, soaked and minced*
¼ *cup medium barley, washed and drained*
2 *cups chicken stock (Page 10)*
2 *cups water*
½ *teaspoon each dried tarragon and basil leaves, crushed*
2 *teaspoons apple cider vinegar*
4 *dashes smoked yeast (Page 6)*
4 *dashes cayenne pepper*
Large bouquet garni

Heat oil until very warm in medium-sized kettle. Add scallion, onion, garlic, shallot, and celery, and sauté until vegetables and garlic are wilted (about 5 minutes over a medium flame). Add chicken stock and balance of ingredients. Bring to a slow boil. Turn flame down. Partially cover and simmer for 45 minutes, stirring from time to time to prevent ingredients from sticking to bottom of kettle. Taste. You may want to add a touch more of smoked yeast or cayenne. Re-cover and continue simmering for another 20 minutes. Turn off flame, and let soup cool, covered, for one hour before serving.

To serve, reheat over a low flame.

Yield: Serves 4
Note: This soup improves in flavor if it is prepared a day ahead, stored in a glass container in your refrigerator, and slowly reheated at serving time.
Variation: At end of cooking time, when soup has cooled down, add 2 heaping tablespoons plain low-fat yogurt and blend. Reheat over very low flame taking care that soup does not boil.

CAL	F	P:S	SOD	CAR	CHO
116	4	4.5:1	44	20	0
With yogurt					
123	2	3.2:1	52	22	1

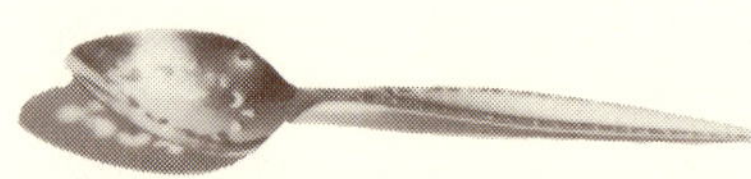

Cabbage Soup—It's A Whole Meal!

There's nothing as welcome as a thick, steaming plate of cabbage soup on a winter's day. It's instant warmth, and packs all the nutrition you've come to expect from the main meal of the day. Serve it with my crusty heated French Bread (Page 135) and there will be calls for seconds.

1 *small head green cabbage, about 1½ pounds, sliced ¼" thick and 2" long*
1 *veal bone*
½ *pound lean soup meat, such as top or bottom round, or shin*
2 *tablespoons corn oil*
5 *cups water*
1 *rib celery, diced*
1 *carrot, peeled and diced*
¼ *cup yellow turnip, peeled and diced*
3 *large fresh mushrooms, trimmed, washed, and coarsely chopped*
3 *large cloves garlic, minced*
1 *large onion, minced*
1 *tablespoon apple cider vinegar*
3 *tablespoons fresh lemon juice*
1 *tablespoon honey*
¼ *cup brown beef stock (Page 13)*
1 *can tomatoes, no salt added (8½ oz.)*
1 *tablespoon tomato paste, no salt added (Page 6)*
1½ *tablespoons regular cream of wheat (optional)*
¾ *teaspoon dried thyme leaves, crushed*
1 *teaspoon caraway seeds*
Bouquet garni, including 1 sprig dill, 1 sprig parsley, and 4 whole cloves, tied together in washed cotton cheesecloth

Pour 3 cups water into a large kettle. Add bouquet garni, veal bone and meat. Bring to boil. Reduce heat, and cook for 2 minutes. Remove scum that rises to top. Cover partially, and simmer for one hour.

While meat is cooking, prepare all the vegetables. Then heat oil in a large iron skillet until very warm. Add garlic, and all vegetables except tomatoes and cabbage. Brown lightly, continually turning with large spoon. Add cabbage, half at a time, and continue to cook until cabbage browns lightly. (Volume will shrink after 5 minutes of cooking and turning.) Add vinegar, lemon juice, and honey, stirring well. Then add brown stock, tomatoes, tomato paste, thyme, and caraway seeds. Cook for 5 minutes.

Pour vegetable mixture into meat which has cooked one hour, and add two more cups water. Bring to boil. Sprinkle cream of wheat into pot and stir. Simmer, partially covered, for one hour, stirring from time to time.

Cool in pot, covered. Remove bouquet garni. If using the same day, reheat and serve.

Yield: Serves 6
Note: Cream of wheat is a thickening agent. The quantity (1½ tablespoons) will just provide a hint of thickening. Omit it if you prefer your soup not thickened at all.

CAL	F	P:S	SOD	CAR	CHO
172	7	3.5:1	74	18	27
Thickened					
176	7	3.5:1	74	19	27

Bracing Fish Chowder

Fresh fish, cooked to perfection with a delicate blend of herbs and spices, comes to the table as a subtle but far from bland chowder. A far cry from the coarse, heavily peppered commercial product.

1 *pound fresh haddock or cod fillets, cut into 2" pieces*
1 *tablespoon corn oil*
2 *medium-sized onions, cut in half, then sliced*
1 *rib celery, diced*
2 *cloves garlic, minced*
1 *large shallot, minced*
½ *carrot, peeled and diced*
2 *small potatoes, preferably Idaho or russet, peeled and diced*
1 *cup fish stock (Page 11)*
1 *cup water*
½ *teaspoon smoked yeast (Page 6)*
2 *sprigs watercress, leaves only, chopped*
1½ *cups non-fat milk, warmed*
1 *bay leaf*
2 *teaspoons regular cream of wheat*
½ *teaspoon dried tarragon leaves, crushed*
4-5 *dashes cayenne pepper*
2 *dashes powdered cloves*
Freshly chopped parsley

Heat oil in heavy-bottomed 2-quart saucepan until warm. Add onions, garlic, shallot, and celery. Sauté over medium heat for 3 minutes, turning constantly. Add wine, and cook for 2 minutes. Add potatoes, carrot, stock, water, cloves, tarragon, bay leaf, cayenne and smoked yeast. Bring to simmering point. Sprinkle with cream of wheat, stirring well. Partially cover, and simmer for 10 minutes.

Add fish and watercress. Simmer until fish flakes easily (about 15 minutes). Add warm milk and stir well. Pour into heated soup dishes. Sprinkle with freshly chopped parsley. Serve with my crackling French Herb Bread, (Page 136).

Yield: Serves 4

CAL	F	P:S	SOD	CAR	CHO
Haddock					
209	4	4.4:1	160	23	80
Cod					
209	4	4.4:1	170	23	80

Fish

Jellied Tile Fish

Go out of your way to find this exquisitely textured fish. It tastes a bit like lobster—and that's a bit of undiluted heaven to fish lovers. Served chilled, it perks up even the most sultry summer day. And for the cool of the evening, try it hot with my creamy sauce.

2 *slices tile fish, 1½ pounds, each slice cut in half*
2 *tablespoons apple cider vinegar*
½ *small carrot, peeled and sliced*
1 *small onion, thinly sliced*
2 *cloves garlic, minced*
1 *large shallot, minced*
4 *dashes cayenne pepper*
½ *cup fish stock (Page 11)*
½ *cup apple juice or cider, no sugar added*
½ *crisp sweet apple, such as Washington State, cored, peeled and diced*
Bouquet garni made up of 1 sprig dill, 1 sprig parsley, 5 whole cloves, ½ teaspoon dried tarragon leaves, 1 small bay leaf, tied together in washed cotton cheesecloth
Freshly chopped parsley and dill

Arrange fish in one layer in a heavy-bottomed saucepan. Add balance of ingredients except freshly chopped herbs. Bring to simmering point. Cover partially and simmer gently for 20 minutes. Let cool in saucepan.

Remove fish with slotted spoon and place in a storage bowl. Remove carrots and add to bowl. Strain liquid into bowl, pressing herbs gently. Refrigerate, and serve sprinkled with freshly chopped parsley and dill. The liquid will jell when cold.

Yield: Serves 4
Variation: After cooked fish has cooled, transfer with slotted spoon to another saucepan. Add a quarter cup of strained cooking liquid. Reheat fish over very low heat.

Remove bouquet garni. Pour balance of cooking liquid with vegetables into blender. Blend for one minute. The liquid will thicken to a creamy consistency. Reheat sauce over low heat and serve in sauceboat with warm fish.

CAL	F	P:S	SOD	CAR	CHO
Jellied or with sauce					
109	0	—	84	3	45

Poached Flounder with Savory Sauce

Flounder is one of those simple fish that needs a deft touch in the kitchen to achieve gourmet status. Here it's tenderly poached in a flavorsome court bouillon and served with a creamy pungent sauce.

For the court bouillon:
1 *leek, white part only, well washed, split lengthwise, coarsely chopped*
2 *large cloves garlic, coarsely chopped*
2 *large shallots, coarsely chopped*
½ *onion, sliced*
1 *rib celery, cut into 1" slices*
1 *carrot, peeled and thinly sliced*
1 *thin slice lemon*
4 *cups water*
4 *dashes cayenne pepper*
4 *whole cloves*
¼ *teaspoon dried thyme leaves*
1½ *cups dry Vermouth or white wine*
½ *cup fish stock or water (Page 11)*
Bouquet garni including ½ teaspoon fennel, tied together in washed cotton cheesecloth

For the fish:
1½ *pounds flounder fillets, cut into serving pieces*
Freshly chopped parsley

For the sauce:
¾ *cup fish stock, room temperature (Page 11)*
½ *cup chicken stock (Page 10)*
2 *tablespoons dry Vermouth or white wine*
1 *small onion, minced*
½ *rib celery, coarsely chopped*
1 *shallot, minced*
1 *large clove garlic, finely minced*
4 *large fresh mushrooms, washed, dried, trimmed and coarsely chopped*
1 *tablespoon non-fat dry milk*
4 *large sprigs fresh watercress, leaves only, washed, dried, and coarsely chopped*
1 *large dollop low-fat plain yogurt*
1 *heaping tablespoon duxelles (Page 13)*

Prepare the court bouillon first. Place all ingredients in large kettle. Bring to boil. Turn heat down, cover, and simmer for 20 minutes. Court bouillon is now ready for poaching.

Prepare the sauce next. Combine fish stock, wine, mushrooms, onion, celery, garlic, and shallot in a heavy-bottomed saucepan, and heat to simmering point. Lower heat and continue cooking for 7 minutes, partially covered, stirring from time to time.

Whisk dry milk into chicken stock until blended. Add to hot mixture and simmer for 2 minutes. Add watercress and duxelles and simmer another minute. Uncover and let stand while you poach the fish.

If you have a poacher. Bring court bouillon to simmering point. Pat fish dry with paper toweling. Place fish on rack and lower into court bouillon. Bring to simmering point again, turn heat down, and simmer, covered, for

12-15 minutes depending upon the thickness of fish.

If you don't have a poacher. Arrange fish on double piece of washed cheesecloth. Fold cheesecloth around fish. Tie ends securely with white thread. Gently lower into simmering court bouillon and continue according to directions given for poacher.

Pour prepared sauce mixture into blender and purée for one minute. Pour back into saucepan. Whisk in yogurt. Reheat over very low heat, taking care that mixture doesn't boil.

Remove fish from court bouillon and drain. Serve on heated individual plates. Pour sauce over fish and serve, sprinkled with freshly chopped parsley.

Yield: Serves 4
Note: Court bouillon can be frozen and used once more.

	CAL	F	P:S	SOD	CAR	CHO
	77	0	—	90	5	61
Sauce	50	2	1.9:1	35	4	0

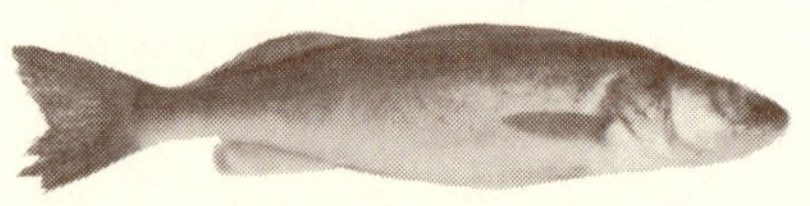

Baked Pike with Mustard Sauce

How do you make an ordinary fish extraordinary? Bake it with flavor-enriching vegetables and herbs, then bathe it in a creamy white sauce accented with the sharp edge of mustard. Totally irresistible!

For the fish:
1 *pike, 3 pounds, cleaned, head left on*
1 *tablespoon corn oil, plus ½ teaspoon to coat baking dish*
2 *large cloves garlic, minced*
2 *shallots, minced*
1 *small onion, finely minced*
¼ *teaspoon dried thyme leaves, crushed*
¼ *teaspoon fennel seeds, crushed*
1 *teaspoon smoked yeast (Page 6)*
2 *dashes cayenne pepper*
2 *sprigs each parsley and dill*

For the sauce:
1½ *tablespoons corn oil*
1½ *tablespoons unbleached flour*
1 *shallot, finely minced*
2 *tablespoons dry Vermouth or white wine*
⅛ *teaspoon ground cloves*
2 *teaspoons dry mustard dissolved in 2 teaspoons water*
½ *cup warmed fish stock (Page 11)*
1¼ *cups warmed non-fat milk*
2 *dashes cayenne pepper*
1 *tablespoon freshly chopped parsley*

Wash fish inside and out under cold running water. Dry well with paper toweling. Make 4-5 diagonal gashes across fish on each side. Combine cayenne, thyme, smoked yeast and fennel. Rub cavity and skin with mixture. Stuff cavity with herb sprigs. Secure with skewers. Cover and let stand at room temperature for one hour before baking.

Heat oil until hot in teflon skillet. Sauté onion, garlic, and shallots until wilted. Spoon over both sides of fish, pressing into gashes. Bake, uncovered, in preheated 400 degree oven for 15 minutes. Baste. Cover and bake for 15-20 minutes, or until fish flakes easily. Transfer to heated serving platter.

While fish is baking prepare the sauce. Heat oil in heavy-bottomed saucepan until hot. Add shallot and sauté until wilted. Add flour and cook for 2 minutes, stirring constantly. Add wine and cook for one minute. Add stock and blend with whisk. Add milk, mustard, cayenne, and cloves, whisking until thickened. Add parsley and stir. Serve immediately (do not reheat) in sauceboat with fish.

Yield: Serves 4

CAL	F	P:S	SOD	CAR	CHO
117	5	3.7:1	68	2	66
Sauce					
48	5	4.5:1	24	5	0

Stuffed Baby Sole Roll-Ups

When is a fillet of sole not a fillet of sole? When it's wrapped around my herb bread stuffing, and bathed in zesty pan juices. A delightfully refreshing departure from high-calorie saline fried fillets.

1½ pounds baby sole fillets (8 fillets)
¼ cup wine vinegar
½ teaspoon ground ginger
1 tablespoon corn oil
2 cloves garlic, minced
2 shallots, minced
1 small green pepper, minced
1½ cups My French Herb Bread for stuffing (Page 136)
½ cup fish stock (Page 11)
¼ cup chicken stock (Page 10)
3 dashes Dr. Bronner's seasoning (Page 6)
4 dashes cayenne pepper
2 tablespoons freshly chopped parsley

Pour vinegar into medium-sized bowl. Add fillets and marinate at room temperature for one hour, turning once.

Now prepare stuffing. Heat oil in small skillet, and sauté garlic, shallots, and green pepper until wilted but not brown. Reserve half sautéed mixture for sauce, and transfer balance to bowl. Break up bread for stuffing into small pieces. Add to half of sautéed mixture and toss together with 2 dashes cayenne and one tablespoon freshly chopped parsley and dill.

In a small saucepan, heat combined stocks until warm. Then add just enough bread mixture to dampen bread and make it spreadable (about 2 tablespoons).

Remove fillets from marinade, reserving marinade. Dry well with paper toweling. Lay each fillet flat. Spoon a tablespoon of stuffing mixture on top of each fillet, and spread evenly. Roll up and secure with toothpicks. Place in lightly oiled casserole large enough to hold fillets in one layer.

Reheat stock. Add 2 tablespoons reserved marinade, balance of sautéed mixture, ginger, Dr. Bronner's seasoning, and balance of cayenne. Stir to blend. Pour over roll-ups. Cover and bake in preheated 400 degree oven for 10 minutes. Remove cover and baste fillets. Return to oven and bake uncovered for another 10 minutes.

Transfer roll-ups to serving platter. Cover to keep warm. Pour cooking liquid and vegetables into blender and blend for one minute. Reheat and pour over fish. Sprinkle roll-ups with fresh parsley and dill, and serve.

Yield: Serves 4

CAL	F	P:S	SOD	CAR	CHO
215	5	3.4:1	201	10	61

Simple Sautéed Fillet of Lemon Sole #1

Fillet of sole is the All-American fried-fish favorite. Here lemon sole—so firmly textured it can be turned successfully in the skillet—is sautéed instead. Enjoy it *au naturel* (this recipe) or lightly coated with flour (the next). Either way, it's a tangy, succulent dish.

1½ *pounds fresh lemon sole, cut into serving pieces*
3 *cloves garlic, minced*
2 *shallots, minced*
2 *tablespoons corn oil*
¼ *teaspoon combined dill and fennel seeds, crushed*
½ *teaspoon combined dried tarragon, basil, and parsley leaves, crushed*
1 *tablespoon wine vinegar*
½ *teaspoon Dr. Bronner's seasoning (Page 6)*

Wipe fish dry with paper toweling. An hour before cooking, sprinkle with herbs and seeds. Press gently into fish on both sides. Cover, and set aside at room temperature.

Cook fish in two batches as follows: Heat half of oil in teflon skillet until hot. Add half of shallots and garlic and sauté for 2 minutes. Spread evenly over skillet. Place half of fish over sautéed mixture and cook over medium-high heat for 5 minutes. Turn carefully with spatula and cook on second side for 3 minutes. Add half of vinegar and cook for one minute. Add half of Dr. Bronner's seasoning, and cook for an additional minute, tilting skillet so that liquid is equally distributed. Transfer to heated serving platter.

Add balance of ingredients to skillet, and cook second batch of fish in the same way. Transfer to heated serving platter, and serve immediately.

Yield: Serves 4
Note: Excellent served on my crisp, heated French Bread (Page 135).

CAL	F	P:S	SOD	CAR	CHO
113	8	4.3:1	52	2	92

Simple Sautéed Fillet of Lemon Sole #2

1½ *pounds fillet of lemon sole, cut into serving pieces*
½ *cup unbleached flour*
¼ *teaspoon combined dill and fennel seeds, lightly crushed*
½ *teaspoon combined dried tarragon, basil, and parsley leaves, crushed*
4 *dashes cayenne pepper*
⅓ *cup non-fat milk*
2 *cloves garlic, minced*
2 *shallots, minced*
2 *tablespoons corn oil*
1 *tablespoon freshly chopped chives or scallion*
Lemon wedges

Combine flour with dried herbs, seeds, and cayenne. Wipe fish dry with paper toweling. Dip into milk and then into flour mixture, coating well. Place on plate in one layer, cover, and refrigerate for one hour before cooking.

Cook fish in two batches as follows:

Heat half of oil in large teflon skillet until hot. Add half of garlic and shallots, and sauté for 2 minutes. Spread evenly over skillet. Place half of fish over sautéed mixture and cook over medium heat for 5 minutes. Turn carefully with spatula, and cook on second side until lightly browned. Don't overcook. Transfer to heated serving platter and keep warm.

Add balance of ingredients to skillet, and cook second batch of fish in the same way. Transfer to heated serving platter. Sprinkle with chives or scallions, garnish with lemon wedges, and serve.

Yield: Serves 4
Note: Fillet of flounder may be substituted successfully for fillet of sole.

CAL	F	P:S	SOD	CAR	CHO
218	8	4.3:1	58	13	92

Flounder
No appreciable difference

Quenelles with Mushroom Sauce

These lighter-than-air dumplings are a combination of ground fish with my version of pate-a-choux (a seasoned egg-flour-oil mixture), subtly accented with herbs and spices, and gently simmered in an herb-enriched stock. Served under a blanket of velvety mushroom sauce, they're pure heaven!

For the quenelles:
1¼ *pounds fillet of lemon sole or pike, cut into 1" pieces*
2 *large eggs, using half of one yolk, and both whites*
1 *cup non-fat milk, extra strength, prepared by using ⅓ less water than called for by instructions*
½ *cup unbleached flour*
¼ *teaspoon ground nutmeg*
½ *teaspoon dried tarragon leaves, crushed*
2 *teaspoons freshly chopped parsley and dill*
¼ *teaspoon powdered thyme*
3 *tablespoons corn oil, plus ½ teaspoon to oil baking dish*
2 *shallots, finely minced*
3 *dashes cayenne pepper*
1 *bay leaf*
5 cups water

For the sauce:
2 *tablespoons corn oil*
1½ *tablespoons unbleached flour*
½ *cup dry Vermouth or white wine*
¼ *pound fresh mushrooms, washed, dried, trimmed, and thinly sliced*
1 *shallot, finely minced*
½ *cup fish stock (Page 11)*
½ *cup chicken stock (Page 10)*
1 *cup non-fat milk, extra strength*
¼ *teaspoon dried tarragon leaves, crushed*
2 *dashes cayenne pepper*

Prepare quenelles first. In a heavy-bottomed saucepan combine egg yolk, flour, 2 dashes cayenne and nutmeg. Whisk well. Add oil and whisk again. Warm ¾ cup milk and pour into saucepan, whisking constantly. Add tarragon and cook over medium heat, continuing to whisk until mixture is very thick (about 5 minutes). Let cool, partially covered.

Grind fish with shallots, balance of cayenne, thyme and balance of milk, using grinder or food processer. Turn into bowl of mixing machine. Add cooled mixture in small amounts at a time, beating well after each addition. Add egg whites, parsley and dill, and beat well.

Lightly oil an oblong baking dish (17" × 11" × 2"). Shape fish into 12 balls, using 2 spoons moistened continually with hot water to prevent sticking, arranging balls in four rows in pan. Cover lightly with waxed paper and refrigerate for one hour.

Quenelles are now going to be cooked in simmering water. Remove waxed paper. Place quenelles on top of stove. Bring 5 cups water to boil in saucepan. Add bay leaf and boil for 2 minutes. Gently pour water around quenelles—never directly on them (they're fragile and break easily). Turn heat on under pan and bring to simmering point. Continue to simmer, very gently, for 12 minutes, basting twice. Quenelles will puff up.

Start to prepare sauce while quenelles are simmering. Heat one tablespoon oil until hot in teflon skillet. Add mushrooms and shallot, and sauté until lightly browned. Add wine, and cook over medium-high heat for 3 minutes. Set aside.

In heavy-bottomed saucepan, heat balance of oil until hot. Add flour and whisk well. Cook for 2 minutes over medium heat. Add stocks, cayenne, and tarragon, whisking continually. Pour in sautéed mixture and stir. Finally, add milk and cook over low heat, stirring frequently, for 10 minutes. Sauce should not boil.

Transfer quenelles with slotted spoon to heated individual plates.

Gently spoon sauce over quenelles, and serve immediately.

Yield: Serves 4 for main course; serves 6 for first course

CAL	F	P:S	SOD	CAR	CHO
First course					
155	9	4.1:1	115	7	61
Sauce					
72	4	4.5:1	27	5	0
Main course					
233	13	4.1:1	172	10	91
Sauce					
108	6	4.5:1	40	7	0

Whiting Baked in Red Wine

Whiting is one of those misunderstood fish that's usually breaded and deep-fried. But once you get to know the sweetness and delicate texture of this favorite of true fish lovers, you'll never want to disguise its charms again. Try this simple recipe for a surprising treat.

- 2 *whitings, $1\frac{1}{2}$ pounds each, cleaned, heads left on*
- ½ *teaspoon each dried thyme and rosemary leaves, crushed*
- 1 *tablespoon corn oil*
- 4 *dill sprigs and 4 parsley sprigs*
- 1 *rib celery, minced*
- 1 *bay leaf*
- 1 *onion, minced*
- 2 *cloves garlic, minced*
- 2 *shallots, minced*
- 1 *carrot, peeled and finely diced*
- 4 *dashes cayenne pepper*
- ¼ *cup water*
- 1 *cup red wine*

Wash fish inside and out. Dry well. Make 3-4 gashes on each side of fish. Rub well with dried herbs. Sprinkle with cayenne. Cover and let stand at room temperature for one hour.

When ready to cook, fill cavities of fish with equal amounts of carrot, parsley and dill sprigs. Close with thin skewers.

Heat oil in small skillet until hot. Sauté onion, celery, garlic, and shallots until wilted but not brown. Add water, wine, and bay leaf. Bring to boil. Reduce heat and simmer, uncovered, for 3 minutes.

Line a rectangular pan, large enough to hold fish flat, with aluminum foil. Place fish on foil. Pour hot vegetable-wine mixture over fish. Cover with another piece of aluminum foil, and bake in preheated 400 degree oven for 10 minutes. Remove from oven, baste, cover, and return to oven for 10-12 minutes. Transfer fish carefully to heated serving platter. Spoon with cooking liquid and vegetables, and serve.

Yield: Serves 4

CAL	F	P:S	SOD	CAR	CHO
181	7	3.0:1	126	4	73

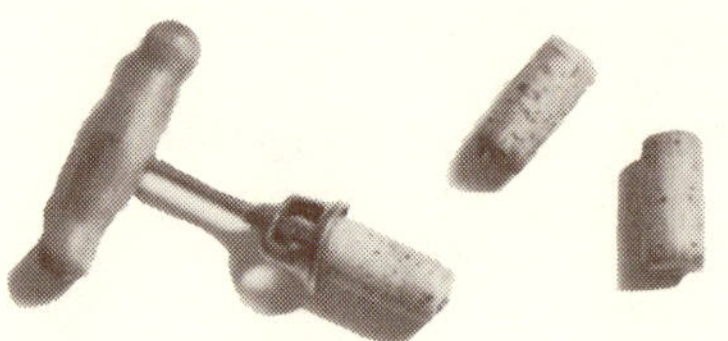

Cod Fish in Court Bouillon

Cod has a special crunchiness that is preserved by poaching (the boiling point, which can wreak havoc with the texture of a fish, is never reached). This sweet-fleshed fish, with its flavor enhanced by court bouillon, emerges from the poacher firm and resistant to crumbling. Feast on it as is, or work it into two versions of artfully simple fish cakes as described in the two recipes that follow.

2 *pounds cod fish, cut into 4 pieces*
1 *rib celery and leaves, coarsely chopped*
1 *large onion, quartered*
1 *cup fish stock (Page 11)*
2 *cups water*
⅓ *cup dry Vermouth or white wine*
1 *carrot, peeled and sliced*
½ *teaspoon vegetable concentrate (Page 6)*
½ *teaspoon dried tarragon leaves*
1 *teaspoon freshly chopped dill, or ½ teaspoon dill weed*
4 *dashes cayenne pepper*
Small bouquet garni
2 *teaspoons arrowroot flour dissolved in 2 teaspoons water (optional)*

Place fish in stainless steel pot or waterless cooker wide enough to hold 4 pieces of fish in one layer. Add balance of ingredients, except flour. Bring to simmering point. Partially cover, and simmer for 15 minutes, or until fish flakes easily. Do not overcook.

Remove cover and let fish cool in liquid. When ready to serve, reheat. Remove fish from liquid with slotted spoon and keep warm. Discard bouquet garni.

Reduce liquid by half over high heat. Pour contents of pot into blender and purée for one minute. Reheat to simmering point. Sauce is now ready to serve. If you prefer a thickened sauce, dribble arrowroot flour into simmering sauce, adding only enough to reach desired consistency.

Yield: Serves 4

CAL	F	P:S	SOD	CAR	CHO
77	0	—	94	5	61
Thickened					
81	0	—	94	6	61

Sautéed Cod Fish Cakes

1 *recipe Cod Fish in Court Bouillon, including puréed sauce, blended but unthickened (Page 48)*
3 *baking potatoes such as Idaho or russet, either baked and mashed with fork, or peeled, cut, boiled and mashed with fork*
2½ *tablespoons corn oil*
2 *shallots, minced*
2 *large cloves garlic, minced*
1 *tablespoon non-fat milk*
½ *cup plus 1 tablespoon bread crumbs (Page 147)*
¼ *teaspoon smoked yeast (Page 6)*
½ *teaspoon dried mustard dissolved in ½ teaspoon water*
1 *egg white, lightly beaten with fork*
½ *teaspoon dried tarragon leaves, crushed*
1 *teaspoon firmly packed freshly chopped parsley*
1 *teaspoon dry sherry*
3 *dashes cayenne pepper*
Lemon wedges (optional)

Reheat cod fish in court bouillon. Remove fish from bones and place in bowl. Combine ⅓-½ cup puréed sauce with fish and mash with fork. Set aside.

Heat one tablespoon oil in teflon skillet until hot. Sauté garlic and shallots until wilted. Combine mashed potatoes with ½ tablespoon oil together with smoked yeast, one tablespoon crumbs, herbs, mustard, cayenne, sherry and egg white. Add potato mixture to mashed fish, together with sautéed garlic and shallots. Add just enough milk to make mixture smooth. Shape into 8 round cakes.

Dip each cake into remaining crumbs, coating evenly. Place on plate in one layer. Cover with saran wrap and refrigerate for at least one hour.

Heat balance of oil in teflon skillet until hot. Sauté cakes on both sides until golden brown. Drain on paper toweling. Serve with lemon wedges or with balance of heated blended sauce.

Yield: Serves 4

CAL	F	P:S	SOD	CAR	CHO
208	9	4.1:1	49	10	61

Broiled Cod Fish Cakes

1 *recipe Sautéed Cod Fish Cakes, using only 1 tablespoon bread crumbs, cakes not breaded (Page 49)*
2 *shallots, minced*
2 *teaspoons fresh lemon or lime juice*
1½ *tablespoons corn oil, plus ½ teaspoon to oil dish*
2 *dashes Dr. Bronner's seasoning (Page 6)*
Lemon or lime wedges

Sprinkle cod fish cakes on both sides with lemon or lime juice. Heat 1½ tablespoons oil in teflon skillet until hot. Sauté shallots until wilted but not brown. Add Dr. Bronner's seasoning, blending well. Spread half of mixture over one side of fish cakes.

Arrange in lightly oiled baking dish in one layer. Broil 1½" from heat until lightly browned. Turn. Spread with balance of mixture and broil until browned. Serve with lemon or lime wedges.

Yield: Serves 4

CAL	F	P:S	SOD	CAR	CHO
248	13	4.4:1	50	4	61

Poached Scrod with Creole Sauce

When a fish doesn't seem to have much flavor of its own, it's usually breaded and deep-fried. And that's the fate of scrod in most kitchens. But that's not really fair to the fish, because scrod has a wonderful potential when treated right. Here it's poached and adorned with a spicy sauce—and a simple fish becomes a sophisticated dish. Reasonable, too!

For the fish:
1½ *pounds fillet of scrod*
1 *recipe court bouillon (Page 48)*
¼ *teaspoon each dried rosemary and thyme leaves, crushed*

For the Creole Sauce:
2 *tablespoons corn oil*
1 *large shallot, minced*
2 *large cloves garlic, minced*
1 *small green pepper, finely minced*
1 *large onion, minced*
¼ *pound fresh mushrooms, washed, dried, trimmed, and sliced*
1 *can tomatoes, (8¼ oz.) no salt added, chopped, ½ liquid drained*
¾ *teaspoon dried tarragon leaves, crushed*
¼ *teaspoon each dried basil and thyme leaves, crushed*
2-3 *dashes cayenne pepper*
¼ *teaspoon dry mustard dissolved in ½ teaspoon water*
¼ *teaspoon smoked yeast (Page 6)*
2 *tablespoons dry Vermouth or white wine*
½ *cup fish stock (Page 11)*
½ *teaspoon curry powder, no salt or pepper added*
1 *bay leaf*
1 *tablespoon freshly chopped parsley and dill*
1 *tablespoon arrowroot flour dissolved in 1 tablespoon water*

Prepare sauce first. Heat one tablespoon oil in large teflon skillet until hot.

Add mushrooms and sauté for 2 minutes. Transfer to bowl and set aside. Heat balance of oil in skillet until hot. Sauté onion, garlic, shallot, and green pepper until lightly browned, turning often. Add wine and cook for one minute. Add stock, herbs, mustard, cayenne, bay leaf, curry, and smoked yeast. Stir well. Add tomatoes. Bring to simmering point, partially cover, and simmer for 45 minutes. Let stand, covered, for one hour.

Prepare scrod for poaching according to directions for Poached Flounder with Savory Sauce (Page 43). Poach fish for 15 minutes. Remove from court bouillon and drain. Arrange on heated individual plates.

Add mushrooms to sauce, and bring to simmering point. Dribble only enough arrowroot flour into sauce to produce a light thickening. Pour over fish, and serve.

Yield: Serves 4

CAL	F	P:S	SOD	CAR	CHO
81	0	—	98	0	64
Sauce					
103	6	4.5:1	17	9	0

Broiled Eastern Halibut with Dill Sauce

Eastern halibut is one of the more delicious denizens of the cold waters of the Atlantic. Here it is broiled simply with just a soupçon of seasoning to accentuate its clear, meaty flavor. Enjoy it as it comes off the broiler, or spoon on my airy, delicate dill sauce.

For the fish and marinade:

- 2 *slices eastern halibut cut into 4 serving pieces, 1¼ pounds*
- 2 *shallots, minced*
- ½ *onion, minced*
- 2 *cloves garlic, minced*
- 4 *dashes cayenne pepper*
- 1 *teaspoon wine vinegar*
- 1 *tablespoon corn oil*

For the dill sauce:

- 1 *tablespoon corn oil*
- 1 *tablespoon unbleached flour*
- ½ *cup chicken or fish stock (Page 10 or 11)*
- ½-¾ *cup non-fat milk*
- 3 *tablespoons fresh dill, minced*
- 3 *dashes smoked yeast (Page 6)*
- 3 *dashes cayenne pepper*

First prepare marinade by combining all ingredients, except fish, in a bowl and blending well. Dip fish in marinade, turning to coat. Let stand, covered, for one hour.

Place coated fish in shallow baking pan. Broil 2″ from heat for 10 minutes. Turn carefully, baste, and broil on second side for 5-10 minutes, or until fish flakes easily when tested with fork. Serve immediately with lemon wedges or dill sauce.

Prepare the sauce while fish is broiling. Heat oil in heavy-bottomed saucepan until hot but not smoking. Add flour and beat with whisk for 2 minutes while mixture bubbles. Pour in stock, whisking constantly as mixture thickens. Add ½ cup milk, cayenne, and smoked yeast, whisking well for one minute. Add dill and continue cooking over very low heat for 5 minutes, stirring constantly. If too thick, thin with a little more milk. Pour over fish and serve immediately. Do not reheat.

Yield: Serves 4

CAL	F	P:S	SOD	CAR	CHO
149	5	3.0:1	48	2	82
Sauce					
72	6	4.5:1	22	4	0

Baked Porgy with Lime Sauce

The mildly sharp lime sauce, creamy-smooth, offers a pleasing counter texture to the firm crunchiness of this sweet-fleshed fish. Baking, my style, retains the full flavorsome succulence of the fish while enhancing its texture.

1 *porgy, 3-3½ pounds, cleaned, head left on*
4 *teaspoons fresh lime juice*
1 *tablespoon corn oil, plus ½ teaspoon to oil baking dish*
2 *fresh mushrooms, washed, dried, trimmed, and coarsely chopped*
2 *cloves garlic, minced*
½ *rib celery, minced*
1 *small onion, minced*
1 *shallot, minced*
½ *green pepper, finely minced*
½ *carrot, peeled and finely diced*
¼ *teaspoon smoked yeast (Page 6)*
2 *sprigs parsley and 1 sprig dill*
1 *teaspoon dried savory leaves, crushed*
4 *dashes cayenne pepper*
½ *cup fish stock (Page 11)*
½ *cup vegetable broth, see Note*

Wash fish well inside and out under cold running water. Pat dry with paper toweling. Make 4-5 diagonal gashes across fish on each side. Sprinkle inside and out with 2 teaspoons lime juice. Cover and refrigerate for 2 hours.

Combine vegetables and garlic. Pat fish dry with paper toweling. Brush with oil. Sprinkle with savory. Fill cavity with dill and parsley sprigs and 3 tablespoons vegetable-garlic mixture.

Lightly oil baking dish long enough to hold fish flat. Spread half of remaining vegetable-garlic mixture into dish. Lay fish on top of mixture. Strew balance of mixture on top of fish. Sprinkle with cayenne.

Combine fish stock, vegetable broth, and smoked yeast. Pour over fish. Cover with aluminum foil and bake in preheated 425 degree oven for 25 minutes. Uncover and baste. Return to oven and bake, uncovered, for 5 minutes.

Transfer fish to heated serving platter and cover to keep warm. Pour vegetables and liquid into blender and purée until smooth. Reheat, adding balance of lime juice, stirring well.

Skin fish, remove from bone, and serve on heated individual plates. Spoon hot sauce over each portion, and serve.

Yield: Serves 4
Note: Vegetable broth is made from leftover juices from cooking such vegetables as string beans, carrots, cabbage, and so on. It works particularly well with this recipe. If, however, you have none on hand, you may substitute chicken stock (Page 10).

CAL	F	P:S	SOD	CAR	CHO
206	9	2.2:1	130	5	79

Baked Striped Bass Steaks

The strong, firm, meaty flesh of this incomparable fish is caressed by tangy herbs and shallots, and cosseted by wine, making a dish of fantastic succulence and flavor. Truly, a four-star experience.

2 *striped bass steaks, cut from large fish, 1½ pounds, each steak cut in half along length of bone*
3 *cloves garlic, finely minced*
3 *shallots, finely minced*
2 *tablespoons freshly chopped parsley*
Juice of ½ lime
½ *teaspoon dried thyme leaves, crushed*
4 *dashes cayenne pepper*
⅓ *cup dry Vermouth or red wine (try it both ways; either will make a delicious dish)*

Wipe fish dry with paper toweling. Rub lime juice into fish on both sides. Sprinkle with thyme and cayenne.

Line shallow baking dish with aluminum foil. Sprinkle half of parsley into pan. Strew half of garlic and shallots over parsley. Lay fish on top of herb-shallot mixture. Sprinkle balance of herbs and shallots over fish. Cover with aluminum foil. Bake in preheated 400 degree oven for 12 minutes.

Remove from oven and pour wine over fish. Re-cover, and bake for 12 minutes. Serve immediately with pan juices spooned over fish.

Yield: Serves 4

CAL	F	P:S	SOD	CAR	CHO
192	2	1.9:1	117	3	75

Chinese Steamed Sea Bass

Sea bass is a Chinese favorite, and deservedly so. It's a sweet firm-textured fish, remarkably suited to steaming. It's simple to prepare, makes use of only a handful of ingredients, and produces a heavenly delight, tangy with the flavors of the Orient.

1 *sea bass, 3-3½ pounds, cleaned, left whole*
2 *teaspoons fresh ginger, peeled and cut into thin slivers*
3 *scallions, thinly sliced for cooking*
2 *scallions, thinly sliced for garnish*
3 *tablespoons dry Vermouth or white wine*
2 *large cloves garlic, cut into quarters*
¼ *cup corn oil*
1 *tablespoon Dr. Bronner's seasoning (Page 6)*

Use a steamer, or devise your own employing a very large pot with a tight-fitting cover, and a slightly narrower and shorter bowl. Pour 1½-2″ of water into pot. Insert bowl. Be sure there is enough room between sides of bowl and pot so that steam can circulate freely.

The special flavor of this dish comes from the fish itself, so it must be fresh—very fresh. Here's how to tell: Underside of gills should be pale pink, flesh should be firm, and fish should have no odor.

Rinse fish inside and out, and dry with paper toweling. Make about 6 diagonal gashes on each side. Dip pastry brush in oil and coat fish lightly. Lay whole fish in steaming bowl. If it doesn't fit, cut it in half. Spoon Vermouth over both sides letting overflow drip into bowl. Sprinkle with ginger and scallions. Bring water to boil, cover pot, and steam for 30 minutes.

Transfer fish to hot serving platter. Heat oil in small heavy-bottomed saucepan until very hot and smoking. Drop garlic into oil for 15 seconds, then remove with slotted spoon. Pour hot oil over entire fish. Spoon with Dr. Bronner's seasoning. Finally, sprinkle with balance of scallions. Serve immediately.

Yield: Serves 4

CAL	F	P:S	SOD	CAR	CHO
281	18	4.1:1	107	4	80

Broiled Red Snapper with Herbs

The soft pastel pinks and reds of its skin promises delectable eating, and the promise is fulfilled, for this is a lovely, sweet, juicy fish. I recommend broiling it whole, accenting its natural goodness with a suggestion of seasoning, and serving with lemon wedges.

1 *red snapper, 3 pounds, cleaned, head left on*
2 *shallots, very finely minced*
2 *large cloves garlic, very finely minced*
1 *tablespoon corn oil*
¾ *teaspoon combined dried tarragon and rosemary leaves, crushed*
1 *large sprig each parsley and dill*
4 *dashes cayenne pepper*
4 *sprigs fresh watercress for garnish*
Lemon wedges

Two hours before cooking fish, wash well under cold running water. Dry inside and out with paper toweling. Rub cavity with a quarter teaspoon crushed herbs. Tuck dill and parsley sprigs inside cavity; secure with skewers.

Score fish 3-4 times on each side. Brush oil over skin. Sprinkle with cayenne, shallots, garlic, and balance of dried herbs. Place on rack in baking dish and cover with waxed paper. Refrigerate for one hour; let stand at room temperature for one hour.

Broil under medium-high heat 2″ from flame for 13 minutes. Turn carefully. Broil another 13-15 minutes, or until fish flakes easily when tested with fork. Do not overcook.

Serve on heated platter garnished with watercress and lemon wedges.

Yield: Serves 4

CAL	F	P:S	SOD	CAR	CHO
224	5	3.7:1	139	0	128

Baked Brook Trout

This simply prepared dish gets its flavor from the natural sweetness of the brook trout itself, pointed up by herbs and tasty homemade bread crumbs. Served with lemon wedges, this is a real treat for the fish lover, and an eye-opener to those of you who think you won't like fish unless it's gussied up.

4 *brook trout, about ¾ pounds each*
¼ *cup non-fat milk*
1½ *tablespoons corn oil*
1 *tablespoon fresh lemon juice*
½ *tablespoon each dried rosemary and sage leaves, crushed*
½ *cup bread crumbs (Page 147)*
3 *dashes cayenne pepper*
½ *teaspoon garlic powder, no salt added*
4 *large sprigs dill*
4 *large fresh mushrooms, washed, dried, trimmed, and sliced*
Lemon wedges

Wash fish thoroughly. Dry with paper toweling inside and out. Make 3 diagonal gashes on each side of fish. Sprinkle inside and out with lemon juice. Cover and refrigerate for 2 hours.

Combine crumbs with crushed herbs, garlic powder, and cayenne pepper. Pat fish dry with paper toweling. Brush fish with milk, using pastry brush. Dip fish into herbed crumbs, coating well. Tuck one dill sprig into cavity of each fish, together with equal amounts of mushrooms.

Choose baking dish large enough to accommodate 4 fish in one layer. Brush bottom of dish with ½ tablespoon oil. Arrange trout in dish and sprinkle with balance of oil. Bake, uncovered, in preheated 425 degree oven until done (25-30 minutes). Fish should be lightly browned, and flake easily. Discard dill sprigs.

Serve on heated individual plates garnished with cooked mushrooms and lemon wedges.

Yield: Serves 4

CAL	F	P:S	SOD	CAR	CHO
234	9	3.0:1	94	4	92

Swordfish in White Wine

Swordfish is generally prepared broiled to dryness and bathed in butter. Here it's cooked instead in one of my versions of a French court bouillon. Result: a fast-cooking easy-to-make dish that's enticingly moist and sparkling with flavor. Serve it *au naturel* or with my creamy sauce.

¾" *thick slice swordfish, to weigh 1½ pounds, cut into four pieces*
2 *cloves garlic, minced*
2 *shallots, minced*
1 *small onion, minced*
½ *cup fish stock (Page 11)*
¼ *cup chicken stock (Page 10)*
¾ *cup dry Vermouth or white wine*
½ *teaspoon dried thyme leaves, crushed*
1 *large bay leaf*
3 *dashes cayenne pepper*

Place onion, shallots, garlic, stocks, bay leaf, wine, thyme, and cayenne in large iron skillet. Bring to boil. Reduce heat, and simmer for two minutes. Add fish in one layer, spooning well with liquid. Cook, uncovered, for 5 minutes, turning once. Cover, and place in 375 degree preheated oven for 15 minutes. Transfer fish to heated serving dish and keep warm.

Place skillet with cooking liquid over medium high heat, and reduce by half. Remove bay leaf, and pour over fish. Serve immediately.

Yield: Serves 4
Note: Sliced salmon steaks can be substituted successfully for swordfish.

Variation: After fish has finished baking, place on heated serving platter. Pour cooking liquid, together with garlic and onion and one teaspoon lowfat dry milk into blender. Blend one minute. Return to saucepan and reheat over very low flame. Thicken with one teaspoon arrowroot flour that has been dissolved in one teaspoon water, using only enough to lightly thicken sauce. Pour over fish or serve with fish in sauceboat.

	CAL	F	P:S	SOD	CAR	CHO
Swordfish	295	9	.8:1	100	3	124
With sauce	307	9	.8:1	110	4	124
Salmon	250	7	.8:1	156	3	124
With sauce	258	7	.8:1	166	4	124

Baked Tuna with Broccoli

Broccoli Magic (Page 18) and the legerdemain of complimentary herbs, spices, and wine, transform an ordinary can of tuna into a wondrous one-dish meal. At long last, the homespun "tuna casserole" earns its third star!

1 *can tuna (6½ oz.) packed in water, no salt added*
1 *tablespoon fresh lemon juice*
2 *whole scallions, minced*
2 *cloves garlic, minced*
1 *shallot, minced*
2 *tablespoons corn oil, plus ½ teaspoon for coating casserole*
2 *tablespoons unbleached flour*
½ *cup fish stock or chicken stock (Page 11 or 10)*
2 *cups cooked broccoli (Page 18)*
3 *tablespoons dry Vermouth or white wine*
1 *cup non-fat milk*
¼ *cup bread crumbs (Page 147)*
½ *teaspoon dried tarragon leaves, crushed*
½ *teaspoon dried mustard dissolved in 1 teaspoon water*
1 *tablespoon freshly chopped dill and parsley*
4 *large fresh mushrooms, washed, dried, trimmed and sliced*
1 *teaspoon tomato paste, no salt added (Page 6)*

Drain tuna. Place in bowl together with lemon juice. Flake coarsely with fork and set aside.

Heat one tablespoon oil in teflon skillet until hot. Sauté scallions, garlic, and shallot until wilted. Add mushrooms and sauté one minute, stirring constantly. Sprinkle flour into skillet, stirring well. Cook one minute. Add stock, mustard and wine, blending well. Add milk, herbs, and tomato paste, and continue stirring while mixture thickens. Cook over very low heat for 3 minutes.

Lightly oil a 2-quart covered ovenproof casserole. Arrange broccoli and flaked tuna in alternate layers. Pour hot sauce over mixture. Sprinkle with bread crumbs and dribble with balance of oil. Bake in preheated 400 degree oven for 20 minutes or until bubbly and lightly brown on top.

Yield: Serves 4
Note: If you like an exotic flavor, substitute one teaspoon curry powder (no salt or pepper added) for tarragon.

CAL	F	P:S	SOD	CAR	CHO
208	7	4:1	67	16	30
With curry					
208	7	4:1	74	16	30

Broiled Salmon with Green Sauce

Salmon is regarded by gourmets everywhere as the king of fish, and rightfully so. It's so basically tasty that broiled *au naturel* it's a wonder. But wonders never cease—and here salmon herbed to piquancy is married to a velvety sauce to create a new gastronomic marvel.

For the fish:
2 *slices fresh salmon, 1½ pounds, each piece sliced in half along length of bone*
1 *tablespoon corn oil, plus ½ teaspoon for coating baking dish*
1 *clove garlic, finely minced*
2 *shallots, finely minced*
2 *tablespoons fresh lemon juice*
3 *dashes cayenne pepper*
½ *teaspoon dried tarragon leaves, crushed*

For the green sauce:
2 *tablespoons corn oil*
2 *tablespoons unbleached flour*
¾ *cup warm fish stock (Page 11)*
¾ *cup warm chicken stock (Page 10)*
2 *cloves garlic, finely minced*
1 *shallot, finely minced*
½ *cup tightly packed parsley, very finely chopped*
4 *dashes cayenne pepper*
½ *teaspoon dried tarragon leaves, crushed*
½ to ¾ *cup non-fat milk*
¼ *teaspoon smoked yeast (Page 6)*

Prepare the fish first. Wipe dry with paper toweling. Combine balance of ingredients in small bowl. Mix well. Place fish in lightly oiled baking dish. Brush half of mixture over top of fish. Broil 3″ from heat for 10 minutes. Turn carefully. Spread with balance of mixture and broil another 7 minutes. Do not overcook. Serve on heated individual plates, spooned with green sauce.

While salmon is broiling, prepare the sauce. Heat oil in heavy-bottomed saucepan until hot. Add garlic and shallot. Cook one minute. Add flour all at once, whisking well. Cook for 2 minutes. Add combined stocks, tarragon, smoked yeast, and cayenne, blending well. Add half-cup milk and parsley. Bring to simmering point and cook for 10 minutes over very low heat, uncovered, whisking often. Add more milk if a thinner sauce is desired. Pour over fish, and serve.

Yield: Serves 4

CAL	F	P:S	SOD	CAR	CHO
192	4	2.4:1	98	2	122
Sauce					
141	11	4.5:1	38	8	0

Baked Bluefish in Red Wine

For lovers of dark fish, and for those who've never had the courage to try it. The flavorful succulence of the meat is pointed up by tangy herbs and spices, savory vegetables and the essence of red wine. One of my most sophisticated dishes, it's wondrously easy to make.

CAL	F	P:S	SOD	CAR	CHO
317	12	2.5:1	124	3	122

1 *bluefish, 3 pounds, cleaned, head left on*
1 *tablespoon corn oil*
1 *small onion, thinly sliced*
1 *large shallot, finely minced*
2 *cloves garlic, finely minced*
2 *sprigs parsley*
1 *sprig dill*
1½ *teaspoons dried rosemary leaves, crushed*
1 *teaspoon each fresh parsley and dill, chopped*
1 *rib celery, including leaves, chopped*
4 *dashes cayenne pepper*
4 *whole cloves*
⅔ *cup red wine*
4 *large sprigs fresh watercress*

Wash fish well under cold running water. Wipe dry with paper toweling inside and out. Rub cavity with three-quarters teaspoon rosemary. Stuff with parsley and dill sprigs. Combine celery, onion, fresh parsley and dill, cloves, shallot, and garlic. Stuff cavity with one-third of this herb-vegetable mixture. Sew up cavity or secure with skewers.

Make four gashes in each side of fish. Brush with half of oil. Then rub with balance of rosemary.

Prepare baking pan by lining with aluminum foil and brushing with balance of oil. Sprinkle one-third herb-vegetable mixture over oiled foil. Add fish. Sprinkle balance of herb-vegetable mixture over fish. Sprinkle with cayenne. Cover pan tightly with aluminum foil and bake in 425 degree preheated oven for 15 minutes. Remove from oven and add wine. Re-cover with foil, and bake 15 minutes. Remove from oven and baste. Bake uncovered for another 10 minutes.

Transfer fish to hot serving platter. Strain juices and serve on the side in sauceboat. Garnish with crisp watercress.

Yield: Serves 4

Sautéed Shrimp— My Style

Quick cooking brings out all the natural flavor, and retains the firmness and crunchiness of these fresh shrimp. Gentle caressing hints of herbs and seasonings make for a flavoring as subtle as it is delicious. Forget about icy cold shrimp in cocktail sauce!

1¼ *pounds fresh shrimp, shelled, deveined, and dried well with paper toweling*
1½ *tablespoons corn oil*
1 *onion, halved then sliced*
3 *cloves garlic, minced*
1 *shallot, minced*
1 *small green pepper, parboiled one minute, cut into slivers*
½ *teaspoon combined dried tarragon, basil, and thyme leaves, crushed*
¼ *teaspoon smoked yeast (Page 6)*
1 *tablespoon apple cider vinegar*
3 *dashes Dr. Bronner's seasoning (Page 6)*
3 *dashes cayenne pepper*
Freshly chopped parsley

Heat oil in large iron skillet until hot. Add onion, garlic, and shallot and sauté one minute. Add green pepper and sauté another minute. Push to side of skillet.

Add shrimp, arranging in one layer, and sauté until bottom is lightly pink (2-3 minutes). Turn and sauté one minute. Add vinegar, and stir sautéed onions, garlic, shallot and green pepper together with shrimp. Add dried herbs, Dr. Bronner's seasoning, smoked yeast and cayenne. Cook for one minute, no longer, over high heat. Serve immediately over a bed of plain boiled rice. Sprinkle with freshly chopped parsley.

Yield: Serves 4

CAL	F	P:S	SOD	CAR	CHO
149	7	2.7:1	152	3	121
Rice					
43	0	—	0	10	0

Sautéed Shrimp— Italian Style

If you like scampi, you'll love this dish. Italian herbs and a bit of Vermouth or white wine are your passport to the Via Veneto.

1¼ *pounds fresh shrimp, shelled, deveined and well dried*
1½ *tablespoons corn oil*
1 *onion, halved and thinly sliced*
3 *cloves garlic, minced*
1 *small green pepper, parboiled one minute, diced*
½ *teaspoon each dried oregano and sweet basil leaves, crushed*
¼ *cup dry Vermouth or white wine*
⅓ *cup tomato juice, no salt added*
3 *dashes cayenne pepper*
2 *dashes Dr. Bronner's seasoning (Page 6)*
Freshly chopped parsley

Heat one tablespoon oil in large iron skillet until hot. Add onion and garlic and sauté one minute. Add green pepper and sauté another minute, stirring constantly. Push vegetables to side of skillet.

Add balance of oil and heat until hot. Add shrimp, arranging in one layer. Sauté until bottom is lightly pink (2-3 minutes). Turn and sauté one minute. Add wine and stir sautéed onion, garlic and green pepper together with shrimp. Cook one minute. Add tomato juice, dried herbs, cayenne, and Dr. Bronner's seasoning, and cook one minute more over high heat.

Serve immediately over a bed of plain boiled rice and top with freshly chopped parsley.

Yield: Serves 4

CAL	F	P:S	SOD	CAR	CHO
151	7	2.7:1	158	4	121
Rice					
43	0	—	0	10	0

Shrimp Paella

Don't look for the traditional copious mélange of ingredients in this mini-paella. It's simply a combination of savory rice with separately quick-cooked shrimp (they retain their original crunchiness this way and never deteriorate to rubberiness). Easier to make than the Spanish national dish which inspired it, my shrimp paella is as light as it's brimful of rich, enticing flavors.

1 *pound fresh shrimp, shelled and deveined*
2 *tablespoons corn oil, plus ½ teaspoon to oil casserole*
1 *onion, minced*
2 *large cloves garlic, minced*
½ *green pepper, parboiled for one minute, cut into thin strips*
2 *shallots, minced*
1 *cup rice*
½ *cup dry Vermouth or white wine*
¼ *cup fish stock (Page 11)*
¼ *cup chicken stock (Page 10)*
½ *cup tomato purée, no salt added (Page 6)*
1 *teaspoon dried tarragon leaves, crushed*
2 *teaspoons freshly chopped parsley and dill*
¼ *pound fresh mushrooms, washed, dried, trimmed, and sliced*
½ *cup tomato juice, no salt added (optional)*
Bouquet garni

Heat ½ tablespoon oil in large teflon skillet until hot. Sauté onion, garlic, and shallots for one minute. Add green pepper and sauté another minute. Add rice and stir well to coat. Cook for 2 minutes. Add wine. Bring to simmering point and cook for 2 minutes. Add balance of ingredients with the exception of shrimp and mushrooms, and heat to simmering point. Pour into lightly oiled 2-quart casserole. Cover and bake in preheated 400 degree oven for 15 minutes.

While rice is baking, heat one tablespoon oil in skillet until hot. Add mushrooms and sauté for two minutes. Transfer to bowl. Heat balance of oil in skillet until hot. Add shrimp in one layer and cook on each side until lightly pink (about 1½ minutes on each side).

Remove casserole from oven. Add shrimp and mushrooms stirring until well distributed. Cover, and return to oven for 7 minutes. Finished rice should be tender and moist. If too dry, add a small amount of tomato juice, stirring well. Serve hot from casserole.

Yield: Serves 4 generously, as a paella is supposed to do
Variation: For an unusual change of flavor, try substituting one teaspoon curry powder (no salt or pepper added) for tarragon.

CAL	F	P:S	SOD	CAR	CHO
353	5	2.5:1	121	49	110
With curry					
353	5	2.5:1	128	49	110
With tomato juice					
359	5	2.5:1	120	51	110

Chicken and Turkey

Poached Chicken Breasts

This is a very simple and quick dish to prepare. Its light mild flavor makes it adaptable to many spin-offs, two of which follow this basic recipe. You'll easily invent more yourself.

4 *boneless chicken breasts, skinned, and pounded to 3/8" thickness (about 1½ pounds)*
1 *small carrot, peeled and diced*
1 *large clove garlic, minced*
½ *leek, white part only, well washed and minced*
1 *small rib celery, minced*
1 *shallot, minced*
1 *cup chicken stock or enough to barely cover chicken (Page 10)*
¼ *cup dry Vermouth or white wine*
3 *large fresh mushrooms, washed, trimmed, and sliced*
3 *dashes cayenne pepper*
Small bouquet garni

Wipe chicken dry with paper toweling. Arrange in one layer in heavy-bottomed saucepan. Combine remainder of ingredients and pour over chicken. Bring to slow boil. Reduce heat and simmer, covered, for 30 minutes, turning once midway. Do not overcook. Turn off heat and let chicken sit in broth and vegetables for at least 30 minutes before serving. Remove bouquet garni.

Reheat and serve as is with boiled parsleyed potato (Page 22) as a simple light lunch or dinner, or serve cold next day, immersed in cooking liquid which will have jelled.

Yield: Serves 4

CAL	F	P:S	SOD	CAR	CHO
214	4	1.8:1	112	4	98

Chicken Breasts with Creamy Sauce

1 *recipe Poached Chicken Breasts (Page 59)*
2 *teaspoons arrowroot flour dissolved in 2 teaspoons water*
Freshly chopped parsley and dill

Prepare Poached Chicken Breasts according to recipe. Transfer chicken to heated serving platter and keep warm.

Reduce unstrained broth by ⅓. Pour into blender and blend for one minute. Pour back into saucepan and reheat. Dribble flour mixture into heated liquid, adding only enough to make a light pourable gravy. Pour over chicken breasts and sprinkle with freshly chopped parsley and dill.

Yield: Serves 4

CAL	F	P:S	SOD	CAR	CHO
218	4	1.8:1	112	5	98

Chicken Divan

Chicken Divan was the inspiration of the master chef of the now regrettably defunct Divan Parisienne Restaurant in New York. It was one of my husband's favorite dishes, and after we met it became one of mine. It consisted of a bed of fresh and sprightly *al dente* broccoli, blanketed with thinly sliced breast of chicken, and bathed in a piquant Mornay sauce. For under $5! My husband exults that my version has all of the taste of the original, with only a suspicion of its calories, fats, and salt. And my chicken divan is still under $5—for two!

3 *cups fresh broccoli, slightly undercooked (Page 18)*
½ *pound cooked chicken breasts, thinly sliced (Page 59)*
1½ *cups chicken stock (Page 10)*
¼ *teaspoon combined ground sage and thyme*
2 *dashes Dr. Bronner's seasoning (Page 6)*
3 *dashes cayenne pepper*
½ *teaspoon smoked yeast (Page 6)*
1½ *tablespoons arrowroot flour dissolved in 1½ tablespoons water*
4 *fresh mushrooms, washed, dried, trimmed, and sliced*
¾ *cup non-fat milk*
¼ *cup grated low-fat cheese (Page 3)*
1 *tablespoon freshly chopped parsley*
½ *teaspoon corn oil for oiling baking dishes*

Lightly oil 4 individual oven-proof baking dishes. Arrange broccoli in equal portions on bottom of each dish. Now prepare the sauce.

Heat stock to simmering point. Add mushrooms, and cook over low heat, covered, for 5 minutes. Add dissolved arrowroot flour, a little at a time, whisking well. Slowly add milk and blend. Add ground herbs, Dr. Bronner's seasoning, cayenne, smoked yeast, and cheese, and bring to simmering point. Spoon half of the hot sauce over broccoli. Arrange sliced chicken over broccoli in equal portions, and spoon balance of sauce over each individual dish. Bake in preheated 425 degree oven for 15 minutes, or until lightly browned. Sprinkle with freshly chopped parsley, and serve.

Yield: Serves 4
Note: Sliced white meat of turkey may be substituted for chicken.

	CAL	F	P:S	SOD	CAR	CHO
	165	12	4.2:1	78	15	10
Turkey	162	12	4.2:1	73	15	10

Chicken Bolognese

This extravagant extension of my recipe for Poached Chicken Breasts (Page 59) is a lighter and more delicate version of the Chicken Bolognese featured in fine Italian restaurants. A superb party dish.

1 *recipe Poached Chicken Breasts (Page 59)*
Smoked yeast (Page 6)
Enough low-fat cheese, sliced 1/8" thick, to cover chicken breasts (Page 3)
1 *tablespoon corn oil, ½ teaspoon oil to coat casserole*
2 *teaspoons arrowroot flour dissolved in 2 teaspoons water*
2 *tablespoons freshly chopped parsley and dill*

Prepare Poached Chicken Breasts according to recipe. Remove from broth and pat dry. Heat oil in teflon skillet until hot. Sauté chicken breasts until lightly browned on both sides, sprinkling liberally with smoked yeast.

Lightly oil an oven-proof casserole. Place browned chicken breasts in casserole in one layer, covering each piece with slices of cheese.

Reduce unstrained broth by ⅓. Pour into blender and blend for one minute. Return to saucepan, reheat, and thicken with only enough dissolved flour to make a light gravy. Spoon half of gravy over chicken pieces, and place under broiler until cheese is melted and lightly browned. Transfer to serving platter and spoon balance of hot gravy over chicken. Sprinkle with freshly chopped parsley and dill.

Yield: Serves 4

CAL	F	P:S	SOD	CAR	CHO
341	15	4.3:1	143	15	109

Simple Broiled Chicken

The emphasis is on simple. Just marinate and broil—that's it. But it's one of the tastiest ways of preparing chicken in any cuisine.

1 *broiling chicken, 3 pounds, cut into serving pieces, skinned*
Marinade (Page 64)
4 *shakes Dr. Bronner's seasoning (Page 6)*
Freshly chopped parsley and dill

Prepare marinade according to recipe, adding Dr. Bronner's seasoning, and stirring well to blend. Place chicken in bowl just large enough to hold all chicken. Pour marinade over chicken, turning pieces to coat evenly. Cover with aluminum foil and refrigerate for 5-6 hours.

Arrange legs and breasts on rack in broiling pan. Broil 3″ from heat for 8-10 minutes. Turn, add smaller chicken parts (they require less cooking time) and broil for 8-10 minutes. Raise pan so that it's 1½″ from heat, and continue broiling and turning chicken until done. Total cooking time is about 30-35 minutes, depending upon weight of bird. Serve immediately sprinkled with freshly chopped parsley and dill.

Yield: Serves 4

CAL	F	P:S	SOD	CAR	CHO
258	8	2.6:1	122	1	98

Broiled Chicken Paprikash

This is a broiled version, sans tomatoes, of one of Hungary's great contributions to the art of haute cuisine, chicken paprikash (Hungarians prefer it as a stew). It's a spicy, full-bodied dish with just a hint of sweetness. As heartwarming as a Gypsy violin.

1 *broiling chicken, 3 pounds, cut into serving pieces, skinned*
1 *tablespoon corn oil*
1 *teaspoon paprika*
2 *large cloves garlic, minced*
2 *teaspoons apple cider vinegar*
2 *dashes cayenne pepper*
Juice of ½ lemon
1 *teaspoon honey*

Pat chicken dry. Make a marinade by combining balance of ingredients. Spoon and spread over chicken. Cover and refrigerate for 3 hours before cooking.

Arrange legs and breasts on rack in broiling pan. Broil 3″ from heat for 8-10 minutes. Turn, add smaller chicken parts (they require less cooking time) and broil for 8-10 minutes. Raise pan so that it's 1½″ from heat, and continue broiling and turning chicken until done. Total cooking time is about 30-35 minutes, depending upon weight of bird. Serve immediately.

Yield: Serves 4
Note: The spiciness of the marinade will depend upon the kind of paprika used. In this recipe I use mild paprika which can be obtained in most supermarkets. If there's a gourmet shop near you, or better still, a Hungarian market, try the full range of paprikas from sweet to hot. If you're using a hot paprika, eliminate cayenne.

CAL	F	P:S	SOD	CAR	CHO
279	9	2.8:1	121	2	98

Simple Sautéed Chicken Rosemary

Rosemary—minty, hearty, fragrant—is a dominant herb. It can be the soloist in a concerto of flavors—and that's how it's used here. The dish is simplicity itself to make.

1 *broiling chicken, 3 pounds, cut into serving pieces, skinned*
2 *tablespoons corn oil*
2 *shallots, minced*
3 *large cloves garlic, minced*
1 *small onion, minced*
½ *carrot, peeled and grated*
3 *dashes cayenne pepper*
¼ *cup dry Vermouth or white wine*
1 *teaspoon dried rosemary leaves, crushed*
⅓ *cup chicken stock (Page 10)*
½ *cup tomato juice, no salt added*
3 *dashes Dr. Bronner's seasoning (Page 6)*
Bouquet garni
Freshly chopped parsley

Pat chicken dry with paper toweling. Combine ½ tablespoon oil with 2 cloves minced garlic. Spoon and rub over chicken. Cover and refrigerate overnight.

Heat ½ tablespoon oil in large teflon skillet until hot. Add half of chicken and sauté on both sides until lightly browned, turning carefully with spatula. Transfer to bowl. Heat ½ tablespoon corn oil until hot. Brown balance of chicken. Transfer to bowl.

Heat balance of oil in skillet until hot. Add onion, shallot, and remaining garlic, and sauté until lightly browned. Add wine and cook for 2 minutes. Add tomato juice, Dr. Bronner's seasoning, stock, cayenne, rosemary, and carrot. Stir. Add browned chicken, turning well to coat. Add bouquet garni. Bring to simmering point, cover, and cook for 45 minutes, turning twice.

Turn off heat, and let stand, covered, for 30 minutes. When ready to serve, reheat over low flame. Sprinkle with freshly chopped parsley, and serve.

Yield: Serves 4

CAL	F	P:S	SOD	CAR	CHO
323	13	3.2:1	132	9	98

Sautéed Chicken Legs with Pimentos

Yes, there *are* dark meat lovers! And if you're not one already, you probably will be when you taste this easy-to-make dish. It's spicy and zesty and hearty. And it's a delight to look at, too.

4 *chicken legs with thighs, skinned, leg separated from thigh (total weight 2 pounds)*
2 *tablespoons corn oil*
4 *cloves garlic, finely minced*
1 *large onion, sliced*
1 *small green pepper, sliced into thin strips*
1 *teaspoon wine vinegar*
¼ *cup chicken stock (Page 10)*
½ *teaspoon dried thyme leaves, crushed*
½ *teaspoon Dr. Bronner's seasoning (Page 6)*
1 *large pimento, no salt added, sliced*
½ *teaspoon ground ginger*
4 *dashes cayenne pepper*

Pat chicken dry with paper toweling. Combine garlic, vinegar, ½ tablespoon oil, ginger, and Dr. Bronner's seasoning in bowl large enough to accommodate all chicken. Add chicken, turning to coat. Cover, and refrigerate for at least 6 hours.

Heat one tablespoon oil in large iron skillet until hot. Add chicken and sauté to a golden brown on both sides, turning carefully with spatula. Skinned chicken must be handled gingerly. Remove from skillet and set aside.

Heat balance of oil until hot. Add onion and green pepper to same skillet and sauté until lightly browned. Add stock, thyme and cayenne, and cook over medium heat, scraping to loosen browned particles (about 2 minutes). Return browned chicken parts and its juices to skillet, turning well. Bring small amount of liquid in skillet to simmering point. Reduce heat, cover, and simmer for 20 minutes.

Turn chicken parts and add pimentos. Bring to simmering point, re-cover, and simmer for 20 minutes, stirring and turning once. Turn off heat and let sit, covered, for 30 minutes before serving.

At serving time, reheat over very low flame and serve piping hot.

Yield: Serves 4
Variation: The marinated chicken may be broiled, and—*voila!*—another dish.

CAL	F	P:S	SOD	CAR	CHO
277	15	3.1:1	91	5	83
Broiled					
256	15	3.1:1	80	2	83

Herb-Flavored Roast Chicken

Roast chicken can be, and generally is, one of the dullest American foods. It's usually prepared by basting with butter or margarine or prepared dressings, sprinkling liberally with salt and pepper, and then cooking on a rotisserie Ho-hum. But just glance over the ingredients for this luscious herb-flavored chicken and you'll agree, chicken can be exciting.

1 *broiling chicken, 3 pounds*
1 *large shallot, minced*
2 *tablespoons freshly chopped parsley and dill*
1 *rounded teaspoon dried rosemary leaves, crushed, or ½ teaspoon each dried rosemary and thyme leaves, crushed*
2 *tablespoons corn oil*
¼ *cup apple cider vinegar*
½ *teaspoon Dr. Bronner's seasoning (Page 6)*
2 *dashes cayenne pepper*

Combine all ingredients, except chicken, in large bowl. Blend well to make marinade.

Lay chicken on its back. Lift skin by gently pushing your finger under skin of breast and then to the thigh and leg. Gently spoon a portion of marinade under skin as far as it will go. Press skin down and skewer in place. With a sharp-pronged fork, prick the skin of wings and back, and spoon with balance of marinade. Turn to coat. Cover with aluminum foil and refrigerate overnight. Remove from refrigerator one hour before roasting.

Place bird on rack in roasting pan. Pour half of marinade over bird. Place in preheated 350 degree oven and roast, uncovered, for 30 minutes. Pour balance of marinade over bird and roast for 45 minutes. Remove from oven and loosely cover with waxed paper. Let stand for 5 minutes before slicing.

Yield: Serves 4
Variation: *Stuffed Herbed Chicken:* Follow stuffing instructions in recipe for Orange-Pineapple Chicken (Page 67), truss, and roast, uncovered. Cooking time 1½ hours.
Note: This marinade is delicious for veal and pork roasts as well.

CAL	F	P:S	SOD	CAR	CHO
351	18	2.7:1	125	1	98
Stuffing					
142	0	—	32	28	16

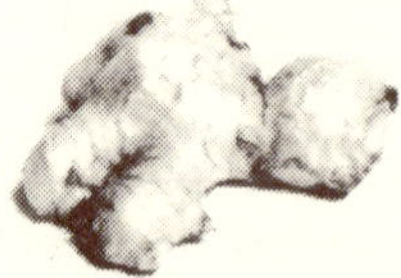

Chicken Tandoori

This dish and the one that follows, are the creation of my son Mitchell, a molecular biologist, who has a passion for exotic food. What he's done—and it's quite a feat—is to fashion unmistakably savory Indian dishes that are yet wondrously light, subtle-tasting, and far from alien to the American palate. Here's where East meets West!

1 *broiling chicken, 3 pounds skinned and left whole*
1 *teaspoon mild paprika*
¼ *teaspoon cayenne pepper*
6 *tablespoons fresh lime juice*
6 *tablespoons wine vinegar*
½ *tablespoon fresh ginger, cut into thin slices*
½ *rib celery, minced*
1 *onion, minced*
1 *large pimento, no salt added, diced (Page 5)*
1 *measure (8 oz.) low-fat plain yogurt*
1 *tablespoon corn oil*
¼ *teaspoon dried rosemary leaves, crushed*
⅛ *teaspoon dried thyme leaves, crushed*
1 *large clove garlic, very finely minced*

Here's how to skin a whole chicken. Start by slipping knife under skin at bottom of breast bone and cutting skin up toward the center of the bird to the neck. Peel skin back off either side of breast, using the knife only to assist the separation of skin from the meat. Skin can be removed from back and legs in similar manner; cut the skin down the backbone and along the thighs, and peel back with one hand assisted by the knife in the other. Skinning the wings is more difficult and not essential, so prick them instead with a sharp-pronged fork.

Wash out cavity of chicken. Pat entire bird dry with paper toweling. Combine cayenne, paprika, lime juice and vinegar. Mix well. Pour this marinade over chicken and rub in and around entire bird. Cover, and refrigerate for 3-4 hours.

Combine one teaspoon oil, dried herbs, and garlic. Remove chicken from marinade. Drain and discard excess. Rub with herb-garlic mixture and return, covered, to refrigerator for another 3-4 hours.

Combine ginger, onion, celery and pimento. Add yogurt and blend well. Coat chicken all over with mixture. Place chicken on rack in shallow roasting pan. Roast, uncovered, in preheated 400 degree oven for 30 minutes. Brush with one teaspoon oil. Roast 15 minutes and brush with remaining oil. Roast 15 minutes. Total cooking time is 60 minutes.

Cut into serving pieces, and serve.

Yield: Serves 4
Note: Typical Chicken Tandoori recipes call for roasting until bird is quite dry. My timetable produces a moister bird.

CAL	F	P:S	SOD	CAR	CHO
340	16	2.8:1	152	8	99

Mogul Chicken with Mushrooms

2 *whole legs (includig thighs) and one whole chicken breast (total weight 2 pounds), skinned*
½ *pound fresh mushrooms, washed, trimmed, and thickly sliced*
3 *tablespoons cold water*
1 *cup cold water*
1½ *teaspoons ground turmeric*
Seeds of 4 cardamom pods, crushed, or ¼ teaspoon ground cardamom
3 *cloves garlic, very finely minced*
3 *tablespoons fresh lime juice, or one tablespoon fresh lemon juice*
¼ *teaspoon mild paprika*
1 *tablespoon freshly chopped chives or freshly chopped parsley*
2 *tablespoons corn oil*

Combine garlic with 3 tablespoons water. Set aside. Combine lime juice with paprika, and set aside. Combine 1 cup water with turmeric. Add mushrooms to soak, and set aside.

Pat chicken dry with paper toweling. Heat oil until hot in large iron skillet. Add chicken, and sauté on both sides until lightly browned (about 15 minutes). Sprinkle with cardamom and continue sautéeing for 5 minutes. Transfer to bowl and cover to keep warm.

Drain mushrooms and add to skillet. Cook over high heat, uncovered, for 2 minutes. Return warm chicken to skillet, and sauté with mushrooms over medium-high heat until all liquid evaporates (about 10 minutes).

In small saucepan, bring garlic and water to boil. Pour over chicken and turn rapidly to coat. Bring lime juice and paprika to boil, and pour this, too, over chicken, turning to coat. Sprinkle with chopped chives or parsley, and serve immediately.

Yield: Serves 4

CAL	F	P:S	SOD	CAR	CHO
210	11	3.2:1	86	1	87

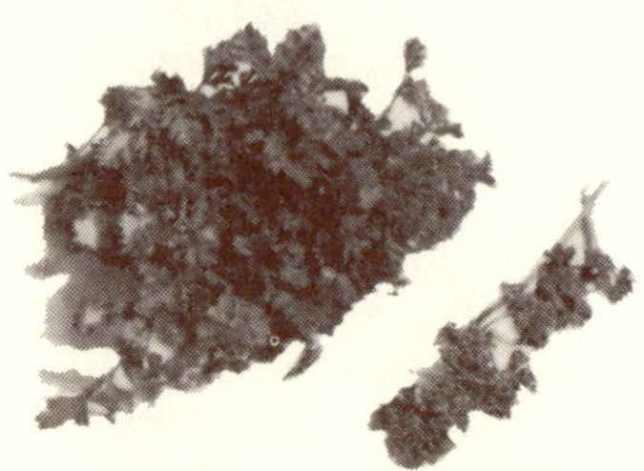

Near-East Chicken

Many Near-East recipes call for buttermilk as an ingredient for their meat and poultry marinades. The liaison of this lean milk product with exotic herbs not only adds an admirable pungency, but also tenderizes the food.

For the chicken:
2 *broiling chickens, 2½ pounds each, skinned, cut into eighths; backs, giblets, and wing tips reserved to make rich gravy*
1 *teaspoon corn oil to coat baking pan*

For the marinade:
¾ *cup buttermilk, no salt added*
1 *small onion, grated*
1 *shallot, finely minced*
3 *cloves garlic, finely minced*
1 *rib celery, finely minced*
¼ *teaspoon each dried sage and thyme leaves, crushed*
3 *dashes cayenne pepper*
1 *tablespoon freshly chopped parsley*

For the breading:
¾ *cup bread crumbs, preferably made from My French Bread (Page 135)*
¼ *cup toasted wheat germ, no sugar added*

For the sauce:
Reserved backs, wings, and giblets (except heart)
½ *rib celery with leaves, coarsely chopped*
1 *small onion, coarsely chopped*
1 *large clove garlic, minced*
1 *large shallot, minced*
½ *teaspoon each dried sage and thyme leaves*
½ *carrot, peeled and sliced*
2 *cups water or enough to barely cover chicken parts*
4 *fresh mushrooms, washed, trimmed, and quartered*
2 *dashes cayenne pepper*
1 *tablespoon freshly chopped parsley*
Small bouquet garni

First prepare marinade by combining all ingredients in large bowl. Stir to blend. Add chicken, turning to coat well. Cover and refrigerate for at least 6 hours, or overnight.

Now prepare broth for sauce. Place reserved chicken parts in waterless cooker or heavy-bottomed covered saucepan. Add water. Bring to boil. Cook, uncovered, for 5 minutes, removing scum that rises to top. Add onion, garlic, shallot, carrot, celery, dried herbs and bouquet garni. Partially cover, and simmer for 45 minutes. Turn off flame and let stand, covered, for one hour. Skim off fat that rises to the top. Add mushrooms. Bring to simmering point, cover, and cook for 15 minutes.

Remove chicken parts from broth with slotted spoon. Reserve for a light lunch. Remove bouquet garni. This broth can be prepared up to this point a day ahead and reheated if desired.

Now prepare and bake the chicken. An hour before baking chicken, remove from marinade. Combine crumbs and wheat germ and blend. Dip each piece of chicken into crumbs, turning well to coat. Place all breaded pieces of chicken on a platter. Cover with plastic wrap, and refrigerate for one hour. Discard marinade.

When ready to cook, arrange chicken in lightly oiled metal baking pan large enough to hold all parts in one layer. Bake in preheated 350 degree oven for 45 minutes, turning carefully with spatula. Chicken will now be ready to serve.

Ten minutes before chicken is done, finish preparation of sauce. Pour broth and vegetables into blender and blend for 2 minutes. Reheat sauce over low flame, adding cayenne and freshly chopped parsley. Stir. Serve in sauceboat with chicken.

Yield: Serves 6
Note: Don't purée the chicken broth and vegetables until 10 minutes before chicken has finished baking. This light, frothy sauce has no thickener and will collapse if prepared in advance of serving time.

CAL	F	P:S	SOD	CAR	CHO
366	6	1.8:1	165	21	108
Sauce					
19	0	—	19	3	0

Orange-Pineapple Chicken

This is a grand dish made with a deliciously herbaceous stuffing, and served with a sweet and pungent sauce.

For the chicken:
1 *3-pound broiling chicken*
1 *tablespoon corn oil*

For the marinade:
½ *cup fresh orange juice*
¼ *cup pineapple juice, no sugar added*
Juice of one large lemon
2 *cloves garlic, finely minced*
1 *shallot, minced*
1 *small onion, thinly sliced*
½ *teaspoon each dried sage and thyme leaves, crushed*
1 *small bay leaf*
2 *dashes cayenne pepper*

For the stuffing:
2 *cups my cubed French Bread for stuffing (Page 147)*
1 *tablespoon corn oil*
1 *onion, minced*
1 *shallot minced*
2 *cloves garlic, minced*
The chicken liver, diced
½ *teaspoon each dried sage and thyme leaves, crushed*
2 *tablespoons firmly packed freshly chopped parsley*
1 *egg white, lightly beaten with fork*
¾ *cup chicken stock, or as much as needed to lightly moisten bread cubes (Page 10)*
1 *tablespoon non-fat milk*
2 *dashes cayenne pepper*

For the sauce:

¼ *cup chicken stock (Page 10)*
Remaining marinade, after chicken is braised, and fat skimmed
3 *large fresh mushrooms, washed, dried, trimmed, and sliced*
1 *tablespoon apple cider vinegar or wine vinegar*
1 *tablespoon honey*
1 *teaspoon arrowroot flour dissolved in one teaspoon water (optional)*
Julienne strips of orange

Julienne strips: Peel off skin from half a navel orange, cutting away white part. Slice skin into very thin slivers and drop into boiling water for 3 minutes. Drain and rinse under cold water. Set aside until sauce is completed.

Mix all ingredients for marinade. Wipe chicken well inside and out with paper toweling. Prick skin with sharp-pronged fork. In a bowl large enough to fit bird, pour marinade over chicken, spooning some into the cavity. Cover with aluminum foil and refrigerate overnight.

To prepare the stuffing: Heat oil until hot in small iron skillet. Sauté garlic, shallot, and onion until lightly browned. Add chicken liver and brown. In a large bowl, pour sautéed mixture over bread cubes. Stir. Add herbs, egg white, chicken stock and cayenne, mixing well. Add milk and mix again. If necessary, add a little more milk so that bread cubes are moistened but not wet.

To prepare the chicken: Remove chicken from marinade, reserving excess marinade. Wipe bird dry. Stuff cavity and truss bird. With pastry brush, lightly oil the bird all over. Brown in cast-iron casserole on top of stove, taking care not to burn skin.

Pour off any oil left in casserole and discard. Pour reserved marinade over bird, cover tightly, and place in preheated 350 degree oven. Bake for 30 minutes. Remove cover and bake for 45 minutes, basting twice. Remove from casserole and keep warm.

To prepare the sauce. Heat chicken stock with mushrooms. Simmer for 3 minutes. Pour into blender together with cooked marinade from which fat has been skimmed. Add vinegar and honey. Blend well. Return to saucepan. Pour juices that have dripped from chicken into saucepan. Reheat and add julienne strips. If you prefer a slightly thicker sauce, dribble tiny amounts of dissolved arrowroot flour into sauce until it is the consistency you like.

Cut chicken into serving pieces and place on serving platter with stuffing in center. Spoon small amount of sauce over chicken, and sprinkle with chopped parsley. Serve balance of sauce in sauceboat.

Yield: Serves 4

	CAL	F	P:S	SOD	CAR	CHO
	278	9	2.6:1	121	9	98
Stuffing	142	0	—	32	28	16
Sauce	16	0	—	3	3	0

Chicken à la Californienne

Juicy sweet-and-tart California navel oranges are the secret ingredient that transforms a simple unadorned barnyard bird into an exquisitely dressed fowl. The velvety yet piquant orange sauce is as California as mission bells and fogs over the Golden Gate. American haute cuisine at its best!

1 *broiling chicken, 3 pounds, cut into serving pieces, skinned*
½ *cup unbleached flour*
2 *tablespoons corn oil*
½ *cup fresh orange juice plus ¼ cup for sauce*
½ *cup chicken stock (Page 10)*
2 *tablespoons brown beef stock (Page 13)*
1 *small green pepper, finely minced*
2 *large cloves garlic, finely minced*
1 *large shallot, finely minced*
1 *small onion, finely minced*
½ *carrot, peeled and finely diced*
1 *small rib celery, finely minced*
3 *sprigs fresh crisp watercress*
2 *tablespoons apple cider vinegar*
¼ *teaspoon dried thyme leaves, crushed*
½ *teaspoon each dried tarragon and marjoram leaves, crushed*
1 *tablespoon freshly chopped parsley*
¼ *teaspoon smoked yeast (Page 6)*
1 *teaspoon Dr. Bronner's seasoning (Page 6)*
2 *dashes cayenne pepper*
1 *navel orange, peeled, sliced, and each slice cut into quarters*
1″ *sliver orange peel*

Combine dried herbs with flour and blend. Dry chicken well with paper toweling. Dredge lightly in flour-herb mixture, shaking off excess. Heat ½ tablespoon oil in large teflon skillet until hot. Add half of chicken and brown lightly. Transfer to covered iron casserole. Heat ½ tablespoon oil in skillet and brown balance of chicken. Transfer to casserole.

Heat balance of oil in skillet, and add garlic and vegetables with the exception of watercress. (Strictly speaking, watercress is a salad green, but most people think it's a vegetable). Brown lightly. Add vinegar and cook for one minute. Add stocks and ½ cup orange juice, together with parsley, Dr. Bronner's seasoning, smoked yeast, watercress, cayenne, and orange peel. Heat to simmering point, and cook uncovered, for 2 minutes. Pour over chicken. Cover tightly and bake for 50 minutes in preheated 350 degree oven, turning once midway.

With slotted spoon, transfer chicken to covered serving dish. Skim off any fat from gravy. Add ¼ cup orange juice. Pour into blender and blend on high speed for one minute. Reheat to simmering point. Pour over chicken. Garnish with fresh oranges and serve.

Yield: Serves 4
Note: If you're very calorie conscious, you can leave out the flour from the recipe. Just rub dried chicken with crushed combined herbs and refrigerate for 4 hours before cooking. Then proceed with recipe. Gravy will be unthickened.

CAL	F	P:S	SOD	CAR	CHO
409	12	3.2:1	156	26	26
Unthickened					
359	12	3.2:1	156	14	26

Sautéed Chicken with Apples

What's a gourmet dish—one that's made with rare, expensive, imported ingredients? Could be, but it usually isn't. The best gourmet dishes are made of high quality local ingredients blended with imagination and tender loving care. The ingredients never scream out, but their identities just quietly meld together to produce a distinctive and unforgettable flavor—such as this one.

1 *broiler, 3 pounds, cut into serving pieces, skinned*
2 *tablespoons corn oil*
2 *large cloves garlic, minced*
1 *large shallot, minced*
¼ *teaspoon each dried sage and thyme leaves, crushed*
¾ *teaspoon ground ginger*
1 *teaspoon fresh lemon juice*
½ *cup apple juice, no sugar added*
½ *cup chicken stock (Page 10)*
2 *sweet, crisp apples, peeled, cored, and diced*
¼ *teaspoon dry mustard dissolved in 1 teaspoon water*
½ *teaspoon Dr. Bronner's seasoning (Page 6)*
¼ *cup dry Vermouth or white wine*
3 *dashes cayenne pepper*
2 *teaspoons sesame seeds, toasted (Page 105)*

Wipe chicken dry with paper toweling. Rub with herbs. Heat one tablespoon oil in large teflon skillet until hot. Sauté half of chicken on both sides until lightly browned, taking care in turning. Remove from skillet and set aside. Heat balance of oil until hot, and brown remainder of chicken. Return first browned batch to skillet. Add garlic and shallot. Brown with chicken for 5 minutes, turning twice. Add wine and cook for 2 minutes, turning chicken to coat.

Combine apple juice, stock, mustard, lemon juice, Dr. Bronner's seasoning, and ginger. Pour over chicken. Sprinkle with cayenne. Heat to simmering point, cover, and simmer for 30 minutes. Add apples. Re-cover, and cook for 10 minutes. Turn flame off and let chicken sit in liquid for 30 minutes before serving.

When ready to serve, reheat, uncovered, over medium flame until simmering, turning chicken pieces once. Transfer chicken, and apples to heated serving dish, using slotted spoon for apples. Cover to keep warm. Turn up heat under skillet and reduce gravy by half. Pour over chicken. Sprinkle with sesame seeds and serve.

Note: Here's how to toast sesame seeds: Heat small iron skillet until hot. Sprinkle seeds into skillet and cook over heat for about 2 minutes, shaking skillet often, until seeds are very lightly browned.
Yield: Serves 4

CAL	F	P:S	SOD	CAR	CHO
331	13	2.7:1	151	8	98

Johnny Appleseed Chicken

In the middle of the last century as America expanded, a larger-than-life character, Johnny Appleseed, journeyed westward, sowing apple seeds everywhere. In his wake, apple orchards sprang up from coast to coast. In honor of Johnny Appleseed, I've invented this pure American dish. It's as adventurous and zesty as Johnny Appleseed himself.

1 *broiling chicken, 3 pounds, cut into eighths, skinned, wing tip removed*
½ *can apple juice concentrate, no sugar added*
1 *teaspoon ground ginger*
¼ *teaspoon ground cloves*
¼ *teaspoon dried marjoram leaves, crushed*
¾ *cup bread crumbs (Page 147) mixed with ¼ cup toasted wheat germ*
2 *dashes cayenne pepper*

In small bowl, combine concentrate with ginger, cloves, marjoram, and cayenne and blend with fork. Pat chicken dry with paper toweling. Dip each piece into mixture, letting excess liquid drain off. Dip into crumbs, covering well. Refrigerate for at least 30 minutes before cooking.

Lightly oil a shallow metal roasting pan large enough to hold entire chicken in one layer. Place chicken in pan. Bake, uncovered, in preheated 375 degree oven for 45 minutes, turning once midway with spatula. Serve immediately. You'll love the golden crunchy crust.

Yield: Serves 4

CAL	F	P:S	SOD	CAR	CHO
419	6	1.8:1	126	39	113

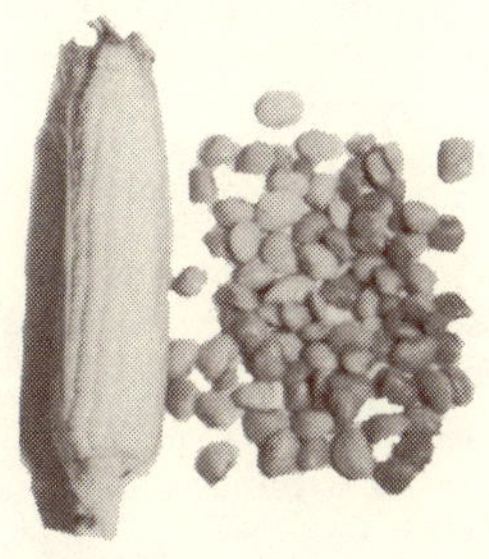

Brunswick Stew

The first settlers in America discovered the potato, the tomato, tobacco, and a fabulous Indian stew called salmagundi. Renamed Brunswick Stew, it became the staple fare of the hardy men and women who brought a new nation out of the wilderness. It's a plethora of sparkling fresh American vegetables, enriching a tender herbed and spiced chicken.

1 *3-pound broiler, cut into serving pieces, skinned*
2 *tablespoons corn oil*
¼ *cup unbleached flour*
2 *teaspoons wine vinegar*
2 *carrots, peeled and diced*
1 *rib celery, diced*
1 *large onion, thinly sliced*
½ *leek, white part only, well washed, and minced*
3 *large cloves garlic, minced*
1 *shallot, minced*
2 *potatoes, peeled and diced*
⅓ *cup yellow turnip, peeled and diced*
1 *fresh corn, kernels removed*
½ *pound fresh lima beans, shelled*
1 *small green pepper, minced*
1 *cup chicken stock (Page 10)*
3 *fresh tomatoes, cored, skinned and chopped, or one 8¼ ounce can tomatoes, no salt added*
1 *teaspoon Dr. Bronner's seasoning (Page 6)*
½ *teaspoon dry mustard dissolved in one teaspoon water*
¾ *teaspoon each dried thyme and rosemary leaves, crushed*
4 *dashes cayenne pepper*
4 *large fresh mushrooms, washed, dried, trimmed and thickly sliced*
1″ *sliver orange peel*
Bouquet garni

Mix flour with herbs. Pat chicken dry with paper toweling. Dredge lightly in flour mixture, shaking off excess. Heat ½ tablespoon oil in teflon skillet. Brown half of chicken on both sides, turning carefully with spatula. Transfer to iron casserole. Add half tablespoon oil to skillet and brown balance of chicken. Transfer to casserole. Heat balance of oil in skillet until hot. Add onions, garlic, celery, shallot, leek, and green pepper. Sauté for 3 minutes. Add vinegar and cook one minute. Add tomatoes, stock, mustard, cayenne, Dr. Bronner's seasoning, mushrooms, carrots, turnip, potato, orange peel and bouquet garni. Bring to boiling point. Pour over chicken. Cover, and bake in preheated 350 degree oven for 40 minutes.

Uncover and add corn and lima beans. Bring to simmering point on top of stove, re-cover, and cook another 15 minutes. Remove orange peel and bouquet garni, and serve.

Yield: Serves 6
Note: Fresh peas may be substituted for lima beans.

CAL	F	P:S	SOD	CAR	CHO
324	9	3.2:1	129	31	65
With peas					
317	9	3.2:1	129	30	65

Chicken Marengo

At Marengo, two victories were won by Napoleon—one on the battlefield, and the other in the kitchen. The results of the battlefield victory are long forgotten, but the culinary triumph still stirs our hearts—and appetites—today. It's Chicken Marengo, that gorgeous stew improvised by Napoleon's chef from whatever he had on hand that day. Here's my version of the dish, so elegantly delectable, it's fit for an Emperor.

- 1 *broiling chicken, 3 pounds, cut into serving pieces, skinned*
- ½ *cup unbleached flour*
- 2 *tablespoons corn oil*
- 2 *large cloves garlic, minced*
- 1 *small onion, minced*
- 1 *shallot, minced*
- 4 *fresh tomatoes, cored, skinned and chopped, or one 8¼-ounce can tomatoes, no salt added, drained*
- ¼ *pound fresh mushrooms, washed, dried, trimmed, and thickly sliced*
- ½ *carrot, peeled and diced*
- ½ *cup chicken stock (Page 10)*
- ½ *cup dry Vermouth or white wine*
- ½ *teaspoon each dried tarragon and rosemary leaves, crushed*
- 3 *dashes smoked yeast (Page 6)*
- 4 *dashes cayenne pepper*
- *Small bouquet garni*
- 1″ *sliver orange peel*
- 1 *tablespoon arrowroot flour dissolved in 1 tablespoon water (optional)*
- *Freshly chopped parsley*
- 2 *dashes Dr. Bronner's seasoning (Page 6)*

Mix dried herbs with flour. Pat chicken dry with paper toweling. Dredge chicken in flour mixture, shaking off excess. Heat ½ tablespoon oil in large teflon skillet until hot. Add half of chicken and brown lightly on each side. Transfer to heavy covered casserole. Heat ½ tablespoon oil in skillet until hot. Brown balance of chicken. Transfer to casserole.

Sauté onions, garlic and shallot in ½ tablespoon oil until wilted (about 3 minutes). Add wine and cook for 2 minutes, scraping skillet gently, if necessary, to remove browned particles. Add tomatoes, stock, Dr. Bronner's seasoning, carrot, cayenne, and smoked yeast. Bring to simmering point, and cook for 2 minutes. Pour over chicken. Add orange sliver and bouquet garni. Cover tightly, and bake in preheated 350 degree oven for 30 minutes.

Meanwhile wash out teflon skillet. Heat balance of oil until hot. Add sliced mushrooms and sauté for 3 minutes, turning constantly. Add to chicken that has baked for 30 minutes. Re-cover and return chicken to oven for 15 minutes, or until fork-tender.

Remove chicken with slotted spoon and keep warm in covered serving dish. Remove bouquet garni and orange peel and discard. Place casserole over medium high heat and bring to boil. Reduce heat, and simmer for one minute. If you'd like a slightly thicker gravy, add dissolved arrowroot flour, a little at a time, to hot gravy, stirring constantly. Pour over chicken. Sprinkle with freshly chopped parsley, and serve.

Yield: Serves 4

CAL	F	P:S	SOD	CAR	CHO
399	10	2.8:1	144	22	98
Thickened					
405	10	2.8:1	144	23	98

Chicken Cacciatore

No chicken cacciatore was ever prepared this way before. In my version, the chicken is sautéed until brown, then baked with rosy, tender tomatoes, snow-white crunchy mushrooms, and the spicy herbs of Italy. Bellisimo!

1 *broiler, 3 pounds, cut into serving pieces, skinned*
1½ *tablespoons corn oil*
1 *large onion, quartered and thinly sliced*
2 *shallots, minced*
3 *large cloves garlic, minced*
½ *green pepper, minced*
1 *rounded tablespoon tomato paste, no salt added (Page 6)*
2 *fresh tomatoes, cored, skinned, drained and chopped*
½ *pound fresh mushrooms, washed, dried, trimmed and sliced*
1 *tablespoon each wine vinegar and apple cider vinegar*
⅓ *cup unbleached flour*
⅓ *cup chicken stock (Page 10)*
1 *teaspoon smoked yeast (Page 6)*
4 *dashes cayenne pepper*
1 *tablespoon combined dried oregano and basil leaves, crushed*
Bouquet garni
Freshly chopped parsley

Pat chicken dry. Rub with dried herbs. Cover and refrigerate for 2 hours before cooking. When ready to cook, dredge chicken lightly in flour.

Heat 1 tablespoon oil in large iron skillet until hot. Add chicken and brown on both sides, turning gently with spatula. Transfer to covered oven-proof casserole.

Add balance of oil to skillet, and heat. Add onions, garlic, green pepper, and shallots. Sauté until lightly browned. Add vinegars and cook for 2 minutes. Combine tomatoes with tomato paste. Add to skillet together with stock, cayenne, smoked yeast and bouquet garni. Bring to simmering point and pour over browned chicken. Cover tightly and bake in preheated 350 degree oven for 20 minutes. Add mushrooms. Re-cover and bake for 25 minutes. Remove from oven. Let casserole stand, covered, for 30 minutes. Remove bouquet garni.

Reheat over low flame. Turn into

serving dish and sprinkle with freshly chopped parsley.

Yield: Serves 4

CAL	F	P:S	SOD	CAR	CHO
395	15	3.5:1	146	19	98

Miracle Chicken

This dish doesn't taste like chicken—and that's a miracle.

1 *broiling chicken, 3 pounds, cut into serving pieces, skinned*
3 *cloves garlic, minced*
1 *small leek, white part only, well washed and minced*
1 *onion, minced*
1 *large shallot, minced*
½ *carrot, scraped and grated*
1 *rib celery, minced*
½ *green pepper, minced*
1 *cup eggplant, peeled, and diced*
2 *tablespoons corn oil*
½ *teaspoon dried thyme leaves, crushed*
2 *tablespoons freshly chopped parsley and dill*
2 *teaspoons wine vinegar*
1 *cup chicken stock (Page 10)*
2 *tablespoons brown beef stock (Page 13)*
¾ *teaspoons curry powder, no salt or pepper added*
1 *sliver orange peel*

Pat chicken dry with paper toweling, and place in bowl. Mix garlic with 1 tablespoon oil and thyme. Coat chicken with mixture and refrigerate for 4-6 hours.

Heat teflon skillet until hot. Add half of garlic-coated chicken, and sauté until lightly browned on both sides. Transfer to iron casserole. Brown balance of chicken. Transfer to casserole.

In same skillet, heat balance of oil until hot. Sauté eggplant until lightly browned, turning constantly. Sprinkle over chicken. In same skillet, sauté all vegetables except carrot, until lightly browned. Add vinegar and cook for 2 minutes. Add stocks, curry and carrot. Heat to simmering point. Cook for 2 minutes stirring well. Pour over browned ingredients in casserole.

Add orange peel, parsley and dill, cover, and bake in preheated 375 degree oven for 30 minutes. Remove from oven, baste, and re-cover. Let stand on top of stove without cooking for 20 minutes. Turn oven up to 400 degrees, return casserole to oven, uncovered, and bake for 10 minutes. Turn chicken and baste. Bake uncovered for another 10 minutes. Liquid will have reduced and chicken will have an all-over brown color. Remove orange peel, and serve.

Yield: Serves 4

CAL	F	P:S	SOD	CAR	CHO
345	12	3.2:1	159	8	98

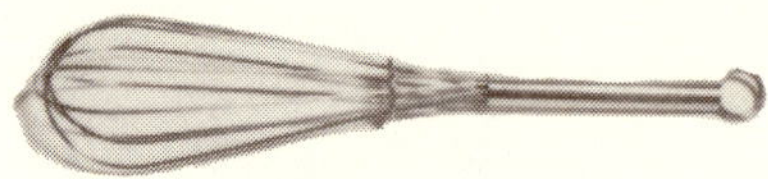

Stuffed Roast Turkey with Giblet Gravy

You don't have to wait for the holidays to enjoy this succulent bird. It's delicious, lower in saturated fats than chicken, and it's economical because you can use leftovers in so many intriguing ways. Any turkey aficionado will tell you it's the stuffing and sauce that make the bird—and here are both prepared with an elegance that lifts them far above the ordinary. Grandma would never recognize this bird!

For the turkey:

1 *6-pound fresh turkey*
1 *tablespoon corn oil*
1 *teaspoon each dried sage and thyme leaves, crushed*
½ *teaspoon dried rosemary leaves, crushed*
Several dashes cayenne pepper
Recipe for stuffing, doubled (Page 67)

For the giblets:

Giblets from turkey, except heart. Set liver aside for stuffing
1 *small whole onion, peeled*
2 *cloves garlic, minced*
½ *teaspoon dried thyme leaves, crushed*
½ *carrot, peeled*
½ *rib celery, cut in half*
Bouquet garni made with 2 sprigs parsley, ½ bay leaf, and ½ teaspoon fennel, tied together in small piece of washed cotton cheesecloth
1 *cup chicken stock (Page 10)*
1 *cup water*

For the gravy:

Chopped cooked giblets
Jelled liquid, fat removed, plus enough chicken stock to equal 2 cups
1½ *tablespoons unbleached flour*
2 *tablespoons corn oil*
3 *dashes Dr. Bronner's seasoning (Page 6)*
3-4 *dashes cayenne pepper*
¼ *teaspoon smoked yeast (Page 6)*
¼ *cup non-fat milk*
½ *teaspoon combined ground sage and thyme*

Remove giblets from cavity. Wash and set aside. Wash turkey inside and out. Dry very well with paper toweling. Prick skin all over with sharp-pronged fork. Rub with combined herbs. Sprinkle with cayenne. Cover with aluminum foil while stuffing is prepared.

Prepare stuffing by doubling recipe. Stuff cavity, packing loosely. Secure with skewers. Truss bird. Place on rack in roasting pan. Dip pastry brush in oil and brush turkey on all sides. Cover with heavy duty aluminum foil. Place in center section of preheated 350 degree oven, and roast for 1½ hours. Remove foil and roast for 45 minutes. Brush again with oil. Roast for an additional 30 to 45 minutes. Test for doneness in the following way: Prick turkey near bottom of thigh. Juices should not run pink. If so, return to oven for another 15 minutes. Let stand for 20 minutes, covered, before carving. Serve with stuffing and giblet gravy.

Cook giblets the day before turkey is roasted so that all fat can be removed. Place giblets in heavy-bottomed saucepan. Add one cup water. Bring to boil. Reduce heat and simmer, uncovered, for 5 minutes, removing scum that rises to top. Add balance of ingredients. Bring to simmering point. Cover partially, and simmer for 2 hours, adding more water, if necessary, so that giblets are barely covered throughout cooking time. Remove giblets with slotted spoon to small bowl. Strain liquid into jar, discarding vegetables and bouquet garni. Cover the giblets and liquid and refrigerate overnight. Next day remove fat that rises to top of liquid. Liquid and giblets are now ready for gravy.

For the gravy, chop up soft section of gizzard and discard balance. Pull off meat from neck and chop. Reheat jelled liquid and set aside. Heat corn oil in heavy-bottomed saucepan until hot but not smoking. Add flour and beat with wire whisk. Turn heat down and cook for one minute. Add reheated liquid to roux (flour and oil) a little at a time, using whisk to blend. Add milk, cayenne, Dr. Bronner's seasoning, smoked yeast, sage, and thyme. Finally, add chopped giblets and simmer, uncovered, for 5 minutes. Serve in sauceboat.

Yield: Turkey serves 8; gravy yields about 2 cups; allow 2 tablespoons per serving

Notes:

1. Say no to frozen birds that are injected with butter, salt, and other ingredients you prefer to avoid.

2. Substitute turkey for chicken in the following recipes: Chicken Divan (Page 60), Chef Salad (Page 104), and Bombay Chicken Balls (Page 119). Turkey Supreme is also made from leftovers (see below).

	CAL	F	P:S	SOD	CAR	CHO
	229	12	2.5:1	186	0	89
Gravy	56	3	4.5:1	32	6	0
Stuffing	142	0	—	32	28	16

Turkey Supreme

There are always leftovers when you serve turkey. Here's a way to use them to make a brightly original dish that may become more popular in your household than the turkey itself.

- 3 *cups cooked turkey, diced*
- 2 *tablespoons corn oil, plus ½ teaspoon to oil casserole*
- 2 *large cloves garlic, minced*
- 1 *large shallot, minced*
- 1 *onion, minced*
- 1 *small green pepper, minced*
- ¼ *pound fresh mushrooms, washed, dried, trimmed, and quartered*
- 3 *cups chicken or veal stock (Page 10 or 11)*
- ½ *cup rice*
- ½ *cup dry Vermouth or white wine*
- 1½ *teaspoons curry powder, no salt or pepper added*
- 2 *tablespoons tomato paste, no salt added (Page 6)*
- ½ *pound fresh peas, shelled and cooked*
- *Small bouquet garni*
- *Freshly chopped parsley*

Heat one tablespoon oil in teflon skillet until hot. Add onion, garlic, shallot, and green pepper, and sauté until tender (about 5 minutes). Add wine. Cook and stir over high heat for one minute. Add rice and stir well to coat. Add stock, tomato paste, curry, and bouquet garni. Bring to simmering point. Pour into lightly oiled 2-quart casserole. Cover and bake in preheated 400 degree oven for 25 minutes.

Meanwhile, wipe out skillet. Heat remaining oil until hot. Add mushrooms and sauté for 2 minutes, turning constantly. Add turkey and sauté only until heated through. After rice mixture has been cooking for 25 minutes, add turkey-mushroom mixture, stirring well. Return casserole to oven, covered, and bake 10 minutes, or until rice is tender and all liquid is absorbed. Uncover, remove bouquet garni, and stir in cooked peas, distributing evenly. Sprinkle with freshly chopped parsley and serve.

Yield: Serves 4

Note: Start to cook peas 15 minutes before you are ready to take casserole from oven. In that way they'll not wrinkle up and they'll retain their bright green color.

CAL	F	P:S	SOD	CAR	CHO
265	6	3.7:1	57	39	17

Meat

Beef Bourguignon

Here's all the heady wine-rich flavor of this classic French gourmet masterpiece with none of the morning-after on-the-scale blues. You'll find my version as authentic in appearance as it is in taste. For true lovers of French food.

1½ pounds beef, top round, cut into 3" chunks
2 tablespoons corn oil
2 onions, minced
3 large cloves garlic, minced
1 large shallot, minced
3-4 tablespoons unbleached flour
1½ cups beef stock (Page 12)
3 tablespoons brown beef stock (Page 13)
1 teaspoon smoked yeast (Page 6)
½ pound fresh mushrooms, washed, dried, trimmed and thickly sliced
½ teaspoon each dried thyme and rosemary leaves, crushed
2 tablespoons dry Sherry
2 tablespoons tomato paste, no salt added (Page 6)
¾ cup Burgundy wine
1 small bouquet garni

Wipe meat well with paper toweling. Dredge in flour, shaking off excess. Heat ½ tablespoon oil in large teflon skillet until very hot but not smoking. Brown half of meat on all sides. Transfer to heavy covered casserole. Add ½ tablespoon oil to skillet, and brown remaining meat. Transfer to casserole.

Add onions, garlic, and shallot to skillet and sauté until lightly browned, adding a drop or two more oil if necessary. Add Sherry, and scrape pan to loosen browned particles. Blend tomato paste with beef stock and brown beef stock and add to skillet. Pour in Burgundy wine and stir. Add herbs and smoked yeast and bring to simmering point. Pour over browned meat in casserole and add bouquet garni. Simmer, uncovered, on top of stove for 5 minutes, stirring well so that meat does not stick.

Preheat oven to 250 degrees. Bake meat, covered, in center section of oven for 1¼ hours. Uncover and stir. If liquid is thickening too fast at this point, add a bit of water. Re-cover and bake another 1½ hours, adding more water, midway, if necessary.

While meat is in the oven, wipe out skillet, and add balance of oil, heating until hot. Sauté mushrooms until lightly browned. After meat has cooked a total of 2½ hours, uncover and add mushrooms. Return covered casserole to oven and bake 15-30 minutes, or until meat is fork-tender, taking care that meat does not stick to casserole. Remove bouquet garni.

Serve immediately with parsleyed potatoes (Page 22) or rice, flecked with a sprinkling of chopped fresh parsley.

Yield: Serves 4 with one leftover

	CAL	F	P:S	SOD	CAR	CHO
	294	12	3.2:1	113	10	81
Rice	43	0	—	0	10	0

Steak Pizzaiola

Start with one of the leanest of all beef cuts, sirloin, brush with a light garlic marinade, and grill to perfection—that's my version of one of the most delectable of Italian dishes. Serve with a risotto (Page 29) and endive and arrugula salad (Page 98), and you'll think you're in a trattoria in Rome.

1 sirloin steak including fillet, sliced 1" thick, to weigh about 3 pounds
1 large shallot, minced
2 large cloves garlic, finely minced
1 tablespoon corn oil
½ teaspoon dried thyme leaves, crushed
1 tablespoon freshly chopped parsley
5 dashes cayenne pepper
½ teaspoon wine vinegar
⅛ teaspoon Dr. Bronner's seasoning (Page 6)

Let steak stand at room temperature for 30 minutes before broiling. Wipe dry with paper toweling. Combine remaining ingredients in a small bowl and blend well. This is your marinade.

Preheat broiler. Brush half marinade over one side of steak. Place under broiler 1½" from flame and broil for 7 minutes. Turn and spread balance of marinade over second side. Broil another 7 minutes. Turn again, basting with marinade, and broil for 10 minutes, 5 minutes on each side. The steak will be medium rare. Serve immediately.

Yield: Serves 6

CAL	F	P:S	SOD	CAR	CHO
314	12	1.6:1	126	0	135

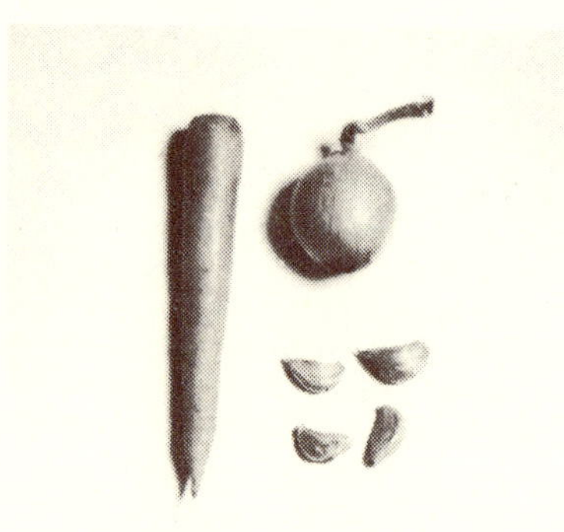

Swiss Steak

Savory slices of lean beef are bathed in a mushroom-enriched gravy in this version of—despite its name—a dish as American as apple pie. It is made to order for contemporary living in the U.S.A., for it freezes like a dream, and is as lovely the second time around.

2½ pounds beef, top or bottom round
About 4 tablespoons unbleached flour
2 tablespoons corn oil
2 onions, minced
3 large cloves garlic, minced
1 large shallot, minced
½ carrot, peeled and grated
½ cup tomato juice, no salt added
1 tablespoon tomato paste, no salt added (Page 6)
2 large fresh tomatoes, cored and skinned, or 1 8¼ oz. can tomatoes, no salt added
¼ cup dry Vermouth or white wine
⅛ cup water
¼ cup beef stock (Page 12)
2 tablespoons brown beef stock (Page 13)
½ teaspoon each dried oregano and basil leaves, crushed
6 large fresh mushrooms, washed, dried, trimmed and sliced
1 teaspoon caraway seeds, lightly crushed
4 dashes cayenne pepper
Large bouquet garni
Freshly chopped parsley

Wipe meat dry with paper toweling. Cut into ⅜" slices. There should be 8 slices in all. (Cutting suggestion: To facilitate easier slicing, freeze uncooked meat. The night before using, remove from freezing compartment and place in *refrigerator* section. Next day, remove from refrigerator and leave at room temperature for one hour. Slice.) Dredge lightly in flour, shaking off excess. Heat enough oil to lightly coat bottom of large teflon skillet. When very warm, brown meat, two to three slices at a time, on both sides, until golden brown, turning carefully with spatula so that coating does not separate from meat. If necessary, add more oil for browning second and third batch. Transfer browned meat to covered cast-iron casserole. (Do not use pyrex. Meat sticks to it.)

Add a few drops more oil to skillet.

Brown onions, garlic, and shallot. Add water and scrape around skillet to loosen browned particles. Add wine and cook over high heat for 2 minutes. Add herbs, tomatoes, tomato paste, tomato juice, stocks, cayenne, carrot, caraway seeds and bouquet garni. Simmer for 5 minutes. Pour over meat and cover tightly. Place in preheated 350 degree oven and bake for one hour, removing from oven once to shift pieces of meat around casserole to prevent sticking. Remove from oven and add sliced mushrooms. Re-cover and bake for another 25 minutes.

Remove from oven and let stand on top of stove, covered, for 15 minutes. Place meat on serving platter without gravy, removing slices with slotted spoon or spatula. Whisk gravy around casserole until well blended. Pour over meat. Sprinkle liberally with freshly chopped parsley.

Yield: Serves 6

CAL	F	P:S	SOD	CAR	CHO
339	14	2.2:1	139	9	133

Sweet and Sauerbraten

In my version of this traditional German dish, lean tender beef is marinated in pickling spices, lemon juice, and—surprise!—apple juice. It's served in a creamy sauce that's as tangy as it's satiny. Preparation is simple, so if you want to show off your mastery of Teutonic cooking effortlessly, this is the recipe for you.

3 *pounds top or bottom round beef*
¼ *cup pickling spices, no salt added*
Juice from 2 lemons
1 *teaspoon grated lemon rind*
1 *cup onion, coarsely chopped*
2 *large cloves garlic, minced*
2 *tablespoons corn oil*
5 *dashes cayenne pepper*
½ *teaspoon thyme leaves, crushed*
2 *ribs celery, minced*
4 *large crisp sprigs parsley, washed and dried*
½ *carrot, peeled and diced*
2 *cups apple juice, no sugar added*
½ *teaspoon smoked yeast (Page 6)*
Enough boiling water to cover meat

In preparing marinade, check pickling spices to see if it includes bay leaf and cloves. If not, add one bay leaf and 8 cloves. Tie spices in small piece of washed cotton cheesecloth. Tie parsley sprigs with white thread in a separate bundle. Set both bundles aside.

Heat 1 tablespoon oil in teflon skillet until hot. Add garlic, onions, celery and carrot. Sauté until lightly browned. Add apple juice and bring to boil. Add cayenne, thyme, lemon juice, rind, pickling spices, and smoked yeast. Turn flame down and simmer for 5 minutes.

Wipe meat dry. Trim away all fat. Place meat in deep, narrow container (stainless steel or glass, not plastic). Pour hot marinade over meat. Add enough boiling water to cover meat. (The narrower the pot the less diluted the marinade.) Cover, and refrigerate for 3 days, turning once daily.

When ready to cook, remove meat from marinade, reserving liquid. Wipe meat dry. Heat remaining oil until hot in covered iron casserole. Brown meat well on all sides. Pour off any unabsorbed oil. Measure out 2 cups of marinade and vegetables and add to casserole. Add parsley bundle. Heat to boiling point on top of stove, skimming off scum that rises to top. Cover, and bake in preheated 325 degree oven for 2½-3 hours. (There should be about 1½ cups of liquid in casserole at all times. If not, add some reserved marinade.) Test with long-pronged fork for doneness. Meat should be very tender.

Remove meat from casserole and slice with very sharp knife. Transfer to serving dish and keep warm. Discard parsley bundle. Pour contents of casserole into blender and purée until smooth. Pour back into a saucepan and reheat. Pour heated gravy over sliced meat, and serve.

Yield: Serves 6
Variations:

1. Dissolve 1 tablespoon arrowroot flour in one tablespoon water. Dribble into hot gravy, whisking constantly until thickened to desired consistency. Pour over meat.

2. Add 3 tablespoons low-fat yogurt to gravy, whisking well. Bring to simmering point, and pour over meat.

CAL	F	P:S	SOD	CAR	CHO
321	14	1.3:1	198	3	135
Thickened					
325	14	1.3:1	198	4	135
With yogurt					
327	14+	1.2:1	198	4	135

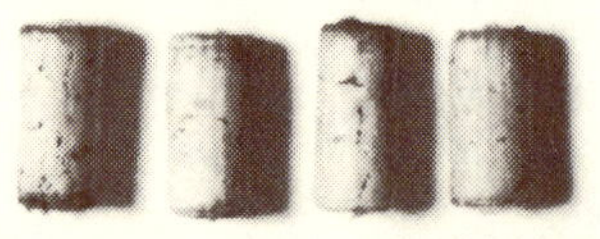

Sautéed Medallions of Veal

If you're in an extravagant mood, splurge with an order to your butcher for three-quarter-inch medallions of veal. This cut is to veal what filet mignon is to beef. Here it's treated with all the grandeur it deserves.

8 *veal medallions, ¾" thick, cut from the eye of round or flank, about 1¼ pounds*
2 *tablespoons corn oil*
2 *large cloves garlic, minced*
1 *large shallot, minced*
½ *rib celery, finely minced*
1 *teaspoon grated carrot*
About 2 tablespoons unbleached flour
¼ *cup dry Vermouth or white wine*
⅔ *cup veal or chicken stock (Pages 11 or 10)*
1 *teaspoon tomato paste, no salt added (Page 6)*
½ *teaspoon dried rosemary leaves, crushed*
1 *large sprig parsley*
1" *slice orange peel*
4 *dashes smoked yeast (Page 6)*
4 *dashes cayenne pepper*
4 *dashes Dr. Bronner's seasoning (Page 6)*
Freshly chopped parsley

Wipe meat dry with paper toweling. Dredge in flour, shaking off excess. Heat oil in large iron skillet until hot. Add veal and sauté on both sides until lightly browned (about 8 minutes). Add garlic, celery, and shallot, and sauté for one minute. Add wine. Cook for one minute. Add balance of ingredients with the exception of chopped parsley. Cover and simmer until tender (about 25 minutes), turning twice. Discard orange peel and parsley sprig.

Place meat on heated individual plates, and spoon with sauce. Sprinkle with chopped parsley, and serve. Delicious accompanied by parsleyed potatoes (Page 22) and any green vegetable.

Yield: Serves 4

CAL	F	P:S	SOD	CAR	CHO
299	15	1.5:1	117	3	103
With veal stock					
299	15	1.5:1	129	3	103

Stuffed Veal

This lowest-calorie of all veal cuts is delectable when it's bathed in an herbaceous marinade and stuffed with savory full-kerneled kasha. A sumptuous looking dish, it more than satisfies the heartiest appetite.

For the meat:

3 *slices boneless veal, cut from the leg, 1/4" thick to weigh 2 pounds, pounded thin*
About 2 cups tomato juice, no salt added
½ *cup veal stock (Page 11)*

For the marinade, combine and mix the following:

3 *tablespoons apple cider vinegar*
1 *tablespoon corn oil*
3 *cloves garlic, minced*
2 *shallots, minced*
1 *teaspoon freshly chopped dill*
½ *teaspoon each dried rosemary and thyme leaves, crushed*
3 *dashes cayenne pepper*

For the stuffing:

1¼ *cups kasha (buckwheat groats)*
1 *onion, minced*
2 *large cloves garlic, minced*
1 *shallot, minced*
½ *teaspoon wine vinegar*
1 *egg white, lightly beaten with fork*
½ *tablespoon corn oil*
¼ *teaspoon smoked yeast (Page 6)*
1 *cup veal stock (Page 11)*
¼ *cup water*
½ *cup dry Vermouth or white wine*
1 *teaspoon freshly chopped dill*
¼ *teaspoon dried thyme leaves, crushed*
½ *carrot, peeled and grated*
3 *dashes cayenne pepper*

Prepare stuffing first. Heat oil in large teflon skillet until hot. Add garlic, onion, and shallot, and sauté until lightly brown. Add vinegar, wine, and water, and cook over medium heat for one minute. Add herbs, pepper, smoked yeast, stock, and kasha, and bring to simmering point. Cover and cook for 6-8 minutes, or until all liquid is absorbed. Uncover and let cool. Add egg white and carrot. Blend. Set aside.

Wipe meat dry with paper toweling. Arrange slices of meat on board alongside each other lengthwise, overlapping edges. Pound seams to hold together. Brush with marinade. Spoon and spread stuffing over meat leaving bare 1" from all edges. Roll up firmly. Tie meat securely in several places. Brush all over with marinade. Place in large iron casserole. Cover and refrigerate for 4-5 hours.

Remove meat from marinade and dry. Pour off marinade and discard. Heat casserole until hot. Add rolled meat and brown lightly on all sides. Add one cup tomato juice and veal stock. Bring to simmering point on top of stove. Cover, and bake in preheated 350 degree oven for 20 minutes. Uncover, and add half cup tomato juice, and return to oven, uncovered. Bake for 40 minutes, basting from time to time, and turning once. Cover, and let stand on top of stove for 20 minutes before carving. Transfer to heated serving platter and keep warm. Pour remaining contents of casserole into measuring cup. Add enough tomato juice to equal one cup. Heat to simmering point.

Slice meat and serve with gravy spooned over each slice.

Yield: Serves 8
Note: This dish is particularly delicious served cold the next day. It can be thinly sliced and served on sandwich bread, or on a bed of Romaine lettuce, as a salad.

CAL	F	P:S	SOD	CAR	CHO
102	5	1.6:1	125	2	85
Stuffing					
80	1	4.5:1	19	15	0

Braised Veal

Serve this delicious dish in three ways. Hot, cold in thin slices, or as a tasty veal salad (Page 103).

1 *2½ pound piece of leg of veal, boned, rolled and tied*
2 *tablespoons corn oil*
3 *cloves garlic, minced*
2 *shallots, minced*
1 *rib celery, minced*
1 *onion, thinly sliced*
1 *small green pepper, minced*
1 *carrot, peeled and thinly sliced*
1 *fresh tomato, cored and coarsely chopped*
2 *tablespoons unbleached flour*
½ *teaspoon each dried rosemary and thyme leaves, crushed*
6 *dashes cayenne pepper*
¼ *teaspoon smoked yeast (Page 6)*
¼ *cup dry Vermouth or white wine*
½ *cup veal stock (Page 11)*
About ¾ cup tomato juice, no salt added
Small bouquet garni

Wipe meat dry with paper toweling. Dredge lightly in flour, shaking off excess. Heat oil in large covered casserole until hot. Add meat and brown on all sides. Remove from casserole.

Arrange onion, shallots, garlic, celery, carrot, and green pepper over bottom of casserole in one layer. Place browned meat on top of vegetable mixture. Sprinkle with cayenne, smoked yeast, and dried herbs. Add chopped tomato and bouquet garni. Pour stock and a ½ cup tomato juice over meat. Bring to simmering point. Cover and bake in preheated 325 degree oven for one hour. Remove from oven and baste, adding more juice if liquid has evaporated. There should be ¾ cup liquid in casserole at all times. Return to oven and bake another hour, basting midway, and adding more juice if necessary. Test for doneness by inserting long-pronged fork into middle of roast. Meat should be tender yet firm. Place meat on platter and cover to keep warm.

Pour remaining contents of casserole into measuring cup. Add enough tomato juice to make 1 cup. Return to casserole together with wine. Bring to boil. Turn flame down and simmer until liquid is reduced to ¾ cup. Pour into blender and purée for one minute. Reheat over low flame.

Slice meat thinly and serve sauce on the side in a sauceboat. Spoon over meat. Serve with risotto or a selection from my recipe for broccoli magic (Pages 18 and 19).

Yield: Serves 6

CAL	F	P:S	SOD	CAR	CHO
201	10	2.8:1	107	7	134

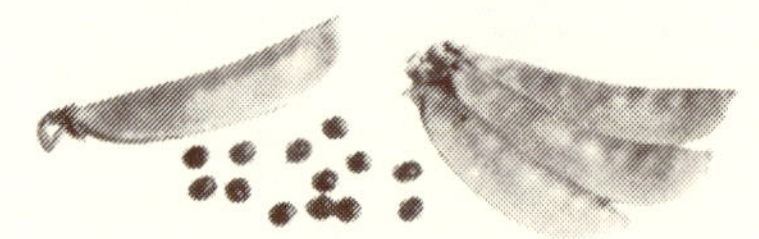

Braised Veal Shanks

The enjoyment of food begins when you look at a dish. And here's one dish with a palette of colors—pink veal, orange carrots, pale red sauce, and bright green peas—that's a delight to the eye. And the delight on the tongue is just as great.

2 *veal shanks, or 3 pounds, cut into 1" slices, well trimmed*
1 *onion, minced*
3 *large cloves garlic, minced*
3 *shallots, minced*
2 *tablespoons corn oil*
4 *miniature carrots, each cut in half*
1 *rib celery, diced*
½ *pound fresh peas, shelled and cooked*
2 *tablespoons unbleached flour*
¾ *cup dry Vermouth or white wine*
¾ *cup tomato purée, no salt added (Page 6)*
1 *rounded tablespoon tomato paste, no salt added (Page 6)*
½ *cup veal stock (Page 11)*
¾ *cup water*
¾ *teaspoon each dried thyme and basil leaves, crushed*
3 *dashes cayenne pepper*
1 *teaspoon dried mint leaves, crushed*
Bouquet garni
Freshly chopped parsley

Wipe meat dry with paper toweling. Dredge lightly in flour, shaking off excess. Heat 1 tablespoon oil in large teflon skillet until hot. Brown meat on all sides, turning carefully with spatula. Transfer meat to iron casserole.

Add balance of oil to skillet, and sauté garlic, celery, onion, and shallots, until lightly browned. Add water, scraping skillet to loosen browned particles. Add wine and bring to simmering point. Cook for 3 minutes. Add carrots, stock, tomato purée, tomato paste, cayenne, thyme and basil, and bouquet garni. Bring to simmering point and cook for 3 minutes.

Pour over meat. Sprinkle with mint leaves. Place in center section of preheated 325 degree oven and bake for one hour, stirring once midway. Meat when done should be fork-tender. Remove from oven and set aside.

Cook shelled peas in rapidly boiling water to cover for 10 minutes. Color should remain bright green. Drain and add to casserole, stirring gently. Sprinkle with freshly chopped parsley.

Yield: Serves 4

CAL	F	P:S	SOD	CAR	CHO
370	15	2.1:1	187	16	159

Veal Birds

My version of this north Italian delicacy is built around a savory mixture of meat, herbs, and bread crumbs sandwiched between thinly pounded slices of lean pink veal. Sautéed to a golden brown, then braised gently in stock, wine, and vegetables, it makes a dish as elegant as it is delectable.

For the stuffing:
1 *tablespoon corn oil*
1 *small carrot, peeled and grated*
¼ *pound lean pork, ground*
¼ *pound lean veal, ground*
2 *cloves garlic, minced*
2 *large shallots, minced*
½ *rib celery, minced*
1 *very small onion, minced*
3 *tablespoons duxelles (Page 13)*
1 *egg white*
3 *tablespoons chopped, drained water-chestnuts, packed in water, no salt added*
¼ *teaspoon dried thyme leaves, crushed*
⅛ *teaspoon dried rosemary leaves, crushed*
1 *tablespoon freshly chopped dill and parsley*
¾ *cup freshly made, very lightly toasted bread crumbs (Page 147)*
¼ *cup non-fat milk*
3 *dashes Dr. Bronner's seasoning (Page 6)*
2 *dashes cayenne pepper*

For the birds:

4 *slices veal, about 1 pound, cut from leg, pounded thin*
1½ *tablespoons corn oil*
1 *small onion, minced*
1 *large shallot, minced*
1 *large clove garlic, minced*
½ *rib celery, finely minced*
2 *teaspoons tomato paste, no salt added (Page 6)*
1 *small bay leaf*
⅓ *cup dry red wine*
2 *dashes cayenne pepper*
2 *fresh tomatoes, peeled, cored, and chopped*
1¼ *cups veal stock (Page 11)*
1 *tablespoon brown beef stock (Page 13)*
2 *tablespoons freshly chopped dill and parsley*
¼ *teaspoon dried thyme leaves, crushed*
⅛ *teaspoon dried rosemary leaves, crushed*

Prepare stuffing first. Heat oil in large teflon skillet until hot. Sauté combined ground meat. Use large metal spoon to break up pieces while cooking. Continue sautéeing, turning often, for 4 minutes, until barely cooked through. Add onion, garlic, celery, and shallots, and cook another 3 minutes, mixing well. Transfer to large bowl.

Add duxelles, waterchestnuts, carrot, Dr. Bronner's seasoning, cayenne, herbs, bread crumbs, egg white, and milk. Blend well.

Wipe veal slices dry on both sides. Cut each slice in half. Place a large mound of stuffing on top of each half, pressing to hold. Cover with another half. Secure each bird with 4 toothpicks. Spoon any leftover stuffing into lightly oiled pyrex dish and set aside.

Heat 1 tablespoon oil in teflon skillet until hot. Sauté birds until lightly browned on both sides. Transfer to oven-proof covered casserole.

Leaving flame on under skillet, add remaining oil and brown onion, garlic, shallot, and celery. Add stocks, wine, herbs, cayenne, tomatoes, and tomato paste. Heat to simmering point. Cook one minute. Pour over meat in casserole, reserving 2 tablespoons for leftover stuffing. Cover tightly. Bake in preheated 350 degree oven for 50 minutes, removing bay leaf when ready to serve.

Serve on 4 heated individual plates, saving leftover stuffing for another light meal.

Yield: Serves 4; 2 leftover portions stuffing

	CAL	F	P:S	SOD	CAR	CHO
	199	12	2.5:1	96	8	105
Stuffing	143	4	4.5:1	96	8	61

Baked Herbed Veal Chops

Veal, the lowest in fat of all meats, can be prepared in many simple yet exciting ways because it so readily takes on the flavors of herbs and spices. If you have an adventuresome streak, there's no reason why you can't add a variety of veal dishes to your menu. But here's one veal dish that's so delicious you might have it more often than any other. We do.

4 *loin veal chops, about 1½ pounds, well trimmed*
1 *tablespoon corn oil*
3 *shallots, minced*
3 *cloves garlic, minced*
1 *onion, minced*
½ *green pepper, parboiled, and minced*
¼ *cup dry Vermouth or white wine*
½ *cup veal stock (Page 11)*
1 *tablespoon tomato paste, no salt added (Page 6)*
2 *dashes Dr. Bronner's seasoning (Page 6)*
1 *bay leaf*
½ *teaspoon each dried thyme and sage leaves, crushed*
3 *dashes cayenne pepper*
Freshly chopped parsley

Wipe chops dry with paper toweling. Rub with dried herbs and let stand, covered, at room temperature for one hour.

Heat half of oil in large iron skillet until hot. Brown chops lightly on both sides. Transfer to shallow roasting pan.

Heat balance of oil in skillet until hot. Add vegetables and garlic and brown lightly. Add wine and cook for 2 minutes. Combine stock with tomato paste. Add to skillet. Add bay leaf, cayenne, and Dr. Bronner's seasoning. Simmer for one minute.

Pour sauce over chops. Cover with aluminum foil and bake in preheated 350 degree oven for 45 minutes, turning once midway. Chops should be fork-tender.

Arrange chops on serving platter. Pour sauce over them. Sprinkle with parsley and serve.

Yield: Serves 4

CAL	F	P:S	SOD	CAR	CHO
366	12	2.0:1	165	4	120

Veal Loaf with Creamy Mushroom Sauce

Of course, there's no cream in it, but why tell your guests? They'll never know. The delicate mushroom sauce with its muted accents of shallot and garlic makes a happy marriage with the herb-flavored veal. For the discriminating palate.

1½ *pounds lean veal, ground*
2 *tablespoons corn oil, plus ½ teaspoon to oil baking dish*
2 *large cloves garlic, minced*
½ *rib celery, minced*
1 *shallot, minced*
1 *onion, minced*
1¼ *cups bread crumbs (Page 147)*
¼ *cup non-fat milk*
¼ *teaspoon each dried basil, thyme, and sage leaves, crushed*
¼ *pound fresh mushrooms, washed, dried, trimmed and sliced*
1 *egg white, beaten lightly with fork*
3 *dashes cayenne pepper*
2 *dashes Dr. Bronner's seasoning (Page 6)*
2 *firmly packed tablespoons freshly chopped dill and parsley*

Heat oil in large iron skillet until very warm but not smoking. Add onion, garlic, celery, and shallot, and cook for 2 minutes, turning constantly. Turn up flame slightly and add mushrooms. Shake around skillet until cooked through lightly (about 3 minutes). Pour into bowl and let cool.

Add veal, crumbs, herbs, and cayenne to sautéed mixture and blend well. Add milk, egg whites, and Dr. Bronner's seasoning and blend again.

Lightly oil a rectangular baking dish. Shape meat into loaf approximately 8″ × 4″, pressing together with hands. Do not use loaf pan. Bake in preheated 350 degree oven for 15 minutes. Remove from oven and pour off any fat that may have dripped from meat. Return to oven and bake another 35 minutes. Let cool for 5 minutes.

Cut into serving slices and serve topped with creamy mushroom sauce.

Creamy Mushroom Sauce:

- *2 tablespoons corn oil*
- *1½ tablespoons arrowroot flour*
- *1¼ cups veal or chicken stock (Page 11 or 10)*
- *2 shallots, finely minced*
- *1 clove garlic, finely minced*
- *¼ pound fresh mushrooms, washed, dried, trimmed and sliced*
- *¼ cup dry Vermouth or white wine*
- *1-1¼ cups non-fat milk*
- *¼ teaspoon each dried basil and thyme leaves, crushed*
- *2 tablespoons freshly chopped dill and parsley*

Heat one tablespoon oil in large teflon skillet until hot. Add shallots and garlic and sauté for one minute. Add mushrooms and sauté for 3 minutes, turning constantly. Add wine and cook over medium high heat until wine is almost evaporated. Pour into bowl and set aside.

Heat balance of oil in heavy-bottomed saucepan until hot. Add flour all at once, beating rapidly with wire whisk until well blended. Lower flame. Add stock and continue whisking until thickened and smooth. Whisk in herbs and milk. Add sautéed mushroom mixture. Bring to simmering point, and simmer very gently for 2 minutes. Serve.

Yield: Loaf serves 6; about 2½ cups sauce; allow 4 tablespoons per serving. There will be leftover sauce.

Notes:

1. This sauce is adaptable to many dishes such as fish, shrimp, and chicken.

2. See note for delicate, airy meat loaf (Page 95).

	CAL	F	P:S	SOD	CAR	CHO
	192	4	1:1	129	9	102
Sauce	54	0	—	22	2	0

Veal Stew with Tomatoes and Mushrooms

This is a light and delicate version of a hearty stew that's popular in the small auberges that dot the French countryside. It has a flavor all its own. It's an excellent dish to make when you're expecting guests because it can be prepared a day in advance and slowly reheated before dinner.

- *2½ pounds stewing veal, cut into 1" chunks, trimmed*
- *2 tablespoons corn oil*
- *1 onion, minced*
- *½ rib celery, minced*
- *3 large cloves garlic, finely minced*
- *2 large shallots, minced*
- *½ green pepper, minced*
- *3 fresh tomatoes, cored, skinned and coarsely chopped, or one 8¼ oz. can tomatoes, no salt added*
- *2 tablespoons tomato paste, no salt added (Page 6)*
- *⅓ cup veal stock (Page 11)*
- *¾ cup dry Vermouth or white wine*
- *½ teaspoon dried thyme leaves, crushed*
- *1 teaspoon dried rosemary leaves, crushed*
- *8 large fresh mushrooms, washed, dried, trimmed, and sliced*
- *2 teaspoons grated orange rind*
- *3 dashes cayenne pepper*
- *Small bouquet garni*
- *Freshly chopped parsley*

Dry meat thoroughly with paper toweling. Trim off fat and membranes. Heat 1 tablespoon oil in covered heavy casserole until hot. Add half of the veal, and brown well on all sides. Transfer to a bowl. Heat balance of oil in same casserole until hot, and brown remaining veal. Transfer to bowl.

Add onion, celery, garlic, green pepper, and shallots to casserole, and sauté until lightly browned, adding a drop more oil if necessary. Add wine, scraping pot with large spoon to loosen browned particles. Return browned meat to casserole, stirring well. Combine veal stock with dried herbs, orange rind, tomatoes, tomato paste and cayenne. Pour over meat. Add bouquet garni, and bring to simmering point. Cover tightly. Place in preheated 325 degree oven, and bake until meat is almost tender (about one hour).

Remove from oven and add mushrooms, stirring well. Bring to simmering point on top of stove. Cover, and return to oven for 30 minutes. Test for doneness with long-pronged fork. Meat should be firm yet tender. If not, return to oven for another 10 minutes.

Serve over a bed of plain boiled rice, and sprinkle with freshly chopped parsley.

Yield: Serves 6

Note: I have found that the flavor of this stew is enhanced if it sits, covered, out of the oven for 30 minutes before serving. It can then be reheated briefly.

CAL	F	P:S	SOD	CAR	CHO
359	16	2.7:1	189	9	171
Rice					
43	0	—	0	10	0

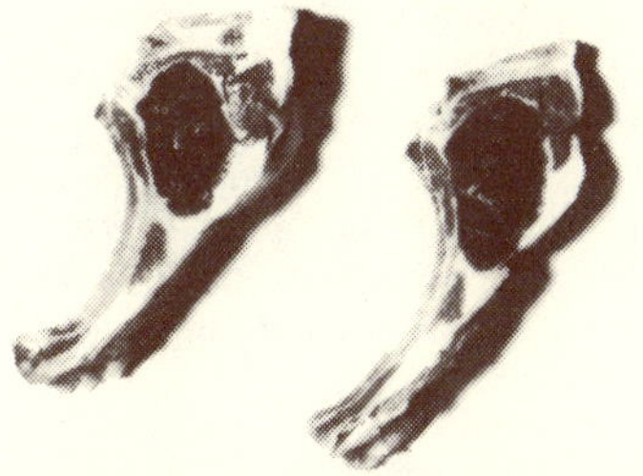

Skillet Pork Chops with Fresh Mushrooms

Here's a pork chop dish that you can prepare rapidly in a single skillet, and everybody will think you slaved over it for hours.

- 4 *center or loin cut pork chops, ½" thick, well trimmed, about 1½ pounds*
- 1 *tablespoon corn oil*
- 2 *shallots, minced*
- 2 *large cloves garlic, minced*
- ½ *green pepper, cut into ¼" strips*
- 1 *tablespoon wine vinegar*
- 1 *tablespoon freshly chopped parsley*
- ½ *teaspoon each dried thyme and basil leaves, crushed*
- ⅔ *cup tomato juice, no salt added*
- 1 *teaspoon tomato paste, no salt added (Page 6)*
- 3 *tablespoons brown beef stock (Page 13)*
- ½ *pound fresh mushrooms, washed, well dried, trimmed, and sliced*

At least 2 hours before cooking time, wipe chops dry with paper toweling, and rub with dried herbs. Cover and refrigerate until ready to cook.

Heat oil until hot in large iron skillet. Brown chops well on both sides (about 12-15 minutes). Lower flame to medium heat. Add garlic and vegetables, and brown together with chops. Add vinegar and cook for 2 minutes.

Combine tomato paste with tomato juice and brown beef stock. Pour over chops. Sprinkle with chopped parsley. Bring to simmering point. Cover, and simmer for 30 minutes, turning chops once. Uncover and add mushrooms. Bring to simmering point. Re-cover and simmer for another 20 minutes, turning once. Chops should be served fork-tender.

Yield: Serves 4

CAL	F	P:S	SOD	CAR	CHO
378	22	2.1:1	106	2	112

Stuffed Pork Chops in Red Wine

This is one of the most spectacular dishes in my new cuisine. It's guaranteed to evoke a chorus of ooh's and aah's when you bring it to the table. It looks and tastes like a million calories. A special treat for hearty eaters.

For the chops and sauce:

4 *loin pork chops, 1¼ pounds*
2 *tablespoons corn oil*
4 *tablespoons unbleached flour*
1 *large clove garlic, minced*
1 *small onion, minced*
1 *shallot, minced*
½ *teaspoon each dried rosemary and thyme leaves, crushed*
2 *dashes cayenne pepper*
Freshly chopped parsley and dill
⅔ *cup chicken or beef stock (Pages 10 or 12)*
¾ *cup dry red wine (we like an Italian Barolo)*
1½ *tablespoons tomato paste, no salt added (Page 6)*
2 *large fresh mushrooms, washed, trimmed and sliced*
1″ *sliver orange peel*

For the stuffing:

1 *cup cubed stuffing bread (Page 147)*
1 *tablespoon corn oil*
1 *clove garlic, minced*
1 *shallot, minced*
2 *tablespoons celery, finely minced*
2 *tablespoons onions, finely minced*
2 *tablespoons duxelles (Page 13)*
¼ *teaspoon each dried thyme and rosemary leaves, crushed*
½ *cup sweet, crisp apple, peeled and finely chopped*
2 *dashes cayenne pepper*
3 *dashes smoked yeast*
2 *teaspoons freshly chopped parsley and dill*
½ *cup hot chicken or beef stock (Page 10 or 12)*

Prepare the stuffing first. Heat oil over medium flame in small skillet until hot. Add garlic, shallot, celery, and onion. Sauté until lightly browned. Place bread in medium-sized bowl. Add sautéed mixture, duxelles, herbs, cayenne, apple, and smoked yeast. Toss well. Add stock to bread mixture and blend. Using a tablespoon, press the bread against the side of bowl, mashing it slightly. The mixture should be damp enough to hold together. Add more stock, if necessary, to accomplish this.

Trim and discard all fat from chop. Make a pocket in each chop as follows: Lay chop flat. With sharp knife cut horizontally from outer edge through center to bone. Open pocket. Fill each pocket with 2 tablespoons stuffing. Sew up pocket. (If you don't have a poultry needle, use a large-eyed needle.)

Mix flour with dried herbs and cayenne. Dredge chops in mixture, shaking off excess. Heat oil in large iron skillet. (An iron skillet is a must because it will later go into the oven.) Add chops, and brown well on both sides. Add minced onion, garlic and shallot just a minute or two before the browning on the second side is done.

Combine stock, wine, and tomato paste in a saucepan and heat. Pour ⅓ cup over browned chops. Cover with aluminum foil and bake in preheated 350 degree oven for 45 minutes, turning once midway.

Add balance of hot stock-wine mixture, together with mushrooms and orange peel. Reheat on top of stove until bubbling, turning meat once. Re-cover and return to oven for 20 minutes.

Transfer to individual heated plates, spooning sauce over chops. Sprinkle with freshly chopped parsley and dill and serve with any of my green vegetables.

Yield: Serves 4

CAL	F	P:S	SOD	CAR	CHO
363	18	2.1:1	95	6	81
With beef stock					
363	18	2.1:1	116	6	81
Stuffing					
134	4	4.6:1	18	12	0
With beef stock					
134	4	4.6:1	26	12	0

Unusual Baked Pork Chops

Pork lends itself to exotic flavors, as every Oriental chef knows. But exotic doesn't necessarily mean Oriental. The exotic flavor of this dish comes from a mixture of familiar spices, acorn squash, and the good old American favorite, apples. If you love the unusual, this one is for you.

4 *very lean center cut pork chops, about 1½ pounds*
1 *tablespoon corn oil*
1 *large shallot, minced*
1 *large clove garlic, minced*
1 *small acorn squash*
½ *cup apple juice, no sugar added*
1″ *slice orange peel*
4 *thin slices orange*
½ *teaspoon ground sage*
1 *teaspoon ground ginger*
¼ *teaspoon ground allspice*
3 *dashes cayenne pepper*
1 *tablespoon honey*
1 *large sweet crisp apple, peeled, cored and thickly sliced*

Wipe meat dry with paper toweling. Rub well on both sides with sage.

Heat oil until hot in large iron skillet. Brown chops lightly on both sides, adding shallot and garlic when you turn meat to second side (about 10 minutes). Pour off any remaining oil.

Cut squash in half, removing seeds. Then cut into quarters. Peel and slice thick. Add to skillet. Combine apple juice, spices, sage, orange peel, and honey. Pour over meat and squash. Bring to boil. Lower flame so that liquid just simmers. Cover with heavy-duty aluminum foil and place in preheated 375 degree oven for 45 minutes, turning once midway.

Add apples. Re-cover, and bake for 7 minutes. Remove from oven and stir well. Remove orange peel.

Serve chops in center of individual heated plates, and top with slice of orange. Spoon gravy over chop and orange, and surround with apples and squash.

Yield: Serves 4

CAL	F	P:S	SOD	CAR	CHO
366	19	2.6:1	94	20	112

Roast Fresh Ham

Only *fresh* ham comes to the kitchen devoid of added salt and sugar. Take advantage of it and enjoy ham transformed into a new kind of gourmet delight by the magic of herbs, wine and the essences of fresh vegetables.

½ *fresh ham (about 7-8 pounds)*
1 *tablespoon corn oil*
½ *teaspoon each ground sage and thyme, and dried rosemary leaves, crushed*
1 *large onion, minced*
1 *rib celery, diced*
3 *cloves garlic, minced*
1 *carrot, peeled and diced*
1 *bay leaf*
6 *whole cloves*
¾ *cup dry Vermouth or white wine*
½ *cup water*

Trim all fat from ham. Wipe dry. Brush lightly with oil. Combine herbs. Sprinkle over meat. Then press into meat with large spoon. Cut three ¼″ slits into surface of each side of meat. Insert cloves in slits. Strew vegetables, bay leaf, and garlic onto bottom of large roasting pan. Place meat on top of vegetables.

Bring Vermouth and water to boil in saucepan. Pour into bottom of pan (not over meat). Cover pan loosely with aluminum foil. Roast ham in preheated 325 degree oven for 45 minutes. Uncover and baste. Re-cover, and roast 30 minutes. Baste again, and return to oven uncovered. Roast for a total of 2½-3 hours (25 minutes per pound, bone in).

Slice thin, and serve with pan juices. Apple relish is a tasty accompaniment (Page 107).

Yield: Serves 8 with half of ham for leftovers

CAL	F	P:S	SOD	CAR	CHO
353	16	1.6:1	125	0	115

Baked Lamb Steaks

Here's a lamb dish that tastes as if it takes a full day to prepare. Actually, it's a quickie. It's the tangy marinade with its adventurously delicious blending of flavors not ordinarily associated with lamb that lifts this dish far out of the commonplace. A must for the jaded palate!

4 *lamb steaks, cut from leg, ½" thick (about 1¼ pounds)*
2 *tablespoons corn oil*
1 *large clove garlic, minced*
1 *shallot, minced*
1 *teaspoon carrot, peeled and grated*
1 *tablespoon apple cider vinegar*
¼ *cup fresh orange juice*
⅓ *cup pineapple chunks, packed in its own juices, no sugar added*
¼ *cup pineapple juice, no sugar added, taken from canned pineapple chunks*
1 *teaspoon ground ginger*
1 *tablespoon honey*
4 *dashes Dr. Bronner's seasoning (Page 6)*
1 *navel orange, peeled, and cut into chunks*
2 *teaspoons arrowroot flour dissolved in 2 teaspoons water*

Place all ingredients, with the exception of meat and fruit chunks, in blender. Purée for one minute. This will be your marinade.

Wipe meat slices dry with paper toweling. Place in shallow baking dish in one layer. Pour puréed marinade over meat. Cover and let stand for 2-3 hours.

Place in preheated 350 degree oven and bake for 45 minutes. Add orange and pineapple chunks. Cover and bake until fork-tender (about 20 minutes).

Transfer meat to serving platter and keep warm. Dribble flour mixture into gravy, a little at a time, stirring well, using only enough to thicken gravy lightly. Pour over meat and serve.

Yield: Serves 4
Note: Lean shoulder lamb chops may be substituted for lamb steaks.

CAL	F	P:S	SOD	CAR	CHO
299	36	1.3:1	112	16	80
Shoulder chops					
325	40	1.2:1	112	16	80

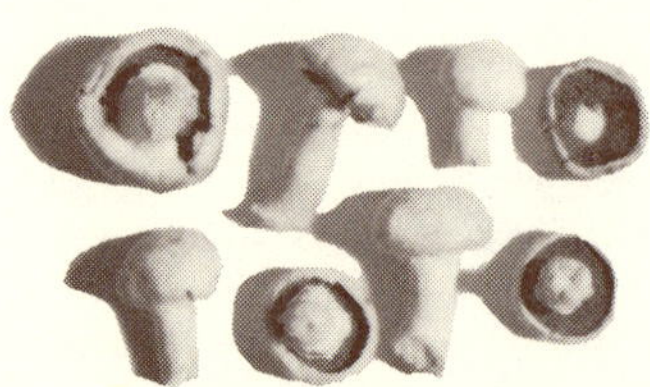

Herb-Broiled Baby Lamb Chops

Lamb without salt? Impossible! Salt, we've all been told, is what removes the lambiness and makes the meat edible. The truth is, it doesn't. Salt just makes lamb salty. But lamb does cry for herbs. Here's a simple way to add just the right herbs and transform an oh-just-another broiled lamb chop into a sublime treat.

8 *baby lamb chops, cut from rib, well trimmed, ends of bone removed, about 1½ pounds*
1 *tablespoon corn oil*
1 *large clove garlic, finely minced*
1 *shallot, finely minced*
1 *teaspoon dried rosemary leaves, crushed*
½ *teaspoon each dried sage and mint leaves, crushed*
Freshly chopped parsley

Wipe chops dry with paper toweling. In a small teflon skillet, heat oil until warm. Sauté garlic and shallot for 2 minutes. Avoid browning. Remove from flame. Transfer to small bowl. Add dried herbs and blend with fork. Spoon half of mixture over one side of chops.

Place chops on rack in shallow roasting pan, and broil 1½″ from flame, coated side up, for 8 minutes. Turn. Spread with balance of herbed mixture. Broil another 5-8 minutes, or until just lightly browned. Meat should remain pink on the inside. Do not overcook. Well-done lamb might just as well be old mutton meat.

Serve immediately, sprinkled with freshly chopped parsley.

Yield: Serves 4
Note: *If you're using shoulder chops:* Shoulder chops are not as tender and, because of the bones between the meat, will require a longer cooking time. Follow the recipe, but turn twice instead of once, so that the meat will have a chance to cook through. Allow one chop per person, total weight 1½ pounds.

CAL	F	P:S	SOD	CAR	CHO
292	12	1.7:1	79	1	100
Shoulder chops					
277	11	1.8:1	79	1	100

French Style Roast Leg of Lamb

We pointed to an item on the menu of a small bistro in Cannes, and asked in our stumbling French, "How is this prepared?" "It's lean, pink leg of lamb," the cheery proprietress answered, "cooked to perfection with slivers of garlic and sprinklings of herbs." Fighting back the gush of salivary juices, we chorused eagerly, "Let's have it." Now we prepare it at home. So can you.

½ *leg of lamb, preferably shank end, about 4 pounds*
1 *tablespoon corn oil*
3 *large cloves garlic, cut into thin slivers*
¼ *teaspoon each, dried sage, thyme, and rosemary leaves, crushed*
1 *teaspoon dried mint leaves, crushed*
3 *dashes cayenne pepper*
2 *fresh tomatoes, cored and chopped*
1 *tablespoon tomato paste, no salt added (Page 6)*
1 *cup veal or chicken stock (Page 11 or 10)*
1 *tablespoon brown beef stock (Page 13)*
½ *cup dry red wine*

Have meat at room temperature before preparing. Trim away all fat. Wipe dry with paper toweling. Cut several ¼″ slits into surface of meat. Insert garlic slivers. Rub meat with crushed herbs and cayenne. Preheat oven to 425 degrees. Place lamb on rack in shallow roasting pan, and roast, uncovered, for 20 minutes. Turn oven down to 400 degrees. Brush meat with oil. Return to oven and roast for 15 minutes.

Heat stock and wine to simmering point and pour over meat. Roast for an additional 40 minutes, basting frequently. Remove from roasting pan to hot platter and keep warm. Remove rack from roasting pan, and place pan on top of stove over medium high flame. Scrape any brown particles into pan juices. Add tomatoes, brown beef stock, tomato paste and mint, and cook until liquid is reduced by a third. Pour into chinois, pressing out juices into saucepan. Return to stove and reheat. Pour juices which have exuded from lamb into saucepan. Taste. Add more cayenne pepper, if desired. Serve hot in sauceboat, and spoon over thinly sliced meat.

Yield: Serves 8

CAL	F	P:S	SOD	CAR	CHO
343	1	1.3:1	160	4	133
With chicken stock					
343	1	1.3:1	154	4	133

Russian Shashlik

Tart-and-sweet and slightly astringent pomegranate juice is the base for the marinade in my recipe for this popular Russian dish. True Russian style? *Da!* True Russian overabundance of calories? *Nyet!*

1½ *pounds lamb, cut from leg*
1 *small onion, finely minced*
2 *large cloves garlic, finely minced*
1 *large shallot, minced*
1 *tablespoon freshly chopped parsley*
1¼ *cups unsweetened pomegranate juice (Page 6)*
2 *tablespoons corn oil*
4 *dashes cayenne pepper*

Trim away all fat from meat. Cut into 2″ chunks. Place in small bowl together with onion, garlic, shallot, parsley, cayenne pepper, and pomegranate juice. Cover and refrigerate overnight.

Remove meat from marinade and pat dry. Skewer the meat, using four substantial skewers. Brush with oil. Broil under very high heat, turning often, until done. I prefer it slightly pink (12 minutes). Well done will take about 20 minutes. Remove from skewers and serve on heated plate with Extraordinary Kasha (Page 26).

Yield: Serves 4
Variation: Include 2 green peppers cut into 12 chunks, 4 tomatoes cut into quarters, and 4 small white onions, peeled and cut in half. Skewer alternate chunks of vegetables and meat chunks. Proceed according to recipe.

CAL	F	P:S	SOD	CAR	CHO
239	12	1.8:1	129	0	120
With vegetables					
289	12	1.8:1	154	12	120

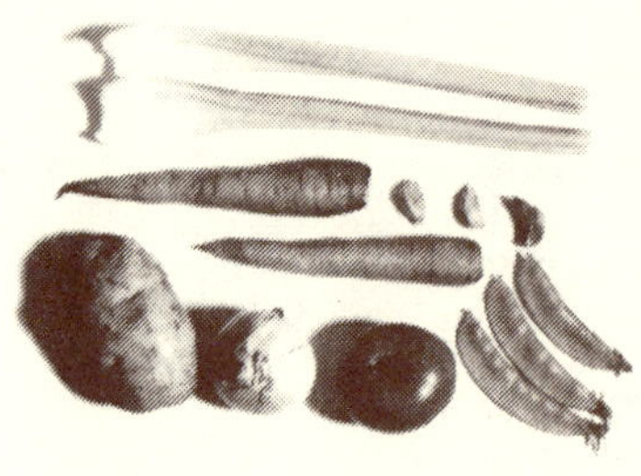

Irish Stew

Don't let the long list of ingredients deter you. You probably have most, if not all, of them in your kitchen right now. And what's an Irish stew anyway without a plethora of garden-fresh vegetables and rich juicy chunks of lamb and beef? My version of this popular dish from the Emerald Isle is light, delicate, subtly flavored and never lamby.

1 *pound lean lamb, from shoulder or leg, cut into 2" chunks*
1 *pound lean beef, such as top round, cut into 2" chunks*
⅓-½ *cup unbleached flour*
2 *tablespoons corn oil*
1 *large shallot, minced*
2 *large cloves garlic, minced*
2 *yellow onions, cut into eighths*
1 *large leek, white part only, well washed and coarsely chopped*
2 *fresh tomatoes, cored and skinned, or 1 can tomatoes (8¼ oz.), no salt added, drained*
2 *carrots, peeled and sliced into 1" pieces*
2 *ribs celery, diced*
2 *large potatoes, preferably Idaho, peeled and cut into 1" cubes*
12 *whole small white onions, peeled*
½ *cup shelled fresh peas*
⅓ *cup yellow turnip, peeled, cut into ½" cubes*
1 *cup beef stock (Page 12)*
1 *cup veal stock (Page 11)*
2 *cups water*
½ *cup dry Vermouth or white wine*
1½ *teaspoons dried rosemary leaves, crushed*
1 *teaspoon dried sage leaves, crushed*
6 *dashes cayenne pepper*
Small bouquet garni
Chopped fresh parsley

Wipe meat dry with paper toweling. Dredge lightly in flour, shaking off excess. Heat half of oil in large heavy casserole. Brown meat, half at a time, on all sides. Transfer to bowl. Heat balance of oil until hot. Sauté garlic, shallot, and leek with balance of meat, and brown lightly. Add wine and cook for 2 minutes. Add stocks, water, bouquet garni, and dried herbs. Return first batch of browned meat to casserole and stir to blend. Bring to simmering point. Cover and cook for one hour, stirring often to prevent sticking.

Add balance of ingredients with exception of peas, white onions and parsley. Bring to simmering point on top of stove. Cover and place in preheated 325 degree oven for ½ hour. Add white onions and peas. Re-cover and return to oven for 40 minutes.

Pour into tureen. Sprinkle with freshly chopped parsley and serve.

Yield: Serves 6

CAL	F	P:S	SOD	CAR	CHO
381	12	2.3:1	183	26	89

Simple Sautéed Steakburger

Once in a while it's nice to make a meal of a simply prepared meat dish, vegetable and salad. For your meat dish, try this gourmet version of a hamburger. Buy your beef pre-ground only if you can rely on its leanness. A good idea is to store frozen chunks of top sirloin in your freezer, and pop them into your grinder or food processer whenever the urge for steakburger grabs you.

1 *pound lean top sirloin of beef, ground*
1 *tablespoon corn oil*
2 *large cloves garlic, minced*
1 *whole scallion, minced*
2 *large shallots, minced*
½ *carrot, peeled and grated*
¼ *teaspoon each dried basil and thyme leaves, crushed*
2 *tablespoons fine bread crumbs (Page 147)*
4 *tablespoons red wine*
3 *dashes cayenne pepper*
¼ *teaspoon smoked yeast (Page 6)*
¼ *teaspoon Dr. Bronner's seasoning (Page 6)*

In large teflon skillet, heat ½ tablespoon oil until hot. Add shallots, garlic, and scallion and sauté one minute.

In small bowl, combine meat, carrot, cayenne, smoked yeast, herbs, Dr.

Bronner's seasoning, crumbs, and wine. Add sautéed mixture and blend. Shape into 4 steakburgers.

Heat teflon until hot, adding remaining oil. Add steakburgers and cook until brown on both sides. Meat should be crisp on outside, and pink on inside. Do not overcook. Serve immediately. Delicious with endive and arrugula salad (Page 98).

Yield: Serves 4

CAL	F	P:S	SOD	CAR	CHO
207	8	2.5:1	85	5	80

Sautéed Steakburger with Mushroom Sauce

This is another gourmet version of a hamburger. It's less strongly spiced than the simple sautéed steakburger (Page 93) because it's accompanied by a creamy mushroom sauce that is as satiny as it is tongue-tingling. Who needs ketchup!

For the steakburger:

1 *pound top sirloin of beef, ground*
1 *tablespoon corn oil*
1 *small onion, minced*
1 *large clove garlic, minced*
1 *shallot, minced*
¼ *cup fine bread crumbs (Page 147)*
⅛ *cup non-fat milk*
¼ *teaspoon dried thyme leaves, crushed*
3 *dashes cayenne pepper*
Freshly chopped parsley

Note: Try to coordinate the cooking of the sauce with the steakburgers so that they're both finished at the same time. After you've done it once, it's easy.

For the sauce:

1½ *tablespoons corn oil*
1 *clove garlic, minced*
1 *shallot, minced*
¼ *pound fresh mushrooms, washed, dried, trimmed, and sliced*
1 *cup beef stock, heated (Page 12)*
2 *tablespoons dry Vermouth or white wine*
1½ *tablespoons unbleached flour*
½ *teaspoon curry powder, no salt or pepper added*
¼ *teaspoon dried thyme leaves, crushed*
2 *dashes cayenne pepper*

In teflon skillet, heat ½ tablespoon oil until hot. Add onion, garlic, and shallot, and sauté until lightly browned.

In the meantime, combine meat, bread crumbs, thyme, milk, and cayenne in small bowl. Blend well. Add sautéed mixture. Shape into 4 burgers about ¾″ thick.

Using the same skillet, heat balance of oil until hot. Add meat. Brown on one side, turn and brown on second side. Meat should be crisp on outside and pink inside. Avoid overcooking.

Begin preparation of sauce about 10 minutes before burger is ready. In a large teflon skillet, heat oil until hot. Add shallot and garlic. Sauté one minute. Add mushrooms. Sauté for 3 minutes until lightly browned. Then sprinkle flour over mixture and cook for 2 minutes, stirring well so that flour cooks through. Combine stock and wine. Add to skillet, stirring continually. Add thyme, cayenne, and curry powder. Let simmer, uncovered, for 2 minutes.

Pour over steakburgers. Sprinkle with parsley and serve.

Yield: Serves 4

CAL	F	P:S	SOD	CAR	CHO
198	8	2.5:1	80	9	80
Sauce					
69	5	4.5:1	24	3	0

Delicate, Airy Meat Loaf

Typical meat loaves, filled with egg yolks, salt, pepper, and fats were never as delectable as my lighter-than-air version. Make the whole recipe, even if you're not serving 4, and have it the next day, hot or cold, served between slices of freshly made bread.

1 *pound top sirloin, ground*
1 *tablespoon corn oil,*
1 *onion, minced*
2 *cloves garlic, minced*
1 *large shallot, minced*
½ *cup bread crumbs, no salt added (Page 147)*
1 *tablespoon tomato paste, no salt added (Page 6)*
1 *cup tomato juice, no salt added*
3 *tablespoons non-fat milk*
2 *tablespoons freshly chopped dill and parsley*
¼ *teaspoon each dried oregano, marjoram, and thyme leaves, crushed*
4 *dashes cayenne pepper*
¼ *teaspoon smoked yeast (Page 6)*
1 *egg white, lightly beaten with fork*
2 *large potatoes, peeled, each cut into 6 pieces*

Boil potatoes for 10 minutes (they should not be fully cooked). Drain and set aside. Heat ¾ tablespoon of corn oil in teflon skillet until hot. Sauté onion, garlic, and shallot until lightly browned.

Place meat in medium-sized bowl together with bread crumbs, smoked yeast, cayenne, milk, egg white and herbs. Combine tomato paste with tomato juice and add to meat. Stir in sautéed mixture, blending well.

Lightly oil a rectangular baking dish. Do not use a loaf pan. Shape meat with hands into a 8″ × 4″ loaf. Place in preheated 350 degree oven, uncovered, and bake for 20 minutes. Remove from oven and pour off any fat that may have dripped from meat. Pour ½ cup tomato juice over loaf. Add boiled potatoes to baking dish and coat with tomato juice. Bake fifteen minutes. Turn potatoes and add balance of tomato juice to baking dish. Return to oven and bake another 15 minutes, or a total of 50 minutes. Do not overcook.

Serve on platter, spooning gravy over meat. Arrange potatoes around loaf, and garnish as desired.

Yield: Serves 4
Note: The reason for not using loaf pan: If meat is placed in loaf pan, there is no way that fat can drip off. It would just go back into meat. Also you would not be able to heat and flavor the potatoes as recommended.

CAL	F	P:S	SOD	CAR	CHO
227	8	2.5:1	104	8	80
Potatoes					
44	0	—	2	6	0

Veal and Spinach Loaf with Potatoes

The test of a great chef is the ability to elevate a meat loaf into a gourmet delight. Follow this veal loaf recipe with tender loving care, and you'll pass the test.

1 *pound fresh spinach, well washed, tough stems removed*
1 *pound ground veal, very lean*
1 *tablespoon corn oil*
2 *large fresh tomatoes, cored, skinned, and drained*
2 *tablespoons tomato paste, no salt added (Page 6)*
½ *cup veal stock (Page 11)*
1 *egg white, lightly beaten with fork*
⅓ *cup bread crumbs, no salt added (Page 147)*
1 *onion, minced*
2 *large cloves garlic, minced*
½ *teaspoon smoked yeast (Page 6)*
¼ *teaspoon dried marjoram leaves, crushed*
¼ *teaspoon each dried basil and oregano leaves, crushed*
¼ *cup non-fat milk*
2 *dashes cayenne pepper*
⅓ *cup fresh parsley and dill, stems removed*
8 *small red-skinned potatoes*

Place spinach in large heavy-bottomed saucepan. Cover and cook over medium-high heat for 4-5 minutes, or until tender. Pour into colander and drain well. Chop.

Boil potatoes in their jackets for 10 minutes. Plunge into cold water and peel. Set aside.

Heat ¾ tablespoon oil in teflon skillet until hot. Sauté onion and garlic until wilted. Transfer to mixing bowl to which veal, spinach, crumbs, egg, dried herbs, smoked yeast, and cayenne have been added. Blend well.

In a blender, combine stock, tomato paste, tomatoes, milk, parsley, and dill, and blend until smooth. Pour half of mixture over veal, blending well. Reserve balance for sauce.

Shape into 8″ × 4″ loaf, and place in lightly oiled rectangular baking dish. Bake in preheated 350 degree oven for 45 minutes. Remove from oven and pour off any fat that may have dripped from meat. Add potatoes, coating well with juices from pan, and bake another half hour. Remove from oven, cover loosely with waxed paper, and let stand for 5 minutes before slicing.

Place on platter surrounded by potatoes. Heat remaining blended mixture to simmering point, and pour over loaf.

Yield: Serves 4
Note: See note for Delicate Airy Meat Loaf (Page 95)

CAL	F	P:S	SOD	CAR	CHO
257	9	2.4:1	228	17	105
Potatoes					
46	0	—	2	11	0

Swedish Meat Balls

Three kinds of tender lean meat, well ground, mixed with tongue-tingling herbs and spices, and gently simmered in a rich stock, produce a meat ball that's as light as it is tasty. Savor a melt-in-your-mouth forkful, close your eyes, and you'll swear you're in Stockholm.

¼ *pound lean veal, ground*
¼ *pound lean pork, ground*
½ *pound beef, top round or sirloin, ground*
2 *tablespoons corn oil*
2 *cloves garlic, finely minced*
1 *large shallot, finely minced*
1 *rib celery, finely minced*
1 *onion, finely minced*
1 *tablespoon freshly chopped parsley and dill*
1 *egg white, lightly beaten with fork*
½ *cup fine bread crumbs (Page 147)*
⅛ *teaspoon ground ginger*
½ *teaspoon ground allspice*
½ *carrot, peeled and grated*
¼ *teaspoon smoked yeast (Page 6)*
⅓ *cup non-fat milk*
1½ *tablespoons unbleached flour*
1¼-1½ *cups beef stock, warmed (Page 12)*
1 *large sprig fresh dill*

Combine meats with herbs and bread crumbs. Mix well with fingers (it's the only way to get a smooth blend). Add milk, egg white, smoked yeast, carrot, and spices. Blend well.

Heat 1 tablespoon oil in large teflon skillet until hot. Sauté onion, celery, garlic, and shallot until lightly browned. Pour into meat mixture and blend. Shape into 24-26 smooth balls. (At this point, you can cover and refrigerate meat until ready to cook.)

Heat ½ tablespoon oil in same large teflon skillet until hot. Brown half of meatballs on all sides, turning carefully with spatula. Transfer to bowl. Add balance of oil, and brown balance of meat balls and return first batch to skillet. Sprinkle with flour and cook for one minute. Add 1¼ cups stock and dill sprig. Bring to simmering point, stirring well. Cover and simmer for 15 minutes.

Uncover, and turn meat balls. If sauce is too thick, add balance of ¼ cup stock. Re-cover, and cook another 15 minutes. Serve immediately with plain parsleyed potatoes (Page 22).

Yield: Serves 4

Note: When you're planning a buffet dinner, why not include hot Swedish meat balls. Shaped into smaller balls, and served with toothpicks, they're also great as hot hors d'oeuvres.

CAL	F	P:S	SOD	CAR	CHO
285	10	2.3:1	226	12	64

Spaghetti and Meat Balls

Here are meat balls, glowingly spiced, satisfyingly hearty, and yet as light as air. They make a perfect match for my incredibly delicious spaghetti with tomato and mushroom sauce.

- 1 *recipe Spaghetti with Tomato and Mushroom Sauce (Page 28)*
- 2 *tablespoons corn oil*
- ¼ *pound ground lean beef*
- ¼ *pound ground lean pork*
- 2 *large cloves garlic, minced*
- 2 *shallots, minced*
- 1 *onion, minced*
- 1 *egg white, lightly beaten with fork*
- ¼ *cup fine bread crumbs (Page 147)*
- 3 *dashes cayenne pepper*
- ½ *teaspoon dried thyme leaves, crushed*
- 2 *tablespoons freshly chopped parsley*

Heat one tablespoon oil in teflon skillet until hot. Sauté onion, garlic, and shallots until wilted. Let cool.

Combine meats, egg white, cayenne, crumbs, and herbs in bowl, mixing well. Add sautéed ingredients and blend. Mixture should hold together when you roll it into small balls. If not, add a bit more bread crumbs. Shape into 12 balls.

Heat balance of oil in skillet until hot. Add meat balls and brown well on all sides. Set aside.

Prepare recipe for Tomato and Mushroom Sauce up to the point where mushrooms are about to be added. Add mushrooms and browned meat balls. Bring to simmering point. Cover and simmer for 45 minutes stirring and turning twice. Spoon sauce and meat balls over cooked spaghetti. Sprinkle with parsley, and serve.

Yield: Serves 6

	CAL	F	P:S	SOD	CAR	CHO
Meat balls	121	6	3.0:1	55	1	27
Spaghetti and sauce	267	3	4.5:1	29	59	0

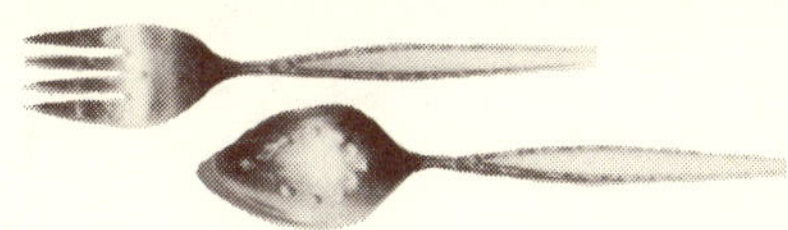

Salads

Green Salad with Flavorful Salad Dressing

There's no end to the variety of greens that can be combined into a salad. But it's not the greens nor the dressing that make a successful salad—it's the freshness of the greens. Avoid brown-edged leaves and leaves that don't feel crunchy to the touch. Serve the crispiest of green salads by following these simple instructions:

Remove each leaf and wash under cold running water. Drain, and refrigerate in an uncovered bowl for one hour before serving. Pat each leaf dry with paper toweling (or use a spinner if you're sure leaves will emerge from it intact). Tear leaves—do not cut—into bite-size pieces.

Here is one of our favorite combination of greens with an herbaceous dressing that's long been a staple in our household.

For the salad:

1 *small head Romaine lettuce (about ¾ pound)*
¼ *pound chicory leaves*
¼ *pound escarole leaves*
½ *bunch watercress, leaves only*
1 *onion thinly sliced*
2 *tablespoons freshly chopped basil, or freshly chopped parsley and dill*
2 *whole scallions, sliced*
8 *crisp radishes, sliced*
1 *endive (optional) to weigh 3 ounces*

For the flavorful salad dressing:

⅓ *cup apple cider vinegar*
⅔ *cup corn oil*
2 *teaspoons dried minced onions*
2 *cloves garlic, minced*
2 *shallots, minced*
¾ *teaspoon combined dried marjoram and tarragon leaves, crushed, and dill and fennel seeds, crushed*
4 *dashes cayenne pepper*
1 *teaspoon freshly chopped chives*

Prepare vegetables and greens according to preceding directions. Combine all ingredients except freshly chopped herbs and refrigerate for one hour.

Prepare salad dressing by combining all ingredients in a jar and shaking well. Let stand one hour before serving. Shake again before serving.

Allow 1½ tablespoons dressing per serving. Pour over dried salad leaves to which freshly chopped herbs have been added. Toss well. Serve immediately.

Yield: Salad serves 4; salad dressing, about 1 cup

Variation: Add 3 tablespoons tomato juice, no salt added, to salad dressing and shake well.

Note: This salad dressing and its variation will keep well in refrigerator for a week. Remove one hour before serving.

CAL	F	P:S	SOD	CAR	CHO
37	0	—	25	14	0
With endive					
38	0	—	26	15	0
With dressing					
129	14	4.5:1	28	16	0
With tomato juice					
130	14	4.5:1	28	16	0

Arrugula and Endive Salad

In posh Italian restaurants, this is often the simplest dish on the menu—and the most sophisticated. Incredibly easy to assemble, it's a study in contrasting textures, colors, and shades of mellowed bitterness. Here's a dramatic curtain riser for your evening's featured dish.

1 *bunch crisp arrugula*
2 *large endives, to weigh about 8 ounces*
Flavorful Salad Dressing (Page 98)

Wash arrugula well under cold running water. Gently pat dry with paper toweling. Never wring dry, since the leaves are very delicate. Clip off and discard long stems.

Gently remove each leaf from endive. Wash and pat dry.

Arrange individual servings by laying equal amounts of endives, hollow sides up on each plate, then doing the same with the arrugula. Spoon enough dressing over each salad to moisten (about 1½ tablespoons per serving). Do not toss. Serve immediately.

Yield: Serves 4

CAL	F	P:S	SOD	CAR	CHO
49	13	4.5:1	12	4	0

Fresh Green Beans with Toasted Coriander

Here's a tantalizingly aromatic salad built around just one green vegetable, tossed in a sweet-and-pungent marinade, and raised far beyond the ordinary by that favored seed of Indian cuisine, the coriander.

1 *pound fresh green beans*
2 *shallots, minced*
1 *large clove garlic, minced*
4 *dashes cayenne pepper*
1 *tablespoon corn oil*
2 *teaspoons coriander seeds, toasted, see recipe*
2 *teaspoons honey*
1 *teaspoon apple cider vinegar*
1 *teaspoon wine vinegar*
1 *tablespoon freshly chopped parsley*

Parboil green beans as described under recipe for Broccoli Magic (Page 18). Avoid overcooking.

Heat oil in heavy-bottomed saucepan until hot. Sauté shallots and garlic until wilted. Add beans and toss well to coat. Remove from heat.

We're now going to toast coriander seeds. Heat small skillet until hot. Add seeds, shaking around in skillet for two minutes. Crush seeds finely in mortar and pestle. Add to green beans together with cayenne and vinegars. Shake saucepan to mix. Add honey and shake to blend.

Pour into small jar or bowl. Chill. Serve cold, sprinkled with freshly chopped parsley.

Yield: Serves 4
Variation: Do not refrigerate. Reheat, and serve hot, sprinkled with freshly chopped parsley.

Yield: Serves 4

CAL	F	P:S	SOD	CAR	CHO
77	4	4.5:1	10	8	0

Tomato and Watercress Salad with Yogurt Dressing

The sharpness of yogurt is mellowed by the sweetness of tomato paste and juice and a suggestion of honey to produce a rich, satiny, herb-accented dressing for this crispy salad.

For the salad:
4 *fresh tomatoes*
1 *bunch watercress*
2 *Kirby cucumbers, peeled and cut into 4 lengthwise sections*

For the yogurt dressing:
1 *cup low-fat plain yogurt*
2 *tablespoons wine vinegar*
4 *tablespoons freshly chopped onion*
4 *tablespoons freshly chopped parsley*
1 *tablespoon tomato paste, no salt added (Page 6)*
4 *tablespoons tomato juice, no salt added*
¼ *teaspoon smoked yeast (Page 6)*
1 *tablespoon honey*
2 *teaspoons freshly chopped basil or chives*

Prepare dressing first. In small bowl, blend tomato juice with tomato paste. Add vinegar, onion, parsley, herbs and honey. Stir well. Add yogurt and smoked yeast. Blend. Let stand while you prepare the salad.

Peel and core tomatoes as described under *Terms* (Page 150).

Wash watercress very well under cold running water. Pat dry with paper toweling. Remove stems and refrigerate. Refrigerate cucumbers until ready to use. Do not peel until ready to cut.

Slice tomatoes and arrange on serving platter. Garnish with watercress. Pour Yogurt Dressing over salad, and serve.

Yield: Serves 4
Note: Use all of the dressing for this salad.

	CAL	F	P:S	SOD	CAR	CHO
	40	0	—	7	9	0
Dressing	70	1	.6:1	36	14	2

European Cucumber Salad

The inspiration for this piquant salad—built around sparklingly crisp cucumber slices marinated in a clear sweet-and-pungent sauce—comes from the Hungarian and German restaurants in our neighborhood where cucumber salad is the invariable accompaniment to all main courses.

4 *Kirby cucumbers, well scrubbed, thinly sliced*
¼ *cup apple cider vinegar*
1 *tablespoon honey*
1 *tablespoon freshly chopped dill*
3 *dashes cayenne pepper*
3 *dashes ground cloves*
3 *dashes smoked yeast (Page 6)*

Combine all ingredients except cucumbers in jar. Cover and shake well. Drop sliced cucumbers into jar, one by one, shaking gently to coat. Cover jar tightly. Turn gently upside down and back several times to distribute liquid evenly. Refrigerate for one day, turning jar upside down from time to time. Serve cold.

Yield: Serves 4

CAL	F	P:S	SOD	CAR	CHO
29	0	—	5	8	0

Cucumber and Onion Salad

Sweet and tart, this easy-to-make salad is just the thing to spark up a meal of simply prepared chicken or chops. Or enjoy it by itself as an appetizing prelude to your main course.

6 *small Kirby cucumbers, peeled, thinly sliced*
1 *large sweet Bermuda onion, peeled, thinly sliced*
2 *tablespoons freshly chopped chives*
Yogurt Dressing (Page 100)

Place onions and cucumbers in bowl. Toss with chives. Add enough dressing to moisten (about ⅓ cup). Cover and refrigerate for at least 3 hours before serving.

Yield: Serves 4

CAL	F	P:S	SOD	CAR	CHO
41	0	—	17	9	0

German-Style Potato Salad

Gemütlich und wunderschön—wonderfully, warmly homespun as only a dish from north of the Rhine can be—this vinegary yet herb-sweetened delicacy is the lightest potato salad extant, and certainly among the world's tastiest.

3 *large potatoes, preferably Idaho, peeled*
1 *small onion, grated*
2 *large cloves garlic, finely minced*
2 *shallots, finely minced*
1 *tablespoon corn oil*
2 *tablespoons wine vinegar*
1 *tablespoon apple cider vinegar*
½ *teaspoon smoked yeast (Page 6)*
¼ *teaspoon each dried thyme and basil leaves, crushed*
4 *dashes cayenne pepper*
2 *teaspoons freshly chopped parsley and dill*

Cut each potato in half. Place in saucepan, adding enough water to cover. Bring to boil and cook, partially covered until tender but still firm. Drain. Let cool.

Cut into ½″ slices and place in bowl. Combine vinegars and oil, and pour over potatoes. Add dried herbs, smoked yeast, cayenne, onion, garlic and shallots, and toss gently. Cover and refrigerate for 4-5 hours before serving, stirring from time to time.

Yield: Serves 4
Variations: Half green pepper, parboiled for one minute and thinly sliced, or one well drained sliced pimento may be added before salad is refrigerated.

CAL	F	P:S	SOD	CAR	CHO
124	4	4.5:1	9	21	0

Variations
No appreciable difference

Cole Slaw

Textured with cabbagy crunchiness, this familiar salad is elevated to new taste heights by a mixture of sweet and pungent vegetables sharpened by the slight bite of my eggless mayonnaise.

¾ *head loose-leafed green cabbage (about 1 pound)*
1 *onion, peeled and grated*
1 *green pepper, finely minced*
1 *carrot, peeled and shredded*
Juice of ½ lemon
4 *dashes cayenne pepper*
1 *tablespoon honey*
¼ *teaspoon smoked yeast (Page 6)*
Eggless Mayonnaise (Page 106)
6 *large crisp radishes, trimmed, thinly sliced*

Cut cabbage in quarters and remove hard section. Slice each quarter into ¼″ slivers. Add carrot, radishes, onion, green pepper, cayenne, smoked yeast, and lemon juice which has been blended with honey. Add enough Eggless Mayonnaise to coat (about ⅓ cup, or to taste). Stir well. Cover and refrigerate several hours before serving, stirring often.

Yield: Serves 4
Variation: Substitute Flavorful Salad Dressing (Page 98) for Eggless Mayonnaise using just enough to moisten (about 5 tablespoons).

CAL	F	P:S	SOD	CAR	CHO
With mayonnaise					
186	15	4.5:1	47	14	0
With salad dressing					
160	11	4.5:1	44	15	0

Russian Salad

What pickles and relishes are to us, Russian salad is to Europeans. My version—a colorful potpourri of raw and cooked vegetables, hard-boiled egg whites, and my mustardy Eggless Mayonnaise—is a zesty delight. No reason why, with slices of one of my breads, you can't relish it as a complete luncheon meal.

½ *pound fresh peas, cooked, drained and cooled*
1 *sweet red onion, thinly sliced*
1 *shallot, finely minced*
1 *rib celery, diced*
2 *whole scallions, diced*
½ *carrot, peeled and thinly sliced*
2 *Kirby cucumbers, well scrubbed, diced*
8 *small red-skinned potatoes, cooked in jackets, peeled and cooled*
3 *hard-boiled egg whites, cooled, cut in half, then cut into quarters*
4 *sprigs watercress*
1 *firm tomato, cored, skinned, and cubed*
¼ *teaspoon ground thyme*
4 *dashes cayenne pepper*
3 *tablespoons Eggless Mayonnaise (Page 106)*
2 *tablespoons low-fat plain yogurt*
1 *tablespoon freshly chopped dill*

Combine all vegetables and egg whites. Sprinkle with herbs and cayenne and toss. Add mayonnaise and gently toss again. Add yogurt and stir well to coat. Refrigerate, covered, until well chilled. Garnish with watercress sprigs, and serve.

Yield: Serves 4, one leftover

CAL	F	P:S	SOD	CAR	CHO
151	7	3.9:1	66	19	0

Cold Bean Salad

For the gourmet with one eye on the budget, here's a main-course salad that's as nutritious and tasty as it's economical. Garnished deftly with glistening fresh vegetables, it looks like it was fashioned for your table by a Madison Avenue caterer. Spectacular—and spectacular savings!

1 *cup red kidney beans*
Flavorful Salad Dressing (about 4 tablespoons) (Page 98)
1 *Bermuda onion, thinly sliced*
¼ *cup freshly chopped dill and parsley*
2 *Kirby cucumbers, peeled and diced*
4 *dashes cayenne pepper*
¼ *teaspoon smoked yeast (Page 6)*
¾ *teaspoon combined dried thyme, oregano, marjoram, and basil leaves, crushed*
8 *Romaine lettuce leaves*
8 *watercress sprigs*
1 *tomato, peeled, cored, and sliced*

Soak beans overnight in water to cover. Drain well. Place beans in heavy-bottomed saucepan. Add enough water to cover and bring to boil. Turn heat down to simmering point, partially cover, and simmer gently for 40-45 minutes, or until tender. Drain and let cool.

Transfer beans to bowl. Add onion, cucumber, herbs, smoked yeast and cayenne. Toss. Pour enough Flavorful

Salad Dressing over beans to moisten (about 4 tablespoons). Cover and refrigerate for 5-6 hours before serving.

Serve on a bed of Romaine lettuce leaves and garnish with tomatoes and watercress.

Yield: Serves 4

CAL	F	P:S	SOD	CAR	CHO
181	9	4.5:1	19	16	0

Lentil Salad

Like cold bean salad, this is an inflation beating one-course meal. The carnivores among us love its meaty taste, and the vegetarians exult in its all-around nutritional goodness—and all revel in its earthy tanginess. The garnish of radiantly fresh raw vegetables gives it an astonishing visual appeal.

1 *cup dried lentils, washed and drained*
½ *teaspoon vegetable concentrate (Page 6)*
1 *bay leaf*
3 *whole cloves*
1 *onion, cut into quarters and sliced*
¼ *teaspoon smoked yeast (Page 6)*
2 *shallots, minced*
2 *whole scallions, minced*
¾ *teaspoon dry mustard dissolved in one teaspoon water*
2 *tablespoons freshly chopped basil or freshly chopped parsley and dill*
3 *dashes cayenne pepper*
Flavorful Salad Dressing (Page 98)
8 *Romaine lettuce leaves, washed and dried*
1 *tomato, cored, skinned, sliced*
8 *crisp radishes, washed, trimmed, cut into flowers*
1 *Kirby cucumber, peeled and sliced*

Soak lentils overnight in water to cover. Drain. Transfer to heavy-bottomed saucepan. Add bay leaf, vegetable concentrate, cloves, and enough water to cover. Bring to boil. Turn heat down, partially cover, and simmer for 30 minutes, or until lentils are tender. Drain well.

Transfer lentils to bowl. Add shallots, smoked yeast, cayenne, freshly chopped herbs, mustard, onion, and scallions and toss well. Add just enough dressing to moisten (about 3-4 tablespoons) and toss. Serve on a bed of Romaine lettuce leaves, garnished with tomato, radishes, and cucumbers.

Yield: Serves 4

CAL	F	P:S	SOD	CAR	CHO
226	7	4.5:1	24	32	0

Veal Salad

With your Braised Veal leftovers, prepare this elegant and colorful main-course salad. It's mildly spiked with curry, sharpened by a touch of lime juice, and textured with crunchy nuts and vegetables.

2 *cups cooked veal, diced (Page 82)*
2 *shallots, minced*
1 *onion, minced*
1 *rib celery, coarsely diced*
½ *carrot, peeled and grated*
1 *whole pimento, no salt added, drained, cut into thin slivers*
2 *teaspoons fresh lime juice*
½ *teaspoon ground thyme*
3 *tablespoons Eggless Mayonnaise (Page 106)*
2 *teaspoons curry powder, no salt or pepper added*
¼ *cups walnuts, coarsely chopped*
8 *Romaine lettuce leaves, washed and dried*

Place meat in large bowl. Sprinkle with lime juice. Add celery, carrot, shallots, and onion, and toss well. Sprinkle with thyme and curry. Add mayonnaise, stirring well to coat. Stir in pimento. Cover and refrigerate for at least 2 hours before serving.

Serve on Romaine leaves. Sprinkle with walnuts.

Yield: Serves 4

CAL	F	P:S	SOD	CAR	CHO
255	16	5.9:1	71	11	39

Turkey Salad— Plus Ultra

Here's a perfect summer meal made with leftover roast turkey accented with herbs and enriched with a subtly spiced dressing. Tangy, crunchy, satisfying—and more sumptuous than any other turkey salad we know.

3 *cups cooked turkey, white and dark meat, cut into ½" cubes*
½ *carrot, peeled and grated*
4 *dashes cayenne pepper*
½ *teaspoon smoked yeast*
¼ *cup dry Vermouth or white wine*
2 *small red-skinned potatoes, cooked in jackets, cut into ½" cubes, cooled*
⅓ *cup celery diced*
½ *teaspoon dried tarragon leaves, crushed*
2 *tablespoons freshly chopped parsley and dill*
½ *pound fresh peas, cooked, cooled*
¼ *pound mushrooms, washed, dried, trimmed, and quartered*
1 *small red onion, thinly sliced*
3 *tablespoons walnuts, coarsely chopped*
2 *navel oranges, peeled, sliced crosswise, then cut into quarters*
½ *cup chicken stock (Page 10)*
2 *tablespoons coriander seeds, toasted and crushed (Page 99)*
8 *Romaine lettuce leaves, washed and dried*
8 *sprigs watercress*
Fruit Dressing (Page 106)

Place turkey in large bowl. Add wine, toss well, and marinate, covered, for one hour.

Pour stock into small saucepan and bring to simmering point. Add mushrooms. Partially cover, and simmer for 2 minutes. Drain, reserving stock to be used again in a soup or gravy. Set aside.

To the marinated turkey, add celery, onion, potatoes, peas, walnuts, oranges, and carrot. Sprinkle with smoked yeast, herbs, cayenne, and coriander seeds, and toss gently. Pour only enough dressing over salad to moisten (about 4-6 tablespoons). Toss well to coat. Chill before serving.

Serve on a bed of Romaine, and garnish with watercress.

Yield: Serves 4, one leftover
Note: Poached Chicken Breasts may be substituted for turkey (Page 59).

	CAL	F	P:S	SOD	CAR	CHO
	297	8	5.0:1	139	21	36
Chicken	290	4	4.3:1	127	23	40

Chef Salad

My version of this classic one-course meal for figure watchers is built around succulent, crisp Romaine and spinach leaves enhanced with an array of hot, mild, sweet and pungent vegetables, and topped off with enticingly fragrant toasted sesame seeds. Not least of its virtues is a flavor-imparting cupful of my toasted French Herb Bread cubes. Every bite as good as it looks!

For the salad:
3 *cups Romaine leaves, washed, dried, and torn into 1" pieces*
5 *cups spinach leaves, washed, dried, and torn into 1" pieces*
1 *whole scallion, finely minced*
1 *small red onion, very thinly sliced*
1 *cup freshly toasted bread cubes (Page 147)*
2 *tablespoons sesame seeds, toasted*
2 *tomatoes, skinned, cored, and cut into wedges*

For the salad dressing:
1 *tablespoon apple cider vinegar*
Juice of ½ lemon
1 *teaspoon Dr. Bronner's seasoning (Page 6)*
2 *teaspoons very flavorful honey, such as thyme*
3 *tablespoons corn oil*
⅓ *cup pineapple juice, no sugar added*
1 *shallot, finely minced*
½ *teaspoon smoked yeast (Page 6)*
1 *clove garlic, finely minced*

Prepare salad dressing first by combining all ingredients in jar, shaking well. Let stand for 30 minutes before serving, shaking again before pouring over salad.

Combine spinach and Romaine with onion, scallion, and bread cubes, tossing well. Add only enough salad dressing to moisten vegetables (about 2 tablespoons per serving).

Toast sesame seeds as follows: Heat a small skillet until hot. Pour seeds into skillet and spread in one thin layer. Continue cooking while shaking skillet at intervals until seeds brown lightly. Sprinkle on top of prepared salad. Garnish with tomatoes, and serve.

Yield: Salad serves 4; dressing, about ¾ cup
Variations:

1. Center a dollop of low-fat cottage cheese on top of salad before adding dressing.

2. Add one cup slivered cooked turkey, veal, or chicken to salad and toss.

3. Add ¼ cup low-fat cheese, cut into thin slivers, and toss (Page 3).

CAL	F	P:S	SOD	CAR	CHO
93	1	4.8:1	48	22	0
Dressing					
56	5	4.5:1	6	2	0
With cottage cheese					
96	1	4.8:1	50	22	0
With turkey					
135	3	3.3:1	78	22	16
With veal					
129	3	3.1:1	66	23	18
With chicken					
129	4	3.0:1	67	25	17
With low-fat cheese					
143	6	1.3:1	49	32	10

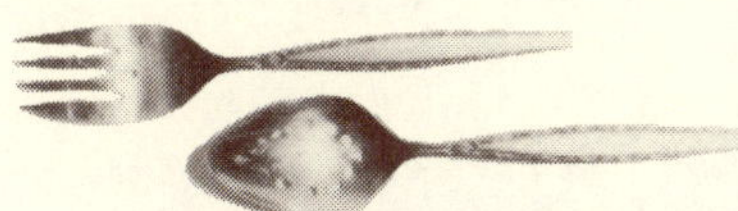

Vegetable-Fruit Salad with Fruit Dressing

Here's an original vegetarian salad devoid of clichés. An unusual combination of dried and fresh fruits, and sweet and tangy vegetables is bathed in an adventurous purée of gingerly spiced fruits to which a touch of carrot has been added. A luncheon dish with a difference!

For the salad:
8 *large Romaine lettuce leaves, washed and dried*
½ *cup seedless raisins*
1 *carrot, peeled and shredded*
3 *crisp sweet apples such as Red Delicious or Golden Delicious, peeled, cored, diced*
1 *rib celery, diced*
1 *banana, sliced*
1 *tablespoon fresh lemon juice*

For the fruit dressing:

½ *banana, sliced*
½ *cup apple juice, no sugar added*
¼ *cup pineapple or orange juice, no sugar added*
¼ *carrot, peeled and shredded*
2 *tablespoons corn oil*
¼ *teaspoon ground ginger*
¼ *teaspoon ground allspice*
1 *tablespoon dry curd cottage cheese, less than ½% milkfat, no salt added*

Combine vegetables and fruit with lemon juice and toss. Arrange Romaine on individual serving plates. Top leaves with vegetable-fruit mixture.

Prepare salad dressing by combining all ingredients in blender and puréeing until smooth. Pour over salad, allowing about 2 tablespoons per serving.

Yield: Salad serves 4; Fruit Dressing, about 1¼ cups

CAL	F	P:S	SOD	CAR	CHO
134	0	—	39	44	0
Dressing					
44	2	4.5:1	2	6	0

Hors D'Oeuvres, Breakfast and Luncheon Dishes, and Relishes

Dinner for most of us is the gastronomic highlight of the day, and too often the little dishes that sustain us for the rest of the day are given short shrift. What a pity! Light, but fulfillingly nutritious, breakfasts and lunches should be every bit as excitingly varied and delectable as your evening repast. Here is a bright array of concoctions to transform the little meals, and the evening's precursor to the grand meal, into small gems. And wonder of wonders, the alchemy is often achieved with humble leftovers.

Of the few condiments in this section, I'm particularly proud of my mayonnaise. It has all of the right flavors and none of the wrong ingredients. And you'll be surprised by my non-saline pickles. They're truly pickley!

Eggless Mayonnaise

½ *teaspoon dry mustard*
1 *tablespoon apple cider vinegar*
1 *teaspoon wine vinegar*
1 *tablespoon fresh lemon juice*
¼ *teaspoon garlic powder, no salt added*
⅓ *cup water*
1½ *teaspoons unflavored gelatin*
¼ *teaspoon dried tarragon leaves, crushed*
½ *teaspoon freshly chopped dill, or ¼ teaspoon dried dill, crushed*
3 *dashes cayenne pepper*
1 *teaspoon honey*
1 *tablespoon non-fat dry milk*
¼ *cup non-fat milk*
¾ *cup corn oil*

Combine vinegars and water in saucepan. Bring to boil. Turn off heat. Add gelatin and stir to dissolve. Let cool to lukewarm.

In small bowl combine mustard, lemon juice, and garlic powder. Beat well with small wire whisk. Add gelatin mixture and blend again with whisk.

In another bowl, whisk together dry and liquid milks, honey, herbs, and cayenne pepper. Dribble into blended gelatin-milk mixture, beating constantly with whisk. Add oil, a little at a time, beating vigorously after each addition, until all oil is absorbed.

Refrigerate until partially set (about 20 minutes). Whisk again until smooth and creamy.

Pile into pint-size jar and refrigerate until set (about 2 hours).

CAL	F	P:S	SOD	CAR	CHO
Per tablespoon					
71	8	4.5:1	4	1	0

Make-Your-Own Pickles

2 *large Kirby cucumbers, well scrubbed, dried, and thinly sliced*
2 *teaspoons pickling spices, no salt added*
2 *teaspoons honey*
1 *teaspoon freshly chopped dill*
3 *tablespoons white vinegar*
1 *tablespoon wine vinegar*
4 *dashes cayenne pepper*

Place cucumbers in small bowl. Combine balance of ingredients in saucepan. Bring to simmering point, and cook for one minute. Pour over cucumber slices. Let stand uncovered until cucumbers have given up some of their juices (about one hour). Transfer to covered jar and refrigerate for 24 hours before serving, turning jar upside down 3-4 times.

Yield: Serves 4

CAL	F	P:S	SOD	CAR	CHO
24	0	—	10	5	0

Apple Relish

6 *crisp apples, such as Red Delicious or Cortland, peeled, cored, and diced*
¼ *cup honey*
¾ *cup apple cider vinegar*
1 *teaspoon freshly chopped parsley*
6 *whole cloves*
1 *teaspoon ground ginger*
¼ *teaspoon garlic powder, no salt added*
1 *medium-sized green pepper, minced*
1 *medium-sized onion, minced*
1 *large shallot, minced*
½ *lime, pitted, sliced, then cubed*
¾ *cup seedless raisins*

Combine all ingredients in waterless cooker. Stir well to blend. Bring to boil. Turn heat down to simmering point. Cover and simmer for 1½-2 hours, until very thick, stirring from time to time. Finished relish should be the consistency of thick sour cream. Partially remove cover and let cool in pot. Transfer to jars and refrigerate. Storage life: about 2 weeks.

Yield: About 1 quart
Note: Delicious served with broilings and roasts.

CAL	F	P:S	SOD	CAR	CHO
Per tablespoon					
34	0	—	2	9	0

Melba Toast

Use any of my firm textured breads such as Pumpernickel, Ryes, Four Flour Bread, Whole Wheat, Cracked Wheat, etc. (see bread section). Slice bread ⅛″ thick, and lay on cookie tin in one layer. Bake in preheated 425 degree oven for ten minutes, or until totally dry. Cool. Store in metal tin.

To prepare melba toast for dips,

cut each slice into quarters before baking.

Yield: As much as you'd like to make

CAL	F	P:S	SOD	CAR	CHO
Per piece (about)					
13	0	—	0	3	0
For dips (about)					
3+	0	—	0	1	0

Three-Flour Griddle Cakes

For breakfast.

½ *cup buckwheat flour*
¼ *cup whole wheat flour*
¼ *cup unbleached white flour*
2½ *teaspoons low sodium baking powder (Pages 4 and 6)*
¼ *teaspoon ground ginger*
1¼-1½ *cups buttermilk, no salt added*
¼ *cup apple juice, no sugar added*
1 *tablespoon corn oil, plus ¼ teaspoon to brush griddle*

Combine flours, baking powder, and ginger in bowl. Stir to blend. Add apple juice and stir. Then add oil and buttermilk and stir again. Mixture should be the consistency of thick sour cream—yet pourable.

Heat teflon skillet until hot. Brush lightly with oil. For each pancake, pour ⅛ cup of batter into skillet, making 3 or 4 pancakes at a time. Cook until top is lightly bubbled and edges are brown. Turn and brown on second side. Serve immediately with dark buckwheat honey, jelly (no sugar added), or sprinkled with cinnamon.

Yield: 12 griddle cakes, 3″ in diameter

CAL	F	P:S	SOD	CAR	CHO
Per griddle cake					
58	1	4.5:1	39	9	0

Blueberry Griddle Cakes

For breakfast.

⅓ *cup buckwheat flour*
⅔ *cup unbleached flour*
2½ *teaspoons low sodium baking powder (Pages 4 and 6)*
½ *cup low-fat plain yogurt*
½ *cup non-fat milk, plus 2 tablespoons*
¼ *cup fresh blueberries*
½ *teaspoon corn oil to coat skillet*

Combine flours and baking powder in bowl. Blend yogurt with half cup milk and add to flour mixture. Stir. The consistency should be thick yet pourable. If too thick, add balance of milk.

Pick over blueberries. Pour into strainer and rinse under cold running water. Drain well. Gently stir into batter.

Heat large teflon skillet until hot enough for a drop of water to bounce off. Coat very lightly with oil for the first batch of griddles. Sauté 3 or 4 griddle cakes at a time. Turn when edges brown and top bubbles (about 3 minutes). Sauté on second side until lightly brown and griddle cakes puff up slightly. Serve with buckwheat honey or your favorite jelly, no sugar added.

Yield: 12 griddle cakes, serves 4

CAL	F	P:S	SOD	CAR	CHO
Per griddle cake					
47	0	—	9	10	0

French Toast

For breakfast

4 *slices my bread, ½" thick, 3" square, including crusts (see Note)*
4 *egg whites*
½ *cup non-fat milk*
2 *dashes cayenne pepper*
2 *dashes smoked yeast (Page 6)*
2 *dashes ground cinnamon*
1 *tablespoon corn oil*

In small bowl, combine egg whites, milk, cayenne, cinnamon, and smoked yeast. Beat until frothy with fork. Soak bread in mixture, one slice at a time, letting it sit until moistened through uniformly. Transfer each slice to plate. Pour any leftover mixture over bread slices.

Heat oil in large iron skillet until hot but not smoking. Add bread, pouring any unabsorbed liquid over bread. Sauté over medium high heat until brown on both sides. Serve immediately, topped with honey, jelly (no sugar added), or sprinkled with cinnamon.

Yield: Serves 4
Note: My breads which are suitable for French Toast are: Featherbread, Cracked Wheat Bread, Cardamom Bread, My French Bread, and My French Herb Bread. If using My French Breads, allow two ½" slices per portion.

CAL	F	P:S	SOD	CAR	CHO
118	4	4.5:1	74	15	0

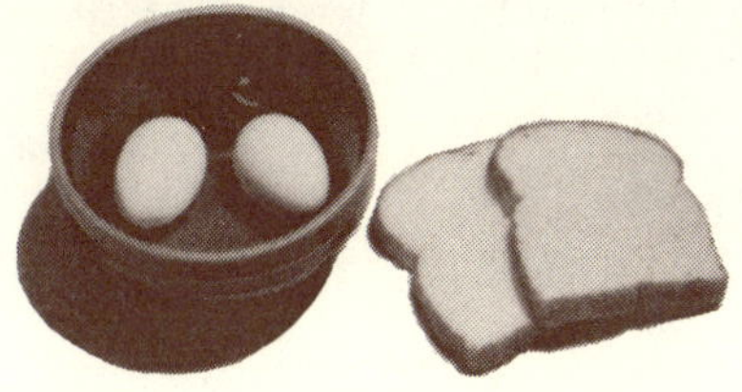

Whole Wheat Crepes with Cheese Filling

For lunch or breakfast. Filling #1 is on the sweet side. Filling #2 is on the spicy side.

For the crepe batter:
3 *egg whites, ½ egg yolk*
¾ *cup non-fat milk*
¾ *cup whole wheat flour*
¼ *cup unbleached flour*
2 *teaspoons toasted wheat germ, no sugar added*
1½ *tablespoons corn oil, plus ½ teaspoon for oiling pan*
½ *teaspoon ground cinnamon*
½ *teaspoon vanilla extract*

Cheese filling #1
1½ *cups dry curd cottage cheese, less than ½% milkfat, no salt added*
1 *tablespoon fresh lemon juice*
2 *dashes ground nutmeg*
1 *small egg (use ½ yolk and all of white)*
½ *teaspoon vanilla extract*
2 *dashes ground cinnamon*
1 *teaspoon honey*

Cheese filling #2
1½ *cups dry curd cottage cheese, less than ½% milkfat, no salt added*
3 *dashes smoked yeast (Page 6)*
1 *tablespoon chopped chives or scallions*
3 *dashes mild paprika*
2 *dashes cayenne pepper*
1 *small egg (use ½ yolk and all of white)*

Prepare batter first. Combine all ingredients in blender and blend for one minute. Cover and let stand at room temperature for one hour.

To prepare fillings: Combine all ingredients in small bowl. Blend well with small wire whisk. Refrigerate until ready to fill crepes.

To cook and assemble crepes: Brush teflon crepe pan lightly with oil for first crepe only. Heat pan until hot. Add ¼ cup batter to center of pan. Tilt so that batter flows to sides and makes complete circle. Cook until lightly brown and edges start to come away from pan. Turn. Cook on second side for just 10 seconds. Stack crepes between alternating layers of waxed paper, first-cooked side down. Continue to cook crepes until all batter is used.

To fill, remove crepes from stack one by one, adding one tablespoon filling to second-cooked side of each crepe. Fold over ends and tuck in sides.

Brush crepe pan lightly with oil. Heat until hot. Place filled crepes in pan, 4 at a time, seam side down, and brown lightly. Turn and brown on other side. Remove to serving platter and keep warm. Repeat cooking procedure for balance of crepes. Serve immediately.

Yield: 8 crepes

CAL	F	P:S	SOD	CAR	CHO
Each crepe					
82	1	2.7:1	32	12	16
Cheese filling #1					
39	0	—	28	4	16
Cheese filling #2					
36	0	—	30	3	16

Corn Muffins

- 1 *cup yellow cornmeal*
- 2½ *teaspoons low sodium baking powder (Page 6)*
- ¾ *cup unbleached flour, plus 1 tablespoon*
- 2 *teaspoons fresh lemon juice*
- 2½ *tablespoons corn oil, plus ½ tablespoon to oil muffin tin*
- ½ *teaspoon ground cinnamon*
- 1 *tablespoon date powder (Page 6) optional*
- ¾ *cup non-fat milk*
- ¼ *cup fresh orange or apple juice, no sugar added*
- 1 *large egg (use ½ yolk and all of the white)*
- 1 *tablespoon honey*

In mixing bowl, combine lemon juice with orange or apple juice. Blend. Add egg, milk, and honey and blend again. Add oil and stir.

Combine cornmeal, flour, baking powder, cinnamon, and optional date powder in one bowl. Stir to blend. Add to liquid mixture, a half cup at a time, blending with wooden spoon after each addition. Mixture should be thick yet pourable. If too thin, add an additional tablespoon flour.

For a crisp crust, lightly oil muffin tin. Place in 425 degree preheated oven for 10 minutes. Remove from oven and fill with batter, filling each cup almost to top. Return to oven and bake for 20 minutes. Remove from oven and let muffins cool for 5 minutes in tin. Remove muffins from tin and serve warm.

Yield: 9 large muffins
Variation: If you prefer smaller muffins, fill each cup ⅔ full. Yield will be 12 muffins.

CAL	F	P:S	SOD	CAR	CHO
Each large muffin					
143	4	4.5:1	17	5	14
Each small muffin					
106	2	4.5:1	12	3	10

Addition of date powder makes no appreciable difference.

Make-Your-Own Granola

For breakfast.

3 *cups old-fashioned rolled oats, toasted*
½ *cup unprocessed bran flakes*
¼ *cup sesame seeds*
½ *cup toasted wheat germ, no sugar added*
¼ *cup chopped walnuts*
3 *tablespoons date powder (Page 6)*
1 *teaspoon ground cinnamon*
¼ *cup dried dates, chopped*
¼ *cup dried apricots, chopped*
½ *cup seedless raisins*

Toss toasted oats with balance of ingredients and store in glass jar in refrigerator.

Yield: About 5½ cups granola
Note: Allow 3 tablespoons per portion

CAL	F	P:S	SOD	CAR	CHO
Per portion					
104	2	7.9:1	4	17	0

Luncheon Omelettes

For each omelette:
2 *egg whites*
½ *teaspoon corn oil*
1½ *teaspoons freshly chopped parsley and dill*
1 *teaspoon onion, finely minced*
1 *small shallot, minced*
¼ *teaspoon freshly chopped chives*
⅛ *teaspoon smoked yeast (Page 6)*
⅛ *teaspoon dried tarragon leaves, crushed*
2 *dashes cayenne pepper*

Drop egg whites into small bowl and beat with fork until frothy. Add one teaspoon parsley and dill and balance of ingredients and beat again with fork.

Brush teflon skillet with oil. Heat until hot but not smoking. Pour egg mixture into pan, tilting pan from side to side so that mixture forms a complete circle. Turn heat down and cook only until lightly browned on one side.The center should remain moist. Slide onto dish, flip half over. Sprinkle with balance of chopped parsley and dill and serve.

Variations:

1. Add 2 tablespoons chopped cooked, drained spinach to uncooked mixture. Blend well with fork.
2. Add 2 tablespoons finely diced warm cooked chicken or veal to center of cooked omelette. Flip sides over and serve.
3. Make basic omelette and pour Creamy Mushroom Sauce over it (Page 86).

Yield: One serving

CAL	F	P:S	SOD	CAR	CHO
62	2	4.5:1	120	2	0
Spinach					
74	2	4.5:1	139	5	0
Chicken					
103	4	3.6:1	139	6	12
Veal					
100	4	3.0:1	135	0	13
Mushroom sauce					
184	9	4.5:1	156	10	0

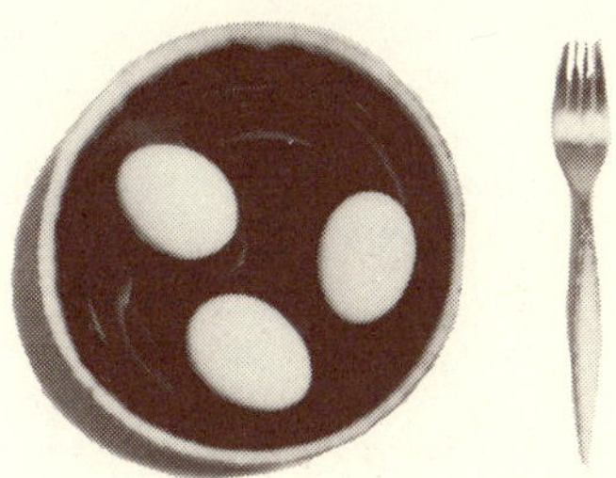

Creamy Mushrooms on Toast

For lunch.

- ¾ *pound fresh mushrooms, washed, dried, trimmed and sliced*
- 2 *shallots, minced*
- 2 *cloves garlic, minced*
- ⅔ *cup chicken stock (Page 10)*
- ¾ *cup non-fat milk*
- 2 *tablespoons unbleached flour*
- 2 *tablespoons corn oil*
- 3 *tablespoons dry Vermouth or white wine*
- ¾ *teaspoon dried tarragon leaves, crushed*
- 3 *dashes cayenne pepper*
- 1 *tablespoon freshly chopped parsley*
- 4 *slices any of my breads, thinly sliced (Pages 135-146)*

Heat oil in large teflon or iron skillet until hot. Add shallots and garlic. Sauté for one minute. Add mushrooms and sauté for 3 minutes, turning constantly. Sprinkle with flour and cook for one minute, stirring well. Add cayenne, wine and stock, and blend. Add tarragon and milk. Simmer until thickened. If too thick to your taste, add a bit more milk and blend well. Do not overcook.

Pour over just-toasted slices of bread. Sprinkle with parsley, and serve.

Yield: Serves 4

CAL	F	P:S	SOD	CAR	CHO
147	7	4.5:1	36	13	0

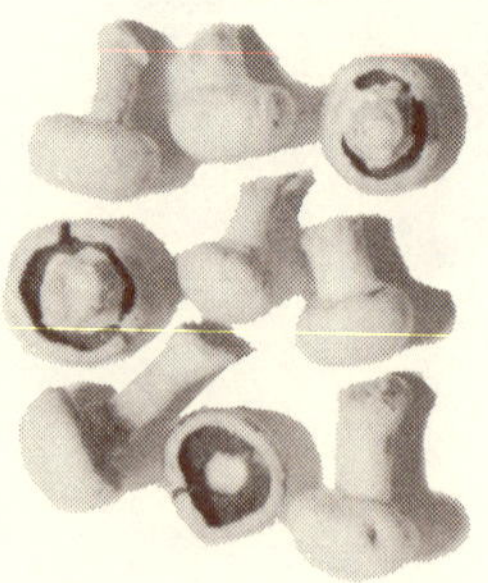

Luncheon Treat with Fruit Juice Dressing

For the salad:

- 1 *large navel orange*
- 1 *large banana*
- 1 *cup dry curd cottage cheese, less than ½% milkfat, no salt added*
- 1 *tablespoon date powder (Page 6)*
- ¼ *cup seedless raisins*
- 8 *large green Romaine lettuce leaves*

For the Fruit Juice Dressing:

- ½ *cup fresh orange juice*
- ¼ *cup apple juice, no sugar added*
- ½ *cup pineapple juice, no sugar added*
- 3 *tablespoons lemon juice*
- 3 *tablespoons corn oil*
- 1 *tablespoon honey*

Prepare the salad dressing an hour before serving. Place all ingredients in pint jar. Cover and shake well. Chill.

Set out 4 salad plates. Wash and pat lettuce leaves dry. Place 2 lettuce leaves on each plate. Spoon ¼ cup cottage cheese per serving on top of lettuce beds. Slice oranges and bananas and distribute equally around cottage cheese. Sprinkle with raisins and then with date powder. Serve with fruit dressing on the side in sauceboat.

Yield: Salad: Serves 4; Fruit Dressing, about 1½ cups—allow 2 tablespoons per serving.

CAL	F	P:S	SOD	CAR	CHO
Salad					
141	0	—	30	29	0
Dressing					
48	4	4.5:1	0	4	0

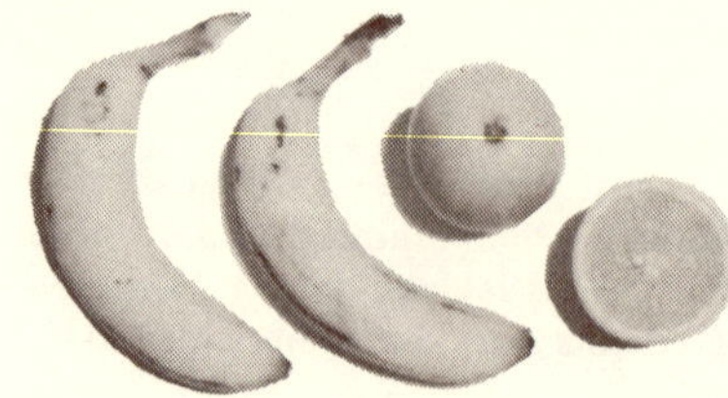

Veal Stuffed Eggs

For luncheon.

6 *hard-boiled egg whites*
⅓ *cup cooked veal, finely diced, leftovers are fine (Page 82)*
½ *crisp apple such as Winesap or Red Delicious, peeled, cored, and finely diced*
1 *tablespoon chopped pickles (Page 107)*
2 *dashes cayenne pepper*
2-3 *tablespoons Eggless Mayonnaise (Page 106)*
8 *crisp Romaine lettuce leaves*
8 *radish roses*

In small bowl, combine veal, apple, and pickles. Add cayenne and enough mayonnaise to bind mixture. Prepare egg whites (Page 125). Lightly stuff egg halves. Arrange on lettuce leaves, surrounded by balance of veal mixture. Garnish with radish roses.

Yield: Serves 4

CAL	F	P:S	SOD	CAR	CHO
106	6	4.5:1	82	1	6

Salmon Stuffed Eggs

For hors d'oeuvres or luncheon.

7 *hard-boiled egg whites*
1 *3½ ounce can salmon, no salt added, well drained*
½ *teaspoon dry mustard dissolved in ½ teaspoon water*
2 *dashes cayenne pepper*
2 *teaspoons finely chopped onion*
1 *teaspoon freshly chopped dill and parsley*
1 *tablespoon Eggless Mayonnaise (Page 106)*
1 *teaspoon fresh lemon juice*

Remove shells from eggs while still warm. Cut eggs in half and discard yolks. Chop 2 halves well, leaving balance of halves intact.

Mash salmon together with mayonnaise and chopped egg white. Add onion, cayenne, mustard, lemon juice and herbs, blending well. Stuff egg halves with mixture. Cover and chill before serving.

Yield: 12 stuffed halves; serves 4

CAL	F	P:S	SOD	CAR	CHO
32	2	3.3:1	98	0	7

Crudités

(colorful, cold vegetable platter)

For hors d'oeuvres or light lunch.

10 *endive leaves, lightly filled with 3 tablespoons dry curd cottage cheese, less than ½% milkfat, no salt added, combined in blender with 2 dashes cayenne pepper, and enough tomato juice (no salt added) to make a spreadable mixture, and sprinkled with chopped parsley*
12 *broccoli flowerettes that have been parboiled for 1 minute, drained in colander, and set under cold running water until cooled*
2 *carrots, peeled and cut lengthwise into thin sticks*
15-20 *cherry tomatoes*
8 *crisp watercress sprigs*
8 *radishes cut into roses*
8 *cauliflower flowerettes that have been parboiled for 2 minutes, drained in colander, set under cold running water until cooled and sprinkled with 1 teaspoon fresh lemon juice*

Arrange all vegetables on platter in attractive pattern and serve with or without dip (Page 118).

Yield: Serves 8 for hors d'oeuvres; serves 4 for light lunch

CAL	F	P:S	SOD	CAR	CHO
For hors d'oeuvres					
39	0	—	38	7	0
For luncheon					
78	0	—	76	14	0

Sardine Canapés

1 *3¾ ounce can Norwegian Dietetic Brisling Sardines, packed in water, no salt or oil added*
2 *teaspoons fresh lemon juice*
3 *hard-boiled egg whites, cooled and mashed*
⅓ *cup finely chopped, drained pickles (Page 107)*
2 *tablespoons Eggless Mayonnaise (Page 106)*
1 *dash cayenne pepper*

Drain sardines. Transfer to small bowl. Add lemon juice and cayenne. Mash well with fork. Add egg whites, pickles and mayonnaise, and blend. Cover and refrigerate until well chilled.

Spread on 5 slices of any of my breads, thinly sliced, each slice cut into quarters (Pages 135-146).

Yield: 20 canapés
Variation: For luncheon. Wash and pat dry 4 large Romaine lettuce leaves. Arrange on luncheon plates. Spoon equal amounts of sardine mixture over lettuce. Garnish with strips of pimento (no salt added), and slices of pickles.

Yield: Serves 4

CAL	F	P:S	SOD	CAR	CHO
Each canapé					
26	1	3.0:1	9	1	3
Luncheon serving					
114	7	3.0:1	48	3	13

Tuna Fish for Canapés

1 *6½ ounce can Albacore white tuna, packed in water, no salt added*
1 *onion, minced*
1 *whole scallion, finely minced*
½ *rib celery, finely minced*
1 *small Italian pepper, sweet variety, finely minced*
Juice of one lemon
2 *dashes cayenne pepper*
2 *tablespoons Eggless Mayonnaise (Page 106)*
2 *teaspoons freshly chopped parsley*

Drain water from can. Transfer tuna to bowl. Add lemon juice and mash well with fork. Add balance of ingredients and blend. Spread on 5 slices of any of my breads, thinly sliced, each slice cut into quarters.

Yield: 20 canapés
Variations: *For luncheon*

1. Sandwiches. Set out 6 slices of any of my breads, thinly sliced (Pages 135-146). Spread ¾ of tuna fish (reserve the balance) on 3 slices of bread. Add a half leaf crisp Romaine lettuce to each sandwich. Spread balance of bread with ½ teaspoon Eggless Mayonnaise per slice and cover sandwich. Cut each sandwich into 4 triangles. Serve 3 triangles per person.
Yield: Serves 4

2. Salad. Spoon all of mixture onto crisp Romaine lettuce leaves. Garnish with watercress, tomato wedges, and radish roses.
Yield: Serves 4

CAL	F	P:S	SOD	CAR	CHO
Each canapé					
26	0	—	7	2	6
Sandwich serving					
171	9	4.5:1	30	15	21
Salad serving					
110	4	4.5:1	35	9	29

My Hot Canapés

Four kinds of canapés: meat, fish, chicken, and gratineed.

- 6 *thin slices of any of my breads (Pages 135-146)*
- 1 *cup cooked meat, finely diced (left-overs are fine)*
- 3 *tablespoons duxelles (Page 13)*
- 1 *teaspoon finely chopped walnuts*
- 2 *teaspoons freshly chopped parsley*
- 3 *tablespoons chicken stock (Page 10)*
- 3 *dashes cayenne pepper*
- ¼ *teaspoon smoked yeast (Page 6)*
- ¼ *teaspoon combined dry thyme and rosemary leaves, crushed*

In food processor or blender combine all ingredients except bread, and blend until smooth. (If using blender, blend small amounts at a time.) Spread over sliced bread. Place in shallow baking pan and bake in preheated 425 degree oven for about 7 minutes, or until heated through. Cut each slice into 4 triangles, and serve.

Yield: 24 canapés
Variations:

1. Substitute fish for meat, fish stock for chicken stock, and crushed fennel seeds for rosemary leaves.

2. Substitute chicken for meat, and sage leaves for thyme leaves.

3. Sprinkle any of heated canapés with 2 tablespoons grated low-fat cheese (the sharper the better), and place under broiler for 2-3 minutes, or until cheese is melted.

CAL	F	P:S	SOD	CAR	CHO
Per canapé, meat					
16	0	—	3	1	2
Per canapé, fish					
14	0	—	2	1	2
Per canapé, chicken					
17	0	—	4	0	2
Cheese, add					
3	0	—	0	0	0

Chopped Egg Hors D'Oeuvres

- 4 *hard-boiled egg whites*
- ¼ *teaspoon smoked yeast (Page 6)*
- 1 *small onion, finely minced*
- 1 *whole scallion, finely minced*
- 1 *teaspoon freshly chopped dill*
- 2 *dashes cayenne pepper*
- 1 *tablespoon Eggless Mayonnaise (Page 106)*
- 1 *pimento, no salt added, well drained, cut into thin strips*

Boiling an egg sounds easy. It is. But if you want a tender egg white, you must boil it with loving care. Here's how.

Bring eggs to room temperature. Fill saucepan with warm tap water. Place eggs in pan and slowly bring water to boil. Turn heat down. Simmer slowly, uncovered, for 15 minutes. Cool eggs under cold running water, and remove shells as soon as eggs are cool enough to handle.

Cut eggs in half, discarding yolks, and mash well with fork. Add balance of ingredients with exception of pimento, and blend well.

Serve spread on 4 thin slices of any of my breads (Pages 135-146). Cut each slice into quarters. Garnish with pimento strips.

Yield: 16 canapés
Variation: For luncheon—open faced sandwiches. Spread on 4 slices of any of my breads, thinly sliced, and garnish with pimento strips.
Yield: Serves 4

CAL	F	P:S	SOD	CAR	CHO
Each canapé					
16	0	—	14	2	0
Each sandwich					
37	0	—	14	7	0

Pineapple-Walnut Cheese Spread

For hors d'oeuvres.

½ *cup dry curd cottage cheese, less than ½% milkfat, no salt added*
¼ *cup crushed pineapple in its own juices, drained, no sugar added*
1 *teaspoon fresh lemon juice*
¼ *teaspoon ground ginger*
2 *dashes cayenne pepper*
2 *dashes garlic powder, no salt added*
1 *tablespoon chopped walnuts*
2 *dashes Dr. Bronner's seasoning (Page 6)*

Combine all ingredients in blender or food processor. Blend until smooth. Spread on 4 slices of any of my breads, thinly sliced (Pages 135-146). Cut each slice into quarters, and serve.

Yield: Enough for 16 canapés
Variation: *For luncheon dish.* Make thin sandwiches using Date-Nut Cake (Page 131). Cut into quarters and serve on a bed of Romaine lettuce. Garnish with radish roses.

CAL	F	P:S	SOD	CAR	CHO
Per canapé					
17	0	0	4	3	0
Per sandwich					
149	2	4.1:1	7	35	10

Apple-Walnut Spread

For hors d'oeuvres.

½ *cup shelled walnuts, finely chopped*
½ *crisp apple, such as Red Delicious or Winesap, peeled and chopped*
1½ *teaspoons fresh lemon or lime juice*
1 *teaspoon corn oil*
2 *cloves garlic, finely minced*
3 *tablespoons bread crumbs (Page 147)*
¼ *teaspoon ground cinnamon*
2 *teaspoons apple juice, no sugar added (optional)*

Using a food processor: Place walnuts, apple, garlic, and bread crumbs in food processor bowl. Blend into paste. Add lemon or lime juice, oil, and cinnamon. Blend until smooth. If too thick to your taste, add optional apple juice and blend again. Pour into jar and chill.

Using a blender: Place chopped walnuts in mortar and pestle and pulverize to a paste. Transfer to blender together with apple, oil, and cinnamon. Blend until smooth. Add crumbs, lemon or lime juice and garlic, and blend. If mixture is too thick to your taste, add apple juice and blend again. Pour into jar and chill.

Cut 6 thin slices of any of my breads (Pages 135-146). Spread one tablespoon mixture over each slice. Cut each slice into 4 triangles. Serve.

Yield: 24 hors d'oeuvres
Variation: Curry powder, no salt or pepper added, or ground ginger can be substituted for cinnamon.

CAL	F	P:S	SOD	CAR	CHO
Each hors d'oeuvre					
36	3	12:1	1	6	0

Variations and option make no appreciable difference.

Mushroom-Egg Spread

For hors d'oeuvres.

4 *hard-boiled egg whites*
3 *tablespoons duxelles (Page 13)*
1 *tablespoon corn oil*
2 *cloves garlic, minced*
1 *onion, minced*
1 *whole scallion, minced*
1 *teaspoon apple cider vinegar*
2 *teaspoons Eggless Mayonnaise (Page 106)*
2 *teaspoons freshly chopped parsley and dill*
¼ *teaspoon dry mustard dissolved in ½ teaspoon water*

Heat oil in small iron skillet until hot. Sauté onion, garlic, and scallion until lightly browned. Add duxelles and stir to blend. Add vinegar and cook for one minute.

In small bowl, mash egg whites to fine consistency. Combine with sautéed mixture, herbs, and mustard, blending well. Add mayonnaise and blend again. Serve immediately, spread on 4 slices of any of my breads, thinly sliced, each slice cut into quarters.

Yield: 16 canapés

CAL	F	P:S	SOD	CAR	CHO
Each canapé					
29	2	4.5:1	15	2	0

Curried Spread

For hors d'oeuvres.

3 *hard-boiled egg whites*
½ *rib celery, diced*
½ *carrot, peeled and sliced*
⅛ *cup shelled walnuts*
1 *whole large scallion, sliced*
1 *teaspoon fresh lemon juice*
¼ *teaspoon smoked yeast (Page 6)*
4 *dashes cayenne pepper*
½ *teaspoon curry powder, no salt or pepper added*
1 *teaspoon freshly chopped parsley and dill*
About 1 tablespoon Eggless Mayonnaise (Page 106)
⅛ *teaspoon dried thyme leaves, crushed*

If you're using a grinder, grind all vegetables and egg. Then add spices and mayonnaise, blending well.

If you're using a food processor, combine all ingredients in processing bowl and blend, using sharp metal knife attachment.

Spread on 4 slices of any of my breads, thinly sliced (Pages 135-146). Cut each slice into quarters, and serve.

Yield: Enough for 16 canapés

CAL	F	P:S	SOD	CAR	CHO
Each canapé					
17	8	—	16	2	0

Cold Fish Spread

For hors d'oeuvres.

¼ *pound cooked fish removed from bone (leftovers are fine)*
Juice of ½ lemon
⅛ *teaspoon dry mustard dissolved in ¼ teaspoon water*
3 *dashes cayenne pepper*
½ *teaspoon finely minced shallot*
1 *tablespoon Eggless Mayonnaise (Page 106), or enough to moisten and make spreadable*
3 *slices any of my breads, thinly sliced (Pages 135-146)*
12 *slivers pimento, no salt added, for garnish*

Sprinkle fish with lemon juice and mash well. Add balance of ingredients, except pimento, and blend. Spread on sliced bread. Cut each slice into quarters. Garnish with pimento and serve.

Yield: 12 canapés

CAL	F	P:S	SOD	CAR	CHO
Per canapé					
21	1	2.5:1	4	2	4

Savory Cheese Dip

1 *cup dry curd cottage cheese, less than ½% milkfat, no salt added*
⅓ *cup low-fat plain yogurt*
1 *shallot, minced*
1 *small onion, minced*
½ *teaspoon dried tarragon leaves, crushed*
3 *dashes cayenne pepper*
1 *teaspoon freshly chopped parsley and dill*
1 *teaspoon fresh lemon juice*
⅛ *teaspoon garlic powder, no salt added*
¼ *teaspoon dry mustard dissolved in ½ teaspoon water*
¼ *teaspoon smoked yeast (Page 6)*
1 *tablespoon tomato juice, no salt added*

Combine all ingredients in blender or food processor and purée until smooth. Serve with melba toast (Page 107), allowing one teaspoon per dip.

Yield: About 1½ cups

CAL	F	P:S	SOD	CAR	CHO
Per dip					
6	0	—	2	1	0

Spicy Hot Cocktail Sausages

¼ *pound ground lean beef, top round or boneless sirloin*
½ *carrot, peeled and grated*
1 *teaspoon freshly chopped parsley*
1 *whole scallion, finely minced*
1 *clove garlic, finely minced*
1 *teaspoon finely chopped celery*
1 *teaspoon bread crumbs (Page 147)*
⅛ *teaspoon dried thyme leaves crushed*
⅛ *teaspoon each ground cloves and allspice*
3 *dashes cayenne pepper*
½ *teaspoon corn oil to oil baking dish*
Moderately hot paprika for sprinkling

Combine all ingredients except paprika in small bowl and blend well. Shape into small sausages by taking one teaspoon of mixture and rolling it between moist palms. Place on lightly oiled baking dish. Sprinkle liberally with paprika. Cover with aluminum foil and refrigerate for 2 hours before broiling.

Broil under medium high heat, turning often, until browned.

Yield: 20 small sausages
Variation: Combine ⅛ pound beef with ⅛ pound pork instead of all beef.

CAL	F	P:S	SOD	CAR	CHO
Each beef sausage					
12	0	—	55	0	6
Each beef-pork sausage					
12	0	—	59	1	6

Hot Stuffed Mushrooms

For hors d'oeuvres.

½ *pound large fresh mushrooms, washed, dried, and trimmed*
1 *tablespoon corn oil*
1 *shallot, finely minced*
1 *clove garlic, finely minced*
¼ *cup bread crumbs (Page 147)*
1 *tablespoon dry Vermouth or white wine*
2 *dashes smoked yeast (Page 6)*
2 *dashes Dr. Bronner's seasoning (Page 6), optional*
2 *dashes cayenne pepper*
½ *teaspoon dried tarragon leaves, crushed*
2 *teaspoons freshly chopped dill and parsley*

Gently separate stems from mushroom caps. Finely chop stems.

Heat ½ tablespoon oil in teflon skillet until hot. Add chopped mushrooms, garlic, and shallot, and sauté until wilted. Add tarragon, smoked yeast, and cayenne. Stir. Pour in wine and cook for one minute. Pour into small bowl. Add bread crumbs and one teaspoon chopped fresh herbs, and optional Dr. Bronner's seasoning. Blend well with spoon. Set aside.

In same skillet, heat balance of oil until hot. Sauté mushroom caps for 30 seconds on each side. Transfer to shallow baking dish. Fill each mushroom with prepared stuffing. Sprinkle with balance of freshly chopped parsley and dill. Bake in preheated 400 degree oven for 10 minutes or until heated through. Do not overbake.

Yield: About 12 stuffed mushrooms

CAL	F	P:S	SOD	CAR	CHO
Each mushroom					
32	0	—	4	4	0

Bombay Chicken Balls

For hors d'oeuvres.

1 *cooked chicken breast, minced (about ¾ cup) or equivalent amount of cooked turkey, white meat only*
1 *tablespoon shallots, diced*
1 *tablespoon onions, diced*
1 *tablespoon celery, diced*
1 *tablespoon carrot, peeled and diced*
1 *tablespoon freshly chopped parsley and dill*
1 *teaspoon curry powder, no salt or pepper added*
1 *tablespoon corn oil*
1 *tablespoon tomato juice, no salt added*
¼ *cup plus 1 tablespoon bread crumbs (Page 147)*
2 *dashes cayenne pepper*
Sprinklings of paprika

This hors d'oeuvre is best made using a food processor, but it can be made successfully with a blender.

If using a food processor, combine all ingredients, except crumbs, in processing bowl. Blend until smooth. If using blender, combine all ingredients except crumbs in blender. Blend for 10 seconds. Stop machine and stir with spoon. Repeat process until mixture is smooth. Turn mixture into bowl.

Scoop up half teaspoon of puréed chicken mixture, and shape into smooth balls by rolling between palms. Roll in crumbs. Then sprinkle with paprika. Arrange in flat dish in one layer. Cover and refrigerate for 2 hours before serving.

Pierce with cocktail picks and serve.

Yield: About 18 balls
Variation: Substitute pineapple juice for tomato juice; add one pineapple chunk from can of pineapple in its own

juices, no sugar added, and blend with balance of ingredients.

CAL	F	P:S	SOD	CAR	CHO
Each ball					
26	1	2.5:1	3	4	2
With pineapple					
27	1	2.5:1	2	5	2
Turkey					
32	1	2.5:1	1	5	2

Desserts

Strawberry Crepes

Make-ahead crepes, airy, light, enrobe a luscious strawberry filling to make the kind of dessert that stirs up memories of champagne and candlelight. A romantic climax to your dinner!

1 *recipe Whole Wheat Crepes (Page 109)*
1 *pint fresh strawberries, washed, hulled and sliced*
1 *teaspoon fresh lemon juice*
⅓ *cup apple juice, no sugar added*
1½ *tablespoons arrowroot flour dissolved in ⅛ cup apple juice*
2 *tablespoons honey*
2 *tablespoons finely chopped walnuts*
½ *teaspoon corn oil to oil baking dish*

Prepare crepes. Set aside.

Combine strawberries with apple and lemon juices in small heavy-bottomed saucepan. Bring to boil. Turn heat down and simmer, uncovered, for 3 minutes. Add dissolved flour mixture and honey and continue cooking for 2 minutes, stirring constantly, until thickened. Cool until just warm.

Spoon one tablespoon warm mixture into center of second cooked side of each crepe. Fold ends over. Arrange in lightly oiled baking dish. Bake in preheated 425 degree oven for 5 minutes. Sprinkle with nuts and serve.

Yield: 8 crepes
Variation: Prepare 8 crepes. Fill each crepe with a tablespoon of your favorite jelly (no sugar added). Fold ends over and proceed as for above recipe, adding ½ teaspoon cinnamon to chopped nuts.

CAL	F	P:S	SOD	CAR	CHO
Each crepe					
82	1	2.7:1	32	12	16
Filling					
29	0	—	0	8	0

Baked Pears in Red Wine

In my version of this masterpiece of Gallic haute cuisine, full-bodied pears are baked to tender perfection and bathed in a rich sauce fragrant with the heady essence of Burgundy brew. Truly, a delectable end to a meal.

4 *firm-skinned pears, such as Winter Bosc or d'Anjou*
1 *cup Burgundy wine*
3 *tablespoons honey*
4 *tablespoons apple juice, no sugar added*
4 *whole cloves*
1 *teaspoon ground cinnamon*
Seeds from 4 pods of cardamom, crushed
4 *dashes ground nutmeg*

Select pears that are not quite ripe, but not rock hard. If necessary, keep them at room temperature until they reach this degree of ripeness. Leaving stems on, gently peel from top to bottom in strips, removing as little skin as possible. Stick a clove onto bottom of each pear, and place, standing up and touching each other, in covered ovenproof casserole.

Combine wine, honey, apple juice, and balance of spices in saucepan. Heat to simmering point. Pour over fruit. Cover and bake in preheated 300 degree oven for 30 minutes, basting twice.

Baste again and return, uncovered, to oven. Bake another 10–15 minutes. Pears should retain shape and not be oversoft. Remove cloves.

Transfer to dish and spoon with wine juices. Cover loosely with waxed paper until cooled. Serve at room temperature or cover tightly and refrigerate. Serve chilled.

Yield: Serves 4
Variation: Serve with one tablespoon Vanilla Sauce spooned over each pear (Page 124).

CAL	F	P:S	SOD	CAR	CHO
113	0	—	7	27	0

Poached d'Anjou Pears

This dessert, light in taste and low in calories, is perfect to top off one of your heavier repasts. What's more, cooked d'Anjou pear has the magical quality of making the meal you've just eaten taste better. One of our favorites, it will likely become one of yours.

4 *d'Anjou pears, not quite ripe*
½ *cup apple juice, no sugar added*
Juice of ½ lemon
¼ *teaspoon ground cinnamon*
3 *dashes nutmeg*
3 *whole cloves, or ¼ teaspoon cardamom seeds, crushed*

Strain lemon juice into wide saucepan. Peel, core, and quarter pears. (If they're rock-hard when you buy them, keep them unwrapped at room temperature for a day or two until they show just some resistence when you press with thumb.) As each pear is cut, drop into lemon juice in saucepan, turning to coat. Lemon juice keeps the fruit from turning brown.

Add balance of ingredients. Bring to simmering point. Partially cover, and simmer for 7–10 minutes, depending upon the ripeness of fruit. Pears when cooked should remain firm yet tender.

Remove cover. Let cool in liquid. Remove cloves. Store in glass jar in refrigerator. Serve, chilled, with cooking liquid poured over pears.

Yield: Serves 4
Note: Two ways to sweeten to taste if desired:

1. Add one tablespoon honey during last 5 minutes of cooking time.
2. Sprinkle with half teaspoon date powder per portion before serving (Page 6).

CAL	F	P:S	SOD	CAR	CHO
76	0	—	2	18	0
With honey					
92	0	—	2	22	0
With date powder					
79	0	—	2	19	0

Apricot-Pineapple Mélange

The old-favorite fruit compote, with sweet spices, apple juice and honey, becomes a triumphant new dessert. For devotees of the sweet and the tart.

11 *ounces dried apricots*
2 *cups apple juice, no sugar added*
1 *cup crushed pineapple in its own juices, no sugar added, drained*
1 *slice lemon*
2 *tablespoons honey*
2 *tablespoons arrowroot flour dissolved in 2 tablespoons water*
1½ *teaspoons unflavored gelatin dissolved in 1 tablespoon boiling water*
1 *teaspoon ground cinnamon*
Seeds from 4 pods of cardamom, crushed

Soak apricots overnight in enough water to cover. Next day pour apricots into strainer and drain, pressing fruit with spoon. Transfer apricots to saucepan. Add apple juice, lemon slice, honey, cinnamon, and cardamom. Bring to boil. Turn heat down, cover, and simmer for about 20 minutes or until tender but firm. Add pineapple and dissolved arrowroot flour. Cook until thickened (about 5 minutes). Add dissolved gelatin and stir to blend. Pour mixture into 8 dessert dishes and let cool to room temperature. Then refrigerate until set.

Yield: Serves 8
Variation: Serve topped with 1 tablespoon Vanilla Sauce per serving (Page 124).

CAL	F	P:S	SOD	CAR	CHO
224	0	—	0	52	0

Spiced Baked Bananas

Here's a sunny touch of the tropics in this off-beat but easy-to-make sweet, redolent of the fragrances of the Spice Islands. Intriguing as it is satisfying.

3 *ripe bananas, peeled, sliced lengthwise, then in half*
1 *teaspoon fresh lemon juice*
⅓ *cup apple juice, no sugar added*
¼ *teaspoon ground cinnamon*
4 *dashes ground mace*
1 *tablespoon seedless raisins*
¼ *teaspoon corn oil to brush baking dish*

In small saucepan, heat apple juice to simmering point. Add lemon juice, cinnamon, and raisins. Bring to simmering point again, and cook, partially covered, for 5 minutes.

Brush shallow baking dish lightly with oil. Place sliced bananas on dish and pour hot apple juice mixture over them. Sprinkle with mace, and bake, uncovered, in preheated 400 degree oven for 15 minutes. Serve warm.

Yield: Serves 4

CAL	F	P:S	SOD	CAR	CHO
97	0	—	2	23	0

Spiced Baked Apples

Prepared with a generous lacing of spiced apple juice—not just plain water—this traditional American dish is transformed into an intriguing delight.

4 *medium-sized baking apples, preferably Roman Beauty*
2 *tablespoons honey*
4 *dashes ground mace*
1 *teaspoon ground cinnamon*
½ *teaspoon ground ginger*
¾ *cup apple juice, no sugar added*
½ *teaspoon fresh lemon juice*

Wash and core apples. Make several slits in skins to depth of one third of apple starting from top center. Arrange in shallow baking dish.

Combine apple juice, honey, spices, and lemon juice in saucepan. Heat to simmering point. Pour over apples. Bake in preheated 350 degree oven for 45 minutes, basting 3 times. Remove from oven. Let cool in baking dish, lightly covered with waxed paper. Serve warm or chilled.

Yield: Serves 4

CAL	F	P:S	SOD	CAR	CHO
129	0	—	3	35	0

Cinderella Applesauce

Applesauce is the homely drudge of the menu—except when it's tapped with the magic wand of exotic spices. Then it becomes a Cinderella at the ball—sassy and sweet, and altogether irresistible.

4 *crisp, sweet apples, such as Washington State*
⅓ *cup apple juice, no sugar added*
¼ *teaspoon ground ginger*
½ *teaspoon ground cinnamon*
3 *whole cloves*
2 *dashes ground nutmeg*
3 *tablespoons very flavorful honey such as thyme*

Combine all ingredients except honey in waterless cooker. Bring to boil. Lower heat. Cover and simmer for 10-15 minutes, or until apples are tender yet firm when pierced with sharp knife. Uncover, and let cool in pot for 10 minutes. Pour into food mill and purée. Add honey to taste, not to exceed 3 tablespoons.

Serve warm or chilled.

Yield: Serves 4 with one leftover portion

CAL	F	P:S	SOD	CAR	CHO
107	0	—	4	26	0

Strawberry Parfait

Pastel pinks and the glorious ripe redness of fresh strawberries make this amazingly low-caloried sweet as colorful as it is delicious. Two textures, one coarse and one smooth, are arranged in alternate layers to provide a series of contrasting taste delights. Use your prettiest parfait glass—and you've created a festive treat!

1½ *cups apple juice, no sugar added*
1¼ *cups sliced fresh strawberries which have been washed and hulled*
3 *teaspoons honey*
½ *cup (4 oz.) low-fat plain yogurt*
2 *teaspoons unflavored gelatin*
4 *drops almond extract*
4 *whole strawberries*
8 *mint leaves for garnish*

Heat apple juice to boiling point. Add gelatin and stir to dissolve. Measure out a half cup of this mixture and set aside, leaving remainder for the next step.

For the smooth-textured part: In a blender, purée half cup strawberries with 2 teaspoons honey. Pour into small bowl. Add remainder of apple juice mixture and stir well. Whisk in yogurt. Pour into an 8¼″ × 9″ loaf pan. Refrigerate until set (about 2 hours).

For the coarse-textured part: Coarsely mash balance of sliced berries. Add balance of honey and cook over very low heat for 2 minutes. Cool. Add almond extract and half cup apple juice mixture which had been set aside. Stir well. Refrigerate until slightly thickened.

When mixture in loaf pan has set, cut into 1″ cubes, and remove from pan with spatula carefully to avoid breaking. In 4 parfait glasses, arrange cubes and slightly thickened strawberry mixture in alternate layers. Refrigerate again until set.

Serve, garnished with one whole strawberry and 2 mint leaves on top of each dessert.

Yield: Serves 4
Note: If strawberries are particularly sweet, you can eliminate the honey. If honey is eliminated, cook the strawberries with 1 tablespoon unsugared apple juice.

CAL	F	P:S	SOD	CAR	CHO
114	0	—	18	27	1
Without honey					
72	0	—	16	16	1

Blueberry Mousse with Vanilla Sauce

The season is short for this delectable berry, so hurry to capture its essence in this blend of sweet creaminess and contrasting tartness. Float a cloud of rich vanilla sauce on its azure blueness, and you have a heavenly finale to your dinner.

For the blueberry mousse:
1 *cup fresh blueberries, washed and picked over*
Juice of ½ lemon
Grated rind of ½ lemon
2 *tablespoons dry curd cottage cheese, no salt added, no more than ½% milkfat*
4 *tablespoons low-fat plain yogurt*
2 *tablespoons honey*
¼ *cup apple juice, no sugar added*
1 *teaspoon agar-agar flakes (Page 6)*
2 *egg whites*
1 *teaspoon Grand Marnier Liqueur (optional) or ½ teaspoon cognac extract*

Combine blueberries, cottage cheese, yogurt, honey, lemon juice, and lemon rind in blender. Purée for 30 seconds. Pour into bowl.

Heat apple juice to boiling point in small saucepan. Sprinkle with agar-agar. Turn heat down to simmering point, and cook, uncovered, for 4 minutes, stirring to blend, skimming foam that rises to top. Let cool. Pour into blended mixture. Add liqueur or extract and blend with whisk.

Beat egg whites until firm but not dry peaks form (Page 125). Whisk one-third of mixture into berries, and fold in balance (Page 128). Spoon into dessert dishes and chill until thickened (about 2 hours). Serve with one tablespoon vanilla sauce spooned over each dessert or to taste.

For the vanilla sauce:
4 *tablespoons non-fat dry milk*
½ *cup water*
1 *tablespoon honey*
1 *tablespoon arrowroot flour dissolved in 1 tablespoon water*
3 *dashes nutmeg*
2 *teaspoons vanilla extract*

Combine milk, water, and honey in blender. Blend for one minute on high speed. Pour into small heavy-bottomed saucepan. Stir in vanilla. Add dissolved flour mixture and cook over very low heat, stirring constantly, until thickened. Sprinkle with nutmeg and stir. Pour through fine-meshed strainer, pressing with spoon. Serve warm or chilled.

Yield: About ¾ cup
Variations:

1. *Almond Sauce:* Substitute ¼ teaspoon almond extract for vanilla extract. Yield: About ¾ cup.

2. *Mocha Sauce:* Dissolve one teaspoon coffee substitute, such as Cafix, in one teaspoon hot water. Add to blender with milk mixture before blending. Yield: About ¾ cup.

3. *Fruit Sauce:* Add ¼ cup fresh fruit to blender with milk mixture. Try berries, sliced ripe peeled peaches, or bananas. Substitute a few drops of almond extract for vanilla extract. Yield: About one cup.

4. *Carob Sauce:* Cook one tablespoon carob powder in ¼ cup water for 5 minutes. Cool. Add to blender with milk mixture and blend. Yield: About one cup.

CAL	F	P:S	SOD	CAR	CHO
97	0	—	35	23	0
With Grand Marnier					
100	0	—	35	23	0
Vanilla sauce					
28	0	—	8	6	0
Almond sauce					
28	0	—	8	6	0
Mocha sauce					
30	0	—	8	6	0

Raspberry sauce					
33	0	—	8	7	0
Peach sauce					
33	0	—	8	7	0
Banana sauce					
34	0	—	8	8	0
Carob sauce					
31	0	—	8	7	0

Prune Mousse

You'll never know it's made from prunes. So even if you've never been a prune fancier, you'll fancy this light and frothy sweet-tooth satisfier. A prune whip must be prepared prior to the making of the mousse, and the whip stands on its own as a dessert or as a routine-breaking breakfast treat.

For the Whip:

Place prunes from a 12-ounce box in a saucepan with enough unsweetened apple juice to barely cover (about 1¼ cups). Be sure that the prunes are unsulphured and unsweetened. Add a large slice of orange, skin and all. Bring to simmering point, cover, and cook for 10 minutes. Turn off heat and let stand in saucepan, covered, until completely cooled.

Purée in food mill. (Do not use blender.) Stir purée to blend. Store in jar in refrigerator.

For the Prune Mousse:

¾ *cup prune whip, room temperature*
⅓ *cup apple juice, no sugar added*
1 *teaspoon agar-agar flakes (Page 6)*
2 *egg whites*
½ *teaspoon ground cinnamon*
2 *rounded tablespoons plain low-fat yogurt*

Heat apple juice in small saucepan. Sprinkle agar-agar into juice and simmer for five minutes, uncovered, stirring often. Skim off foam. Let cool.

Prune whip should have the consistency of thick, pourable sour cream for this recipe. If too thick, thin down with small amount of apple juice before proceeding with recipe. Pour ¾ cup prune whip into large mixing bowl. Add cooled agar-agar mixture, together with cinnamon, and blend with whisk.

To beat egg whites, start mixing machine on medium speed. As egg whites begin to congeal, turn speed up gradually to top speed and beat until firm but not dry peaks form. Add egg whites to prunes as follows:

Blend ⅓ of egg whites into prune mixture with whisk. Then with wooden spoon, fold balance of whites (Page 128) into prunes. Spoon into dessert dishes. Refrigerate for 2 hours before serving.

Yield: Prune Whip: about 1 cup, serves 4. Prune Mousse: serves 4

CAL	F	P:S	SOD	CAR	CHO
Whip					
229	0	—	11	55	0
Mousse					
250	0	—	39	58	0

Banana Whip

Light, frothy, fruity, with just a touch of tartness, this multi-flavored version of the familiar banana whip is as different as it's delicious. Pretty to serve, too.

1 *large ripe banana, plus ½ small banana for garnish*
1 *cup apple juice, no sugar added*
⅓ *cup combination of raisins and unsweetened chopped dates*
1½ *teaspoons agar-agar flakes (Page 6)*
4 *tablespoons low-fat plain yogurt*
⅛ *teaspoon almond extract*
¼ *teaspoon vanilla extract*
2 *egg whites*
4 *dashes ground cinnamon*

In small saucepan, combine date-raisin mixture and apple juice. Bring to boil. Turn heat down, and simmer for 5 minutes. Add agar-agar, and simmer for 5 minutes, skimming foam that rises to top. Let cool. Pour into blender and purée for 30 seconds. Pour into bowl.

Mash one banana with fork. Combine with apple juice mixture. Add extracts and cinnamon, stirring to blend. Whisk in yogurt.

Beat egg whites until stiff but not dry peaks form (Page 125). Drop ⅓ of egg whites into banana mixture blending well with whisk. Fold in balance of egg whites (Page 128). Pour into 4 dessert dishes. Top each serving with 2 slices of banana.

Yield: Serves 4

CAL	F	P:S	SOD	CAR	CHO
138	0	—	59	30	0

Harold's Delight

A creation of my husband, it's stunningly simple to prepare. Try it, and come away as open-mouthed with surprise—and delight—as I did.

16 *pitted California dates*
8 *very thin slices of Danish Muenster or Lorraine Swiss, or other low-fat sliceable cheese (Page 3)*
Cinnamon sprinkled to taste

Set out 4 oven-proof dessert dishes. Place a slice of cheese in bottom of each dish. Add 4 dates. Top with a slice of cheese over each dessert. Sprinkle with cinnamon.

Bake in preheated 350 degree oven for 10-15 minutes or until cheese is melted and dates are well heated. Let cool for 2 minutes before serving.

Yield: Serves 4

CAL	F	P:S	SOD	CAR	CHO
75	6	.6:1	0	35	14

Honeydew Sherbert

Can you imagine the pure fruit essence of honeydew or pineapple captured in a frozen dessert almost as light as a meringue? If you can't, dip into the two after-meal treats that follow, and enjoy new heights of taste-consciousness. And, on the practical side, you don't need an ice cream machine to make them.

2½ *cups puréed ripe honeydew melon (about ¾ of average size melon) plus honeydew balls for garnish*
2 *tablespoons honey*
Juice of one lemon
Grated rind of ½ lemon
3 *egg whites*

Cut and dice honeydew. Purée in blender. Pour into mixing bowl. Add lemon juice and rind and blend with whisk. Add honey and blend again.

Beat egg whites (Page 125) until firm but not dry peaks form. Whisk ⅓ of egg whites into the puréed melon; then fold in the balance (Page 128). Pour into 9″ × 5″ loaf pan that has been rinsed in cold water and dried. Cover with aluminum foil and place in freezer compartment of refrigerator.

Remove from freezer after 45 minutes. At this point, top has started to solidify and the bottom has become watery. Fold bottom over top with wooden spoon until most of liquid is absorbed. Return, covered, to freezer.

Repeat the freezing, stirring, and folding process twice more. After 3 hours, remove from freezer, and using wire whisk or portable mixing machine, beat until smooth. At this point, the dessert will look and taste like sherbert. Return, covered, to freezer.

Sherbert will be fully ripened in flavor in about 5 hours from starting time. Remove from freezer 20 minutes before serving if you prefer a softer consistency. Serve in parfait or dessert dishes, garnished with two honeydew balls on top of each dessert.

Yield: Serves 4, and one leftover
Note: If melon is very sweet, honey may be eliminated.

CAL	F	P:S	SOD	CAR	CHO
72	0	—	47	15	0
Without honey					
47	0	—	47	9	0

Pineapple Sherbert

1 *20-ounce can pineapple chunks, in their own juices, no sugar added*
Juice of 1/2 lemon
2 *tablespoons honey*
3 *egg whites*

Pour contents of one can pineapple into blender, together with lemon and honey. Blend at high speed for one minute. Pour into large mixing bowl.

Beat egg whites (Page 125), folding them into fruit (Page 128), following directions for Honeydew Sherbert (Page 126).

Yield: Serves 6
Note: If you're fortunate enough to find a very ripe Hawaiian pineapple (outer skin brown, and fruit soft to touch), by all means use it. Replace canned pineapple with 2½ cups cubed fresh pineapple, plus juices. (Catch them while you're cutting.) Very ripe Hawaiian pineapple is as sweet as sugar, so eliminate the honey.

CAL	F	P:S	SOD	CAR	CHO
88	0	—	29	20	0
Fresh pineapple					
40	0	—	29	7	0

Pineapple Chiffon Pie

Inevitably there will come a time when you feel the urge to binge. This extravagant dessert was cunningly prepared for just that moment. It's a bonanza of crust-and-filling richness that satiates your most compulsive craving for sweets.

For the pie crust:
½ *cup rye flour*
1 *cup whole wheat flour*
½ *cup buckwheat flour*
2 *tablespoons date powder (Page 6)*
¼ *cup finely chopped walnuts*
½ *teaspoon ground cinnamon*
½ *cup corn oil*
About 3 tablespoons ice water

In medium-sized bowl, combine flours, date powder, walnuts, and cinnamon. Add oil, a little at a time, and blend with fork. Finally, dribble ice water, a tablespoon at a time, into mixture, blending with fork, using enough water to hold the mixture together.

Turn into an 8″ or 10″ aluminum pie pan (not glass), and press even amounts against bottom and sides of pan. Bake in preheated 375 degree oven for 35–40 minutes until lightly browned. Cool pan on rack.

Note: If there are some white beans on hand, strew a cupful over unbaked shell so that dough won't swell while baking. When fully baked, remove beans and save for next baking.

For the filling:
6 *ounces dry curd cottage cheese, no salt added, less than ½% milkfat*
½ *cup low-fat plain yogurt*
2 *pre-measured envelopes unflavored gelatin, or 2 tablespoons gelatin*
1 *12-ounce can crushed pineapple in its own juices, no sugar added*
Grated rind of ½ lemon
1½ *teaspoons vanilla extract*
4 *drops almond extract*
2 *tablespoons honey (optional)*
2 *large egg whites*
2 *tablespoons walnuts, coarsely chopped*
About 1 cup fresh orange juice

Add enough orange juice to juice from can of pineapple to equal 1½ cups liquid. Pour into saucepan together with honey. Bring to simmering point. Add gelatin, stirring to dissolve. Let cool to room temperature.

Combine cottage cheese, yogurt, and pineapple in blender. Add extracts and lemon rind, and purée on low speed for one minute. Pour into cooled gelatin mixture, and refrigerate until mixture begins to thicken.

Beat egg whites until firm but not dry peaks form (Page 125). Drop one third beaten egg whites into cheese mixture. Blend well with whisk. Pour balance of egg whites into mixture and fold gently using wooden spoon. Folding is done by making a down motion with the spoon, and then a scooping up and folding over motion. In this way, all the egg white is incorporated into the mixture while air bubbles remain intact. Don't overfold. Cool in refrigerator until almost set. This will take about 45 minutes.

Turn cooled filling into baked pie shell. Sprinkle with coarsely chopped nuts and refrigerate. Allow 2 hours to set.

Yield: Serves 10
Variations:

1. Alternate pie crust:

Crunchy Rolled Oats Pie Shell
1 *cup old fashioned rolled oats*
4 *tablespoons honey*
½ *cup finely chopped walnuts*
¼ *cup corn oil*
2 *tablespoons date powder (Page 6)*

Toast oats by spreading them on cookie sheet and baking for 10 minutes. Transfer to plastic bag. Press all air out of bag. Then tie securely. Roll oats with rolling pin until they are broken up but not pulverized.

In a bowl, combine oats with date powder and nuts. Add oil, a little at a time, mixing with spoon. Lift mass into center of 8″ ungreased pie pan and press to bottom and sides of pan. Dribble honey onto crust and gently spread along sides and bottom of crust. Refrigerate for at least one hour before filling.

2. The filling alone makes a superb dessert. Just pour into 8 dessert dishes and chill until firm. Sprinkle with chopped nuts and serve.

CAL	F	P:S	SOD	CAR	CHO
Crust					
123	4	5.4:1	0	42	0
Filling					
71	0	—	25	13	0
Filling with honey					
86	0	—	25	16	0
Rolled oats crust					
117	7	4.5:1	0	14	0

Apple Coffee Cake

This cake, and the one that follows, are our favorites. They are, to put it in the simplest possible way, delicious. Quality cold-pressed corn oil (lighter by far than commercial corn oils) is a must, and so is an authoritatively flavored honey. Wild thyme honey, our choice, is a miracle maker.

For the cake:

- 1/4 *cup corn oil, plus ½ teaspoon for oiling baking pan*
- 4 *tablespoons honey*
- 3 *egg whites*
- ½ *egg yolk*
- 2¼ *cups unbleached flour, sifted*
- 3 *teaspoons low sodium baking powder (Pages 4 and 6)*
- 1 *measure low-fat plain yogurt (8 oz.) room temperature*
- 1 *teaspoon vanilla extract*

For the topping:

- 4 *crisp apples, such as Washington State*
- 1 *small lemon, including grated rind of ½ lemon*
- ½ *teaspoon cinnamon, plus several sprinklings*
- 4 *dashes ground cloves*
- 1 *teaspoon corn oil*
- 2 *tablespoons honey*
- 2 *tablespoons coarsely chopped walnuts*
- ⅛ *cup seedless raisins*

Cut apples into quarters, peel and core. Slice lengthwise a quarter inch thick. Place in bowl, together with lemon juice and rind, turning to coat. Add combined oil and honey, tossing gently. Add cinnamon and cloves, and toss again. Set aside.

Sift flour and baking powder into mixing bowl. Combine oil, honey, and eggs. Beat lightly with fork. Add to dry ingredients. Blend on medium speed of mixing machine for one minute. Add yogurt and vanilla and blend again. Pour into 9″ square lightly oiled baking pan, spreading mixture evenly.

Arrange coated apples close together in a neat pattern on top of batter. Sprinkle with raisins and nuts, pouring any leftover juices over cake as well. Press entire mixture slightly into batter, using spatula. Sprinkle with cinnamon.

Bake in preheated 350 degree oven for 50 minutes. When cake is fully baked, the batter should come away slightly from sides of pan, and be lightly browned. Remove from oven and place pan on rack to cool. Cut into 8 serving pieces. Remove carefully with spatula, and serve slightly warm.

Yield: Serves 12
Note: If all cake isn't used on baking day, wrap each piece in aluminum foil and freeze. When you want a slice of this delicious goodie, reheat in foil in 350 degree preheated oven for 15 minutes. Serve warm.

Variation: Fresh peaches or blueberries can be substituted for apples. If either are used, add ⅛ teaspoon almond extract to topping mixture.

CAL	F	P:S	SOD	CAR	CHO
215	8	4.7:1	26	37	11
Peaches					
208	8	4.7:1	26	35	11
Blueberries					
218	8	4.7:1	26	38	11

5-Minute Spice Cake

Fast to make but long-lingering in your memory, this zesty cake replete with rich spice flavors makes a simple—in the sense of simply wonderful—finale to your meal. And with no beating, just stirring, it's almost effortless to make.

- 1 *cup unbleached flour*
- 1½ *teaspoons low sodium baking powder (Pages 4 and 6)*
- 1 *teaspoon ground cinnamon*
- 1 *teaspoon ground ginger*
- ¼ *teaspoon ground nutmeg*
- 1 *large egg (use ½ of the yolk)*
- 1 *tablespoon buckwheat honey*
- ¾ *cup buttermilk, no salt added*
- 3 *tablespoons corn oil, plus ¼ teaspoon to oil pan*
- 3 *tablespoons date powder (Page 6)*
- 1 *teaspoon grated orange rind*

Sift flour, baking powder, and spices into a bowl. Add date powder and stir.

In another bowl, combine egg beaten lightly with fork, honey, rind, buttermilk and oil. Stir to blend. Pour liquid ingredients into bowl with flour mixture. Stir well with wooden spoon to blend.

Turn into lightly oiled small loaf pan (7⅜″ × 3⅝″ × 2¼″), and bake in preheated 350 degree oven for 45–50 minutes, or until toothpick inserted through center of cake comes out dry.

Place pan on rack to cool for 15 minutes. Using blunt knife, loosen around sides and invert. Serve slightly warm.

Yield: 1 loaf, serves 6

CAL	F	P:S	SOD	CAR	CHO
131	7	4.1:0	47	19	16

Banana Crazy Cake

It's not a cake, though it looks like a cake. It's not a pudding, though it tastes like a pudding. What is it? A candy? A confection? A banana brownie? It's crazy! Hence, its title. But whatever it is, you'll be crazy about it.

- 2 *small ripe bananas*
- ¼ *cup chopped dates, no sugar added*
- ½ *cup apple juice, no sugar added, brought to boiling point*
- ¼ *cup unprocessed bran flakes (Page 6)*
- ¼ *cup whole wheat flour*
- 1½ *cups unbleached flour*
- 1 *teaspoon low sodium baking powder (Pages 4 and 6)*
- ½ *teaspoon ground cinnamon*
- ¼ *teaspoon ground allspice*
- *Juice of ½ lemon plus rind from ½ lemon*
- ¼ *cup finely chopped walnuts*
- 1 *egg, half yolk removed*
- 1 *tablespoon date powder (Page 6)*
- 3 *tablespoons corn oil, plus ½ teaspoon to oil baking pan*
- ⅓ *cup low-fat plain yogurt*
- 1 *tablespoon honey (optional)*
- 1 *teaspoon vanilla extract*

Place dates in small bowl. Pour boiling apple juice over them. Stir with fork to separate. Add lemon juice and rind. Stir. Let cool.

Combine flours with baking powder. Sift once into bowl. Add bran flakes and date powder. Stir to blend. Set aside.

Slice bananas and place in mixing bowl together with oil, honey, and egg, beating well. Add yogurt, vanilla, cooled date mixture, and spices. Blend with wooden spoon. Finally, add flour mixture, ⅓ at a time, beating with wooden spoon after each addition. Stir in chopped nuts.

Pour into lightly oiled 9″ square aluminum baking pan (preferable to glass because the bottom of cake will brown more evenly), and bake in preheated oven for one hour. Let pan cool on rack. Cut into 16 squares, then remove from pan carefully with spatula.

Yield: 16 squares

CAL	F	P:S	SOD	CAR	CHO
101	4	4.2:1	7	16	8
With honey					
105	4	4.2:1	7	17	8

Carob Swirl Cake

For the cake:

2½ *cups unbleached flour, sifted*
3 *teaspoons low sodium baking powder (Pages 4 and 6)*
¼ *cup corn oil, plus ½ teaspoon to oil baking pan*
4 *tablespoons very flavorful honey, such as thyme*
½ *cup low-fat plain yogurt (4 oz.)*
¼ *cup non-fat milk*
3 *egg whites*
½ *egg yolk*
1 *teaspoon vanilla extract*

For the carob mixture:

3 *tablespoons carob powder, no sugar added (Page 6)*
¼ *teaspoon vanilla*
½ *cup water*
½ *teaspoon arrowroot flour dissolved in teaspoon water*

Prepare carob mixture first. Combine carob, water, and vanilla in small saucepan. Bring to boil. Turn heat down and simmer, uncovered, for 3 minutes. Add flour mixture and continue cooking for 2 minutes more, or until slightly thickened, stirring constantly with wooden spoon. Let cool.

To prepare the cake, sift flour and baking powder together into small bowl. Combine oil, honey, eggs, milk and yogurt in mixing bowl. Blend on medium speed of mixing machine for 2 minutes. Add dry ingredients, a half cup at a time, beating well after each addition. Add vanilla, and blend for 30 seconds.

Pour half of batter into lightly oiled 7⅜″ × 3⅝″ × 2¼″ loaf pan. Combine balance of batter with cooled carob mixture and stir to blend. Pour over batter in loaf pan. With knife, using a digging-in and turning-over motion, swirl light mixture over dark mixture in several places. Place in center section of preheated 350 degree oven, and bake for one hour. Tests for doneness: When inserting toothpick into center of cake, it should come out dry; the cake will come away from sides of pan and will be lightly brown.

Remove from oven and let cool in pan on rack for ten minutes. Loosen with blunt knife, and turn onto rack to cool completely.

Yield: Serves 8
Variation: Can be embellished with sugar-free jellies to make an extravagant dessert.
Note: This cake freezes very well. It can be frozen whole; or it can be sliced, reshaped to loaf, and frozen—so slices can be flipped off, one at a time, and reheated.

CAL	F	P:S	SOD	CAR	CHO
Per slice					
182	8	4.0:1	29	34	13

Date-Nut Cake

This is one of the look-forward-to treats of my childhood. The recipe, a family heirloom, has been altered to meet the lighter requirements of my new cuisine; and the result is even more irresistible than I remember it. This cake—and the dreamy date candy bar that follows—are confections to satisfy the most insatiable lust for sweetness.

1 *8-ounce package dates, no sugar added chopped (Dromedary brand works well for this recipe)*
1 *cup boiling water*
1 *tablespoon corn oil plus ½ teaspoon to oil baking pan*
3 *tablespoons honey*
1 *egg, using ½ yolk and all of egg white*
1½ *cups unbleached flour*
1½ *teaspoons low sodium baking powder (Pages 4 and 6)*
⅓ *cup chopped walnuts*
1 *teaspoon ground cinnamon*
¼ *teaspoon ground cloves*
1 *tablespoon grated orange rind*

(Here's an easy way to chop sticky dates. Open box, turn upside down onto board, and remove dates intact. Using sharp moistened knife, cut vertically into 1/4" slices; then cut horizontally into 1/4" slices. Transfer to small bowl.) Pour boiling water over dates, stirring well to separate fruit. Let stand for 10 minutes. Then add oil, honey, rind, cloves, and cinnamon, stirring to blend.

In large mixing bowl, beat egg with fork until light and frothy. Pour date mixture into eggs, and blend on medium speed of mixing machine.

Sift flour and baking powder together into small bowl. Add to mixing bowl, a third at a time, mixing only until all flour is absorbed. Add nuts and stir.

Pour into lightly oiled small loaf pan (7 3/8" × 3 5/8" × 2 1/4"). Bake in preheated 350 degree oven for 55–60 minutes, or until toothpick inserted into center of cake comes out dry.

Yield: 1 loaf, 12 servings

CAL	F	P:S	SOD	CAR	CHO
133	2	6.3:1	3	33	10

Date Dreams

- 1 *8-ounce package dates, no sugar added, chopped (Dromedary brand works well for this recipe)*
- 1/2 *cup chopped walnuts*
- 1/2 *cup toasted wheat germ, no sugar added*
- 1/2 *cup date powder (Page 6)*
- 3 *egg whites*
- 1/2 *egg yolk*
- 3/4 *teaspoon ground cinnamon*
- 1 *tablespoon corn oil, plus 1/2 teaspoon for oiling baking pan*
- 1/2 *cup unbleached flour*
- 1 *tablespoon grated orange rind*
- 2 *tablespoons apple juice, no sugar added*

Place chopped dates in large mixing bowl together with nuts. Beat eggs lightly with fork and add to mixture.

Combine wheat germ, cinnamon, and date powder in blender and pulverize to a powder. Pour over date-nut-egg mixture. Beat with wooden spoon until blended.

Combine apple juice, rind, and oil, beating lightly with fork. Pour over dry ingredients and beat with wooden spoon. Add flour and mix with wooden spoon until all flour is absorbed. Mixture will be thick.

Spread into lightly oiled 9" square baking pan. Bake in preheated 350 degree oven for 30 minutes. Cool pan on rack for 10 minutes. Cut into 12 bars while still slightly warm. Remove from baking pan with spatula, and let cool completely on rack before serving.

Yield: 12 bars

CAL	F	P:S	SOD	CAR	CHO
139	3	6.5:1	15	32	10

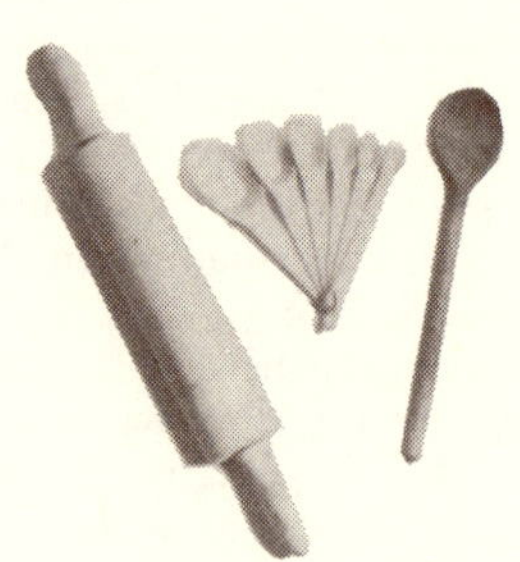

Apple-Oatmeal Cookies

The perfect cookie for the dieting cookie addict. So long-lastingly chewy, just two of them will satisfy your mad, mad craving. Extravagantly delicious, as well.

1 *cup old fashioned rolled oats*
¾ *cup unbleached flour*
1½ *teaspoons low sodium baking powder (Pages 4 and 6)*
¼ *cup seedless raisins or chopped dates*
¼ *cup chopped walnuts*
2 *tablespoons corn oil*
¼ *cup date powder*
¾ *teaspoon ground cinnamon*
¼ *cup non-fat milk*
¼ *cup apple juice, no sugar added*
1 *teaspoon vanilla extract*
1 *egg white, lightly beaten with fork*
1 *sweet, crisp apple, peeled, cored, and finely diced*
1 *teaspoon grated orange rind*
2 *tablespoons honey (optional)*

Place date powder in blender and pulverize. Combine with flour, baking powder, and cinnamon, and sift into small bowl. Add nuts, and raisins or dates. Stir. Set aside.

In large bowl, combine rolled oats with milk and apple juice. Stir well. Add egg white, orange rind, vanilla, optional honey, and oil to oatmeal mixture and stir. Add flour mixture, beating well with wooden spoon. Add apples and stir. Mixture will be quite thick.

Drop by spoonfuls, an inch apart, onto ungreased cookie sheet. Bake in preheated 375 degree oven for 20 minutes. Remove from oven and place on rack to cool. Let cookies dry out thoroughly for several hours before storing in a tightly covered tin.

Yield: 25–30 cookies

CAL	F	P:S	SOD	CAR	CHO
Per cookie					
45	1	5.5:1	4	9	0

Carob-Honey Cookies

These chocolaty goodies make a scrumptious snack or a light, yet satisfying, dessert after an elaborate entrée. The emphasis is on *chocolaty.*

¼ *cup honey*
¼ *cup corn oil, plus ½ teaspoon to oil cookie sheet*
¼ *cup apple juice, no sugar added*
2 *tablespoons carob powder, no sugar added (Page 6)*
½ *teaspoon ground cinnamon*
½ *teaspoon ground allspice*
¼ *cup unbleached flour*
1 *cup whole wheat flour*
1½ *teaspoons low sodium baking powder (Pages 4 and 6)*

Heat apple juice in small saucepan. Add carob. Cook over low heat for 3 minutes, stirring well to blend. Let cool.

Sift flours, baking powder, and spices together. Set aside.

Combine honey and oil in mixing bowl, and whisk briefly. Add cooled carob mixture and whisk again. Add dry ingredients, a little at a time, and beat with wooden spoon after each addition. Mixture will become very thick and fall away from side of bowl.

Gather up batter with fingers, and pressing together well with hands, shape into a large frankfurter 1½″ in diameter and 6″ long, smoothing out ends. Lay on a sheet of waxed paper and roll up tightly, twisting ends of waxed paper. Place in freezer for 4-6 hours, or overnight.

Preheat oven to 375 degrees. Roll dough out of waxed paper. With a very sharp knife, cut dough into ⅜″ slices. Place on very lightly oiled cookie sheet. Bake in center section of oven for 18–20 minutes, taking care not to burn. With spatula, very gingerly transfer cookies to rack. Cool thoroughly before serving.

Yield: 20 cookies

CAL	F	P:S	SOD	CAR	CHO
Per cookie					
46	3	4.5:1	0	5	0
With dates					
No appreciable difference					

Rich Carob Pudding

Midas-rich with chocolaty flavor, this melt-in-your mouth sweet is totally satisfying even in small portions.

4½ *tablespoons carob powder, no sugar added, (Page 6)*
2 *cups non-fat milk*
1½ *tablespoons coffee substitute, such as Cafix (Page 6)*
¼ *teaspoon ground cinnamon*
2½ *tablespoons arrowroot flour dissolved in 2 tablespoons water*
1 *tablespoon unbleached flour*
¼ *cup water*
1½ *teaspoons vanilla extract*
1 *tablespoon honey*

Combine carob, coffee substitute, cinnamon and water in small heavy-bottomed saucepan. Heat to simmering point, stirring to dissolve. Add honey and milk. Stir to blend. Bring to simmering point again. Add arrowroot flour mixture, blending with whisk as mixture thickens. Lower heat. Sprinkle flour into mixture, a little at a time, whisking after each addition. Continue to cook and whisk for 3 minutes. Let cool, uncovered, for 5 minutes. Stir in vanilla.

Pour into 4 small dessert dishes. Cover each dish with aluminum foil and refrigerate for at least 2 hours before serving.

Yield: Serves 4
Variation: Delicious sprinkled with one tablespoon chopped walnuts which have been blended with ½ teaspoon ground cinnamon.

CAL	F	P:S	SOD	CAR	CHO
90	0	—	58	18	0
With nuts					
135	1	12.5:1	58	19	0

Apple-Rice Pudding

Delicately light, spiced with cinnamon, and flecked with coriander, this is a wondrous dessert. Tangy and chewy apples—a surprise in a rice pudding—accentuates this sweet's smooth-as-velvet consistency.

¼ *cup uncooked rice, washed and drained*
3 *cups non-fat milk*
1 *cup apple juice, no sugar added*
4 *dashes ground nutmeg*
½ *teaspoon ground cinnamon*
2 *teaspoons coriander seeds, finely crushed and sieved*
½ *teaspoon vanilla extract*
1 *sweet, crisp apple, such as Washington State, peeled, cored, and diced*
½ *teaspoon corn oil to oil casserole*
2 *tablespoons very flavorful honey*

In large saucepan heat milk and apple juice to simmering point. Add rice, nutmeg, cinnamon, coriander, honey, and vanilla, stirring to blend. Pour into lightly oiled 2-quart casserole and bake, covered, in preheated 325 degree oven for one hour, stirring once. Turn oven down to 300 degrees. Add apples, stir, and return to oven. Bake, uncovered, until all liquid is absorbed, stirring every 15 minutes, folding crust that forms into pudding. Serve warm or chilled.

Yield: Serves 6
Variation: A quarter cup of either seedless raisins or chopped dates may be added after rice has cooked for one hour.

CAL	F	P:S	SOD	CAR	CHO
133	0	—	61	24	0
With raisins					
152	0	—	62	27	0
With dates					
154	0	—	61	27	0

Wish-I-Had-A Milk Shake

And here's your wish come true in a frothy, velvety, ever-so-chocolaty drink that you can imbibe without guilt. You'd never know you're on a diet!

To make one milk shake:

- 4 *ounces non-fat milk*
- 1 *tablespoon carob powder, no sugar added (Page 6)*
- ¼ *cup apple juice, no sugar added*
- 4 *crushed ice cubes*
- ½ *teaspoon vanilla extract*
- 1 *tablespoon flavorful honey*

Combine carob and apple juice in small saucepan. Heat to boiling point and stir to blend. Turn heat down and simmer, uncovered, for 3 minutes. Let cool.

Combine ice, milk, honey, and vanilla in blender. Add cooled carob mixture and blend on high speed for 2 minutes.

Yield: One tall glass milk shake

Variations:

1. Add ½ teaspoon coffee substitute, such as Cafix, to saucepan when heating carob.

2. Replace carob with ¼ cup mashed fresh berries (blueberries, strawberries, raspberries). Boil with apple juice for 2 minutes. Use 4 drops almond extract in place of vanilla.

CAL	F	P:S	SOD	CAR	CHO
151	0	—	9	53	0
With Cafix					
158	0	—	9	53	0
With berries					
150	0	—	9	53	0

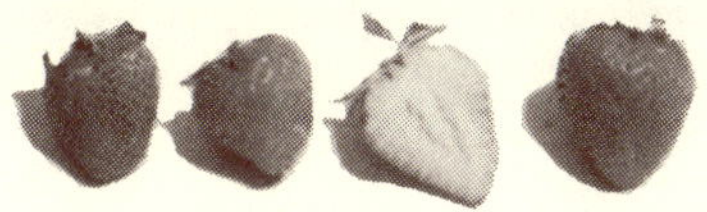

Breads

My French Bread

This is a very light-textured bread, unusually flavored. It derives its special taste from crushed coriander or cardamom seeds plus a small amount of rye flour combined with unbleached flour. It's delectable eating, and particularly good when used for stuffings and bread crumbs.

- 1 *tablespoon dry yeast, or one premeasured package*
- 2½ *cups warm water (105 to 115 degrees)*
- 1 *tablespoon honey*
- 1 *tablespoon coriander seeds, pan toasted, finely crushed (Page 99)*
- 1 *cup medium rye flour*
- 5½–6 *cups unbleached flour*
- 1 *egg white, lightly beaten with fork*
- ½ *tablespoon corn oil to oil baking pans*
- 1 *tablespoon sesame seeds to sprinkle on top of loaves*

Combine honey, water and seeds in mixing bowl. Sprinkle in yeast, blending with fork until dissolved. Add 2 cups unbleached flour and all rye flour. Beat on medium speed of mixing machine for two minutes, or with wooden spoon until smooth.

Add 3 cups flour, a cup at a time, mixing with wooden spoon after each addition. Turn out on a lightly floured board and knead (see Note 2) until smooth and elastic, adding small amounts of flour until dough is no longer sticky. If kneading with dough-hook, follow directions given in manual. If you've never made bread before, I recommend that you start by kneading your first loaves by hand. This is the only way you can learn how bread changes in texture as it's kneaded. After that, you'll be able to use a doughhook successfully.

When kneading is completed, shape dough into a ball, and drop into a large straight-sided bowl. Cover with plastic wrap, and let rise at room temperature (70–80 degrees) until double in bulk. A straight-sided bowl makes it easier to judge when dough has doubled in bulk. Rising takes about 1½–2 hours depending upon the temperature and humidity in your room and the freshness of the yeast. Many recipes recommend at this point covering with damp towel, or placing bowl in warm water to stimulate the rising process. Don't do it. This produces a yeast-tasting loaf, and you don't want to taste the yeast; you only want to benefit from its magic qualities. To test if bread has fully risen, poke one finger into dough. If it springs back, it's not fully risen; if the indentation remains, you're ready for the next step.

Punch dough down and knead briefly, popping out all air bubbles. Cut into 4 equal pieces and let rest, covered, for 5 minutes. With very lightly floured hands, shape into four slender loaves the length of the French baking pans (about 14″). Place in lightly oiled pans. With sharp knife, make four diagonal slashes across each loaf. Dip pastry brush into egg white and paint each loaf around the sides and top. Cover loosely with waxed paper and let rise until dough has risen above the edges of pans (about one hour).

Sprinkle with sesame seeds and bake in preheated 425 degree oven for 15 minutes; then at 400 degrees for an additional 20 minutes. Immediately slide loaves out of pans and place each loaf back in oven on racks. Bake for 5 minutes. Remove from oven. Cool *completely* on rack before slicing. The full flavor of the bread cannot be enjoyed until it's completely cooled, which takes 2–3 hours.

Yield: Four 14″ loaves, 14 one-inch slices per loaf

Notes:

1. This bread is best on the day it's baked. Preserve the fresh-baked taste by cutting each loaf in half, wrapping in aluminum foil and freezing. When ready to use, bake in preheated 350 degree oven for 15 minutes without removing foil. Remove foil and let cool before slicing. Frozen properly, it will keep for several months.

2. How to knead: Push the dough down and then forward with heel of your hand, then fold the dough over towards you. Make a quarter turn, and push and fold as before. Repeat turning, pushing and folding until the texture of dough becomes smooth and elastic, and dough can be easily shaped into a ball.

CAL	F	P:S	SOD	CAR	CHO
Per slice					
54	0	—	2	13	0

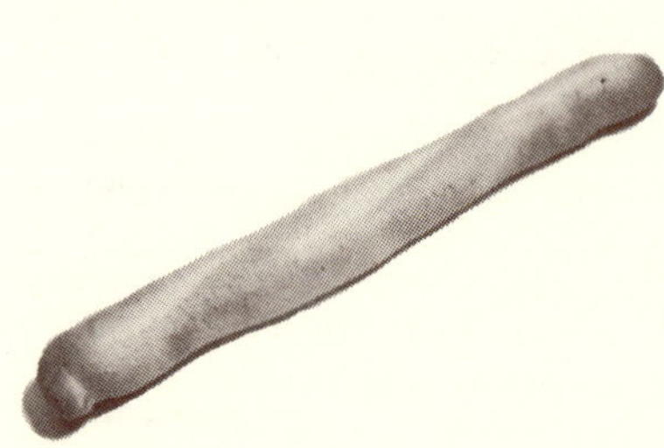

My French Herb Bread

This herb-flavored multi-floured bread baked in French loaf pans makes a deliciously crunchy accompaniment to soups and salads. Use it as a flavor-booster in recipes calling for stuffing and crumbs.

1 *tablespoon dry yeast, or 1 pre-measured package*
6 *cups unbleached flour*
½ *cup rye flour*
½ *cup whole wheat flour*
¼ *cup non-fat dry milk*
1¾ *cups water*
¾ *cup chicken stock (Page 10)*
½ *teaspoon each dried rosemary, thyme, and basil leaves, crushed*
1 *tablespoon dried minced onion*
1 *egg white mixed with 1 tablespoon water*
½ *tablespoon corn oil to oil baking pans*

In large mixing bowl, combine yeast, 5½ cups unbleached flour, rye and whole wheat flours, dry non-fat milk, minced onions, and herbs. Stir to blend.

Heat water and stock until warm (110–115 degrees). Pour over the mixed dry ingredients and beat with wooden spoon. When dough can no longer be handled with spoon, scoop up with hands, and turn onto lightly floured board and knead (Page 136), adding balance of flour if necessary, until dough is smooth and elastic. Shape into ball and drop into a straight-sided bowl. Cover with plastic wrap. (Transparent wrap works best because you can see exactly how your dough is progressing without lifting off its cover, thereby retaining necessary moisture.) Let rise at room temperature (70–80 degrees) until double in bulk (about 2 hours).

Punch dough down and knead out all air bubbles. If dough feels sticky, knead briefly on lightly floured board for one minute. Cut into 4 equal pieces. Cover loosely with waxed paper and let rest for 5 minutes.

Prepare French loaf pans according to instructions for My French Bread (Page 135). Shape each piece into long slender loaves almost the length of pans, and place in pans. Slash loaves diagonally in four places and brush with egg white mixture which has been lightly beaten with fork. Cover loosely with waxed paper, and let rise until well above sides of pans (2–2½ hours).

Bake in preheated 425 degree oven for 15 minutes. Turn heat down to 375 degrees, and bake for 20 minutes. Immediately slide loaves out of pans and place back in oven on rack. Bake for 5 minutes more. Remove from oven. Cool thoroughly on rack before slicing.

Yield: Four 14″ loaves, fourteen 1″ slices per loaf

CAL	F	P:S	SOD	CAR	CHO
Per slice					
54	0	4.8:1	2	13	0

Sourdough Rye Bread

Unless you're an experienced bread-maker, you'll never be able to identify the ingredients in this hearty, yet light-textured bread. Made with sourdough starter and just a soupçon of buckwheat and rye flours, this is a highly versatile bread, equally as good with meat as with cheese and jellies. It's a good toaster, and when sliced very thin can be converted to melba toast. A good keeper at room temperature, too.

I use a rye starter for this bread, and for all my breads calling for starters, because rye flour's flavor and texture eliminate any sense of salt deprivation. Please do not use ready-made starters. Mine is easy to make, produces a delicious loaf—and you know what's in it.

For the Sour Rye Starter:
2½ *cups medium rye flour*
2 *cups warm water (105–115 degrees)*
1½ *tablespoons dry yeast, or 1½ pre-measured packages*

Dissolve yeast in warm water. Add flour and blend well. Cover tightly with plastic wrap and let stand at room temperature (70–80 degrees) for 4 days. Mixture will become bubbly and develop a slightly sour aroma. After using starter, replenish with equal amounts of flour and water. Example: If you've taken out a cup, replace it with a cup of water and a cup of flour. Stir, re-cover, and let stand again until bubbly (about 8 hours). Stir down and refrigerate in tightly closed glass jar for next use.

To keep starter alive, use at least once in 10 days. If not used within that time, remove from jar, pour off half and discard. Pour remainder in bowl, and replenish with equal amounts flour and water. Cover and let stand at room temperature until bubbly (about 8 hours). Stir down, return to glass jar, and refrigerate.

For the bread:

1½ tablespoons dry yeast, or 1½ pre-measured packages
½ cup non-fat milk
½ cup buckwheat flour
½ cup rye flour
4–4½ cups unbleached flour
2 tablespoons buckwheat honey
1 tablespoon corn oil, plus ½ teaspoon for oiling bowl
2 teaspoons each caraway and poppy seeds
1¼ cups warm water (105–115 degrees)
1½ cups sour rye starter, room temperature
1 tablespoon white cornmeal to sprinkle on baking sheet

In large mixing bowl, combine one cup unbleached flour, all of buckwheat and rye flours, yeast, milk and seeds. Blend.

Combine water, honey, and oil, stirring well. Pour over dry ingredients, and beat on medium speed of your mixing machine for 2 minutes. Add starter and continue beating for another 2 minutes. Add 3 cups flour, a cup at a time, beating well after each addition with wooden spoon. Turn out on lightly floured board and knead (Page 136) until smooth and elastic, adding a small amount of flour, if necessary, until dough is no longer sticky. This is a lovely dough to handle. It's smooth and silky to the touch and doesn't stick to your hands.

Lightly oil a large straight-sided bowl. Shape dough into a smooth ball, and drop into bowl, turning to coat. Cover with plastic wrap, and let rise at room temperature (70–80 degrees) until double in bulk (about 2 hours).

Punch dough down, kneading briefly until all air bubbles are dispelled. Cut in half and shape into 2 smooth, round balls. Sprinkle jelly roll sheet with cornmeal, and place each loaf in opposite corners. Cover loosely with waxed paper and let rise until double in bulk (about 1 hour).

Place in preheated 375 degree oven and bake 40 minutes, spritzing twice during baking time with water, and again when bread is removed. Bread is fully baked when tapping bottom with knuckles produces a hollow sound.

Yield: 2 loaves; each quarter loaf makes eight ½″ uneven slices.
Note: Make your own handy spritzing gadget by sterilizing an empty windex bottle and setting it aside just for bread-making.

CAL	F	P:S	SOD	CAR	CHO
Average slice					
49	1	4.6:1	2	24	0

Cardamom Bread and Rolls

Any of my bread recipes can be converted easily into recipes for rolls. Here's how it's done for a sourdough bread flavored with the elusive sweetness of cardamom. Use it as the master plan, and regale your taste buds with crackling crunchiness no matter which of my doughs you start with. Superb for sandwiches, my rolls also make an excellent light breakfast accompanied by sugar-free jelly or cheese and your favorite herb tea. This recipe makes two loaves and 12 rolls.

½ *cup Sour Rye Starter (Page 137)*
2¼ *cups warm water (105–115 degrees)*
1 *tablespoon dry yeast, or 1 premeasured package*
1 *tablespoon corn oil, plus 2 teaspoons to oil utensils*
1 *tablespoon honey*
¼ *cup non-fat dry milk*
7–7½ *cups unbleached flour*
2½ *teaspoons cardamom seeds, crushed*
1 *egg white mixed with 1 tablespoon water*

The day before baking, combine starter, 2 cups flour, and one cup warm water in large bowl. Stir to blend. Cover with plastic wrap and let stand at room temperature.

Next day, stir mixture down. Sprinkle with yeast and stir. Add milk, 2 cups flour, and 2 teaspoons cardamom seeds. Blend with wooden spoon.

Combine balance of water, honey, and one tablespoon oil in saucepan, and heat until warm (105-115 degrees). Pour over starter mixture. Beat with wooden spoon for one minute. Then beat with mixing machine on medium speed for 2 minutes. Stop machine.

Add all but half cup flour, a cup at a time, beating well with wooden spoon after each addition. When dough can no longer be handled with spoon, scoop up and turn onto lightly floured board and knead (Page 136), using balance of flour, if necessary, until dough is smooth and elastic.

Shape into ball. Drop into lightly oiled straight-sided bowl. Turn to coat. Cover with plastic wrap and let rise at room temperature (70–80 degrees) until double in bulk (1½–2 hours). Punch dough down, knead briefly, and shape into ball. Cut into thirds. Cover with waxed paper and let dough rest for 3 minutes.

Shape into 3 loaves. Place in lightly oiled loaf pans (7⅜″ × 3⅝″ × 2¼″). Brush lightly with egg white mixture which has been lightly beaten with fork. Cover with waxed paper and let rise at room temperature until double in bulk (about one hour). Brush again with egg white mixture. Sprinkle with balance of cardamom seeds. Bake in preheated 375 degree oven for 40 minutes. Remove from pans. If bottoms of loaves are not well browned, place back in oven directly on rack for 5 minutes. Bread is fully baked when you tap bottom with knuckles and hear a hollow sound. Let cool on racks thoroughly before slicing.

Yield: 3 loaves; twenty ⅜″ slices per loaf.
Note: This recipe, which uses more flour than most recipes, can produce 2 loaves and 12 rolls; or each third can produce one loaf or 12 rolls. Rolls can be formed into a variety of shapes. My two favorites are round twists with a lot of crust, and plain round rolls like balls, which have a soft interior.

To make a dozen rolls, cut ⅓ of dough into 12 equal parts. Let rest, covered with waxed paper, for 3–4 minutes.

To make round rolls, tuck together edges of each piece to form a rough ball. You will now have a fairly smooth side and a puckered side. Squeeze puckers together to hold, and refine shape of ball. Place puckered side of balls onto a cookie sheet which has been sprinkled with 2 tablespoons white cornmeal, arranging the balls in 4 parallel rows of 3 rolls each. Brush with egg white mixture. Cover loosely with waxed paper and let rise at room temperature (70–80 degrees) until double in bulk (about one hour). Brush again with egg white mixture, sprinkle with seeds, and bake in center section of preheated 400 degree oven for about 20 minutes. Shift rolls at the end of 12 minutes to obtain uniform brownness. Finished rolls should be golden brown.

To make twisted rolls, start by cutting ⅓ of dough into cylinders resembling bread sticks 5″ long. Lay 2 cylinders parallel to each other pinching together at one end. Starting from pinched end, twist cylinders around each other until both cylinders are completely twisted. Pinch bottom end. With twist lying on a board, start at one end and fold portion into the side of twist; then with a rolling motion continue to fold until the entire twist has been formed into a circle. Pinch the loose end into the dough.

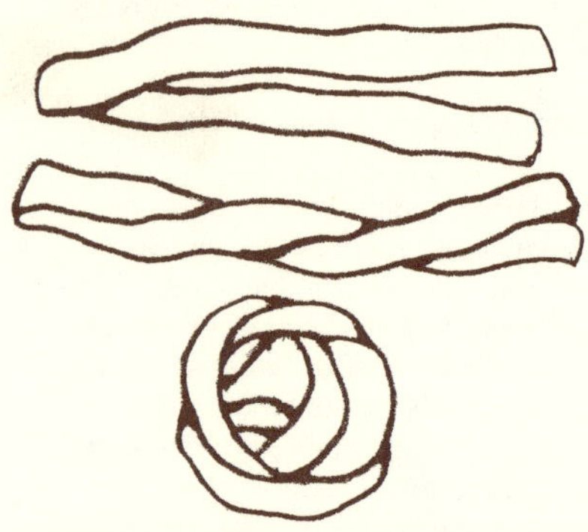

Yield: 3 loaves, or 2 loaves and 12 rolls

CAL	F	P:S	SOD	CAR	CHO
Per slice					
60	1	4.6:1	2	13	0
Per roll					
97	1	4.6:1	3	21	0

Apple Juice Rye Bread

This bread is a delight to make. You'll fall in love with the oh-so-easy-to-knead dough, and you'll be entranced by the aromatic fragrance of toasted coriander. Three risings make exceptionally fine textured loaves, and apple juice gives them a subtle sweetness.

- 2 *tablespoons dry yeast, or 2 premeasured packages*
- 1¼ *cups warm water (105–115 degrees)*
- 1 *cup apple juice, no sugar added*
- ¼ *cup non-fat dry milk*
- ½ *cup gluten flour*
- 2½ *cups rye flour*
- 3½–4 *cups unbleached flour*
- 1 *tablespoon corn oil, plus ½ teaspoon for oiling bowl*
- 2 *tablespoons coriander seeds, toasted, finely crushed (Page 99)*
- 1 *tablespoon poppy seeds*
- 1 *tablespoon buckwheat honey*
- *Grated peel of ½ navel orange*
- 2 *tablespoons white cornmeal to sprinkle on baking sheet*

Combine rye flour with 2 cups unbleached flour, milk, poppy and coriander seeds.

In large bowl, dissolve yeast and honey in ¼ cup warm water (105–115 degrees), blending with fork. Let stand for 5 minutes.

Heat apple juice, water, orange peel, and oil in saucepan until warm (105–115 degrees). Pour into dissolved yeast mixture and stir. Add flour mixture, and beat with wooden spoon until all flour is absorbed. Add gluten flour and 1½ cups unbleached flour, beating well. When mixture becomes too difficult to handle with spoon, scoop up and turn onto lightly floured board. Knead (Page 136) adding balance of flour if necessary until smooth and elastic.

Shape into ball and drop into lightly oiled straight-sided bowl. Cover with plastic wrap and let rise at room temperature (70–80 degrees) until double in bulk (about one hour). Punch down to original size and knead briefly in bowl. Let rise again, covered, until double in bulk (about 40 minutes).

Punch dough down and shape into ball. Cut in half. Shape into 2 round smooth loaves. Sprinkle jelly roll pan with cornmeal and place each loaf in opposite corners of pan. Spritz with water (Page 138). Cover with waxed paper and let rise until double in bulk.

Bake in preheated 375 degree oven for 45 minutes. Bread is fully baked when tapping bottom with knuckles produces a hollow sound. Spritz again with water. Place on rack and cool thoroughly before slicing.

Yield: 2 loaves; each ¼ loaf makes eight ½″ uneven slices

CAL	F	P:S	SOD	CAR	CHO
Average slice					
49	0	—	1	10	0

Norwegian Rye Bread

Norwegian rye bread derives its world-renowned qualities from a combination of rye and other flours, butter, seeds, sugar and molasses. In my version, I've added an adventurous mélange of different ingredients to the flours to produce a moist, light, butternut brown loaf with a crackling crust.

2 *tablespoons dry yeast, or 2 pre-measured packages*
¼ *cup warm water (105–115 degrees)*
2 *cups unbleached flour*
2 *cups rye flour*
1¾ *cups whole wheat flour*
½ *cup gluten flour*
¼ *cup date powder (Page 6)*
1 *tablespoon corn oil, plus ½ tablespoon to oil utensils*
½ *cup non-fat milk*
1½ *cups apple juice, no sugar added*
1 *teaspoon cardamom seeds, crushed*
1 *tablespoon caraway seeds, partially crushed*
1 *tablespoon honey (optional)*
1 *egg white mixed with one tablespoon water*

In large mixing bowl, dissolve yeast in warm water, beating lightly with fork. Let stand for 5 minutes.

In another bowl, combine all flours, seeds, and date powder, stirring to blend.

Heat apple juice together with milk, oil and honey until warm (105–115 degrees). Pour into dissolved yeast, stirring to blend. Add half flour mixture and beat well with wooden spoon until all flour is absorbed. Add all but half cup of balance of flour mixture, a cup at a time, beating well after each addition. When dough becomes too difficult to handle with spoon, turn onto lightly floured board and knead (Page 136), adding balance of flours, if necessary, until dough is smooth and elastic (about 10 minutes). Shape into a ball and drop into a lightly oiled straight-sided bowl, turning to coat. Cover with plastic wrap and let rise at room temperature (70–80 degrees) until almost double in bulk. Punch down, knead briefly in bowl, and let rise, covered, a second time until double in bulk (about one hour).

Shape into ball, cut in half, and shape into 2 loaves. Place in lightly oiled small loaf pans (7⅜″ × 3⅝″ × 2¼″). Cover with waxed paper and let rise until double in bulk (45 minutes). Brush with egg white mixture. Bake in preheated 375 degree oven for 45 minutes. Remove from pans. Breads should be crisp and butternut brown. If not, return to oven on rack, and bake another 5 minutes. Cool thoroughly on rack before slicing.

Yield: 2 loaves; twenty ⅜″ slices per loaf

CAL	F	P:S	SOD	CAR	CHO
Per slice					
77	0	—	37	18	0

Honey
Makes no appreciable difference

Buckwheat Rye Bread

Do you like buckwheat griddle cakes? Then you'll love this bread. Buckwheat isn't a wheat at all. It's an herb. And it adds that special kind of flavor that only an herb can impart. Here that flavor is sharpened by a contrasting hint of the sweetness of coriander. A bread for connoisseurs.

2 *tablespoons dry yeast, or 2 premeasured packages*
1 *cup buckwheat flour*
2 *cups dark rye flour (see Note for Pumpernickel, Page 147), or medium rye if dark variety isn't available*
3–3½ *cups unbleached flour*
½ *cup gluten flour*
1 *tablespoon corn oil, plus ½ teaspoon to oil bowl*
2 *tablespoons buckwheat honey*
1½ *cups warm water (105–115 degrees)*
½ *cup low-fat plain yogurt*
2 *teaspoons caraway seeds, partially crushed*
1 *teaspoon caraway seeds, uncrushed, to sprinkle on loaves*
1 *tablespoon coriander seeds, toasted, finely crushed (Page 99)*
1 *egg white mixed with 1 tablespoon water*
2 *tablespoons white corn meal to sprinkle on baking sheet*

Combine all flours. Measure out 2 cups and place in large mixing bowl, together with crushed seeds and yeast. Stir to blend.

Heat water with one tablespoon oil and honey until warm (110–115 degrees). Add to flour mixture and beat with wooden spoon or on medium speed of mixing machine for 3 minutes. Add yogurt and beat another minute. Add all but half cup of balance of flours, a half cup at a time, beating well with wooden spoon after each addition. When dough starts to come away from side of bowl and becomes too difficult to handle with spoon, turn onto lightly floured board. Knead (Page 136), adding balance of flour if necessary until dough is smooth and elastic.

Shape into ball. Drop into lightly oiled straight-sided bowl, turning to coat. Let rise at room temperature (70–80 degrees) until double in bulk (about 1¾ hours). Punch down, knead briefly, and shape into ball. Cut in half and shape into 2 round smooth loaves. Sprinkle jelly roll sheet with cornmeal. Place loaves in opposite corners. Brush with egg white mixture that has been lightly beaten with fork. Cover loosely with waxed paper, and let rise until double in bulk (about one hour). Brush again with egg white mixture. Sprinkle with uncrushed caraway seeds, and bake in preheated 375 degree oven for 45 minutes. Test for doneness: Thump the bottoms of loaves with your knuckles. You should hear a hollow sound. Let cool on rack thoroughly before slicing.

Yield: 2 loaves; each quarter loaf makes eight ½″ uneven slices

CAL	F	P:S	SOD	CAR	CHO
Average slice					
49	0	—	2	10	0

Featherbread

This bread is so light it seems to float in air. It's textured like that masterpiece of Jewish breadmaking, the challah, but has none of the challah's overabundance of eggs, sugar and oil. This is the angel cake of breads.

2 *tablespoons dry yeast, or 2 pre-measured packages*
5–5½ *cups unbleached flour*
1 *cup whole wheat flour*
⅓ *cup non-fat dry milk*
1 *measure (8 oz.) low-fat plain yogurt*
1½ *tablespoons corn oil, plus 1 teaspoon for oiling utensils*
1 *cup apple juice, no sugar added*
1¼ *cups water*
1 *tablespoon honey*
1 *tablespoon anise seeds, crushed*
1 *egg white combined with 1 tablespoon water*
2 *teaspoons sesame or poppy seeds to sprinkle on top of loaves*

In large mixing bowl combine yeast, milk, whole wheat flour, anise seeds, and 2 cups unbleached flour. Stir to blend.

Combine water, apple juice, honey, and 1½ tablespoons corn oil in saucepan and heat until warm (105–115 degrees). Pour over dry ingredients and seeds, stirring with wooden spoon. Beat with wooden spoon, or with mixing machine on medium speed for 2 minutes. Add yogurt, and continue beating for one minute. Add all but half cup flour, a half cup at a time, beating well with wooden spoon after each addition. When mixture becomes too difficult to handle with spoon, turn onto a lightly floured board and knead (Page 136), adding balance of flour if necessary, until dough is smooth and elastic. Shape into ball and drop into a lightly oiled straight-sided bowl. Turn to coat. Cover with plastic wrap and let rise at room temperature (70–80 degrees) until more than double in bulk.

Punch dough down. Knead briefly and shape into ball. Cut into thirds. Shape into 3 loaves. Place in lightly oiled small loaf pans (7⅜″ × 3⅝″ × 2¼″). Brush with egg white mixture that has been lightly beaten with fork. Cover with waxed paper, and let rise until double in bulk (45–60 minutes). Brush again with egg white mixture, sprinkle with seeds, and bake in preheated 375 degree oven for 40 minutes. Remove from pans. If bottom of loaves are not well browned, place loaves back in oven on rack on their sides and bake for 3 minutes. Turn on other side and bake an additional 3 minutes. Cool on rack thoroughly before slicing.

Yield: 3 loaves; twenty ⅜″ slices per loaf

CAL	F	P:S	SOD	CAR	CHO
Per slice					
54	0	—	4	12	0

Whole Wheat Bread

Commercial bakers rely on huge quantities of sugar and other sweetening agents to make whole wheat bread palatable. My version employs fruit juice, cinnamon, herbs, and little more than a touch of honey (not the half cup called for by most recipes for home-made bread), to produce an utterly delectable loaf. The dough will delight you with its tantalizing aromas and the ease with which it can be handled. Let it rise three times, not twice, to bring out its full-bodied flavor.

2 *tablespoons dry yeast, or 2 pre-measured packages*
3½ *cups whole wheat flour*
3 *cups unbleached flour*
2 *tablespoons toasted wheat germ, no sugar added*
¼ *cup non-fat dry milk*
1 *teaspoon ground cinnamon*
4 *teaspoons coriander seeds, toastd and finely crushed (Page 99)*
1 *teaspoon anise seeds, crushed*
¼ *cup apple juice, no sugar added*
¼ *cup fresh orange juice*
1¾ *cups warm water (105–115 degrees)*
2 *tablespoons honey*
1 *tablespoon corn oil, plus 1 teaspoon for oiling utensils*
1 *tablespoon non-fat milk to brush on loaves before baking*

In the large bowl of your mixing machine, combine 2 cups unbleached flour, yeast, wheat germ, milk, and cinnamon. Stir to blend. Heat juices, water, oil, and honey until warm. Pour over flour mixture and beat with wooden spoon or mixing machine at medium speed for 2 minutes. Add seeds, and all but ½ cup flour, a half cup at a time, beating well with wooden spoon after each addition. When mixture becomes too difficult to handle with spoon, scoop up with hands and turn onto lightly floured board. Knead for 8–10 minutes (Page 136), adding a small amount of flour if necessary, until dough is smooth and elastic and no longer sticky. Shape into a ball. Drop into a lightly oiled straight-sided bowl. Turn to coat. Cover with plastic wrap and let rise at room temperature (70–80 degrees) until double in bulk (about 1 hour). (Hint for faster rising: Warm your rising bowl by filling with hot tap water and drying well before coating with oil.) Punch dough down, knead briefly to original size, and let rise again until double in bulk.

Punch dough down. Shape into ball. Cut into thirds. Shape into 3 loaves and place in lightly oiled small loaf pans (7⅜" × 3⅝" × 2¼"). Cover loosely with waxed paper and let rise until double in bulk. Brush with milk. Bake in preheated 375 degree oven for 45 minutes.

Remove from pans. Place loaves back in oven on rack on their sides and bake for 4 minutes. Turn on other side and bake another 4 minutes. The crusts will be brown and crisp. Cool on rack.

Yield: 3 loaves; twenty ⅜" slices per loaf

CAL	F	P:S	SOD	CAR	CHO
Per slice					
56	0	—	1	11	0

Cracked Wheat Bread

Breakfast toast aficionados—here's your bread! This light cracked wheat bread turns into a crunchy delight in the toaster. It's a perfect foil for jellies (unsugared, of course) and cheese (low-fat, naturally). The dough is particularly easy to handle, so you'll probably want to make up a batch and keep reserves in your freezer.

½ *cup uncooked cracked wheat cereal*
2 *tablespoons dry yeast, or 2 pre-measured packages*
1 *cup apple juice, no sugar added*
2 *cups warm water (105–115 degrees)*
⅓ *cup non-fat dry milk*
½ *cup rye flour*
½ *cup whole wheat flour*
4–4½ *cups unbleached flour*
1 *tablespoon corn oil, plus 2 teaspoons for oiling utensils*
1 *tablespoon anise seeds, crushed*
1 *egg white mixed with 1 tablespoon water*
2 *teaspoons sesame seeds to sprinkle on loaves*

In small saucepan, combine cracked wheat and apple juice. Bring to boil. Turn heat down and simmer, partially covered, for 15–20 minutes, or until all water is absorbed. Let cool to room temperature.

In small bowl, dissolve yeast in ½ cup warm water (105–115 degrees), blending well with fork. Let stand for 5 minutes.

In large mixing bowl, combine whole wheat and rye flours, non-fat milk, and one cup unbleached flour. Combine balance of warm water with 1 tablespoon oil. Pour over flour mixture. Stir with wooden spoon. Add dissolved yeast mixture, and anise seeds. Beat with wooden spoon until blended. Add cooled cracked wheat and beat with wooden spoon, or on medium speed of mixing machine, for 3 minutes. Add 3 cups flour, half cup at a time, beating with wooden spoon after each addition. When dough gets too difficult to handle with spoon, scoop out of bowl onto lightly floured board. Knead (Page 136) adding balance of flour if necessary until dough is smooth and elastic.

Drop into lightly oiled straight-sided bowl, turning to coat. Cover with plastic wrap and let rise at room temperature (70–80 degrees) until double in bulk (1½–2 hours).

Punch down. Shape into ball. Cut into 3 equal pieces and shape into loaves. Place in lightly oiled small loaf pans (7⅜″ × 3⅝″ × 2¼″). Cover with waxed paper and let rise until double in bulk. Beat egg whites briefly with fork. Brush over loaves. Sprinkle with sesame seeds and bake in preheated 375 degree oven for 45 minutes. Loosen around edges of pans with blunt knife and remove loaves from pans. Place loaves on their sides directly onto rack in oven. Bake for 4 minutes; turn on other side and bake for an additional 4 minutes. Let cool on rack before slicing.

Yield: 3 loaves; twenty ⅜″ slices per loaf

CAL	F	P:S	SOD	CAR	CHO
Per slice					
57	0	—	2	11	0

Four-Flour Bread

This hearty nutritious bread is an appetite-satisfier by itself, and it's impeccably textured for sandwiches. Its prime virtue: it sticks with you.

2 *tablespoons dry yeast or 2 premeasured packages*
2 *cups rye flour*
2 *cups whole wheat flour*
2 *cups unbleached flour*
½ *cup gluten flour*
¼ *cup toasted wheat germ, no sugar added*
1 *cup low-fat plain yogurt, room temperature*
1½ *cups warm water (105–115 degrees)*
1 *tablespoon dried minced onion*
1 *tablespoon caraway seeds*
1 *tablespoon corn oil, plus ½ teaspoon for oiling bowl*
2 *tablespoons honey*
1 *tablespoon white cornmeal to sprinkle on baking sheet*

Combine four flours and wheat germ. Place 2 cups combined mixture together with yeast in mixing bowl. Combine water, onion, seeds, honey, and oil and add to dry ingredients. Stir well with wooden spoon. Add yogurt and stir again to blend. Beat with wooden spoon for 3 minutes or with mixing machine on medium speed for two minutes. Add 4 cups of flour mixture, a cup at a time, beating after each addition. Turn out on board which has been lightly sprinkled with some of the balance of flour mixture, and knead (Page 136) until smooth and elastic. The dough will be sticky at first because of the rye and wheat flours which contain more moisture than white flour.

Stay with it and the stickiness will disappear. Dough is fully kneaded when it reaches a fine-textured smooth consistency.

Shape into a ball, and drop into a lightly oiled straight-sided bowl. Turn to coat. Cover with plastic wrap and let rise at room temperature (70–80 degrees) until double in bulk (1½–2 hours). Punch dough down, knead for one minute. Divide in half, cover and let rest for 5 minutes. Shape into two round balls. Sprinkle jelly roll sheet with cornmeal, and place each ball in opposite corners. Cover loosely with waxed paper and let rise until double in bulk (about an hour).

Bake in preheated 375 degree oven for 40–45 minutes, spritzing (see page 138) twice during baking time with water, and again when bread is removed from oven. Tap bottom with knuckles. If bread is completely baked, you should hear a hollow sound. Let cool completely on rack before slicing.

Yield: 2 loaves; each ¼ loaf makes eight ½″ uneven slices

CAL	F	P:S	SOD	CAR	CHO
Average slice					
52	1	3.1:1	2	9	0

Pumpernickel

Pumpernickel's pleasingly rough texture sets it apart from other breads, not its brown color. In commercial pumpernickels, the color comes from caramel syrup, chocolate and coffee—and who needs them? Here's a pure pumpernickel that's as right cut thick for hearty sandwiches as it is cut paper-thin for canapés. It's a good keeper, too.

- ½ *cup Sour Rye Starter, room temperature (Page 137)*
- 2 *tablespoons dry yeast, or 2 premeasured packages*
- 2 *cups dark rye flour (see Note)*
- 1 *cup whole wheat flour*
- 2 *cups unbleached flour*
- 1 *cup warm water (105–115 degrees)*
- ½ *cup apple juice, no sugar added, warmed*
- 1 *tablespoon corn oil, plus ½ teaspoon to oil bowl*
- 1 *tablespoon buckwheat honey*
- 1 *teaspoon poppy seeds*
- 1 *teaspoon caraway seeds*
- 1 *teaspoon anise seeds, partially crushed*
- 1 *tablespoon white cornmeal to sprinkle on baking sheet*

The night before baking, in large mixing bowl, combine starter, one cup rye flour, one cup warm water, poppy, caraway, and anise seeds. Stir well. Cover with plastic wrap. Mixture will appreciably expand and bubble during the night.

Next day, stir mixture down. Sprinkle with yeast, add apple juice and stir well. Add honey and one tablespoon oil, and beat with wooden spoon.

Combine balance of flours, stirring to blend. Add to starter mixture, a half cup at a time, beating well with wooden spoon after each addition. When dough becomes too difficult to handle with wooden spoon, turn onto lightly floured board and knead until smooth and elastic (Page 136). This will take a little effort because of the dark flours. When dough is fully kneaded, shape into ball. Drop into lightly oiled straight-sided bowl. Turn to coat, cover with plastic wrap, and let rise at room temperature (70–80 degrees) until almost double in bulk (about 1½–2 hours). Pumpernickel never rises the first time with the same gusto as white bread. Punch down, shape into ball, re-cover, and let rise again until double in bulk (about 1½ hours). The dough will rise more rapidly the second time. Punch down again, knead briefly, and shape into 2 smooth balls.

Place in opposite corners of jelly roll pan which has been sprinkled with cornmeal. Spritz with water (Page 138). Cover loosely with waxed paper, and let rise a third time until loaves double in bulk (about 1 hour). Spritz with water again. Bake in preheated 375 degree oven for 45–50 minutes. Bread is fully baked when tapping bottom with knuckles produces a hollow sound. Cool on rack thoroughly before slicing.

Yield: 2 loaves; each ¼ loaf makes eight ½″ uneven slices
Note: Dark rye flour can be found in ethnic markets and grain stores. Medium rye flour is stocked in most supermarkets. Dark rye produces a more dense, coarse, and darker bread,

CAL	F	P:S	SOD	CAR	CHO
Average slice					
37	0	—	0	9	0
With medium rye flour					
48	0	—	0	11	0

Bread for Stuffing

Bread for stuffing and bread crumbs (the recipe follows) should be kept in your refrigerator at all times. Mine are child's play to make, add herbaceous flavors to many of my dishes, and are amazingly low in calories.

Cut one loaf of My French Bread into ½″ slices (Page 135), and then into cubes. Spread cubes on cookie sheet in one layer. Bake in preheated 425 degree oven for 10 minutes, turning cubes with spatula after 5 minutes. Cool. Store in glass jar in refrigerator until ready to use.

Yield: About 4 cups
Note: Any yeast bread can be made similarly into bread for stuffing.

CAL	F	P:S	SOD	CAR	CHO
Per cup					
190	2	4.6:1	6	47	0

Fine Bread Crumbs

1 *loaf My French Bread, cut into cubes and toasted (Page 135)*

Place cubes in blender, half at a time, and blend until smooth. Store in glass jar in refrigerator.

Yield: 1 cup
Variation: Combine ¾ cup bread crumbs with ¼ cup wheat germ, no sugar added, and blend.
Yield: 1 cup

CAL	F	P:S	SOD	CAR	CHO
Per cup					
760	6	4.6:1	25	186	0
Per tablespoon					
48	0	—	2	12	0
Variation:					
Per cup					
680	8	4.8:1	20	153	0
Per tablespoon					
43	0	—	1	10	0

About Wine

Wine has heightened the enjoyment of food since Biblical times, and now comes news that wine drinking is not only one of the great joys of the table but it's salubrious as well. At a recent meeting of the American Medical Association, Dr. Arthur L. Klatsky announced a study of some 87,000 hospital patients showing that people who drink alcohol moderately are not likely to suffer from hypertension, and are less likely to become a victim of heart attack. Dr. Klatsky conjectured that alcohol is related to high density lipoprotein, HDL, a type of cholesterol that apparently protects people from heart disease. (Dr. Klatsky warned that people who are taking medication should consult with their physician on how much and when they can drink.)

I cook with wine and we drink it at dinner because it marries so felicitously with my new gourmet cuisine. Eight ounces of red wine or dry white wine contribute about 168 calories. But since most of those calories are derived from alcohol, and since alcohol evaporates in cooking leaving only the flavorsome essence of the wine, about 85 percent of those calories disappear. A half cup of wine as a recipe ingredient adds only about 13 calories to a dish, plus 3 grams of carbohydrate, 4 milligrams of sodium, and no fats or cholesterol.

White wine—that is wine made from white-skinned grapes *(blanc de blanc)* or from the pulp of white or red grapes—when it's used for cooking must be dry (not sweet) and assert its flavor authoritatively. I prefer dry Vermouth, an herbaceous wine, either from Italy (Stock) or from France (Noilly-Prat). Not quite as flavorsome, and a bit more expensive, is a French Macon or an American Chardonnay or Pinot Noir.

Red wine for cooking has to be exuberantly vigorous, so full-bodied younger wines get my nod. A French Beaujolais, Burgundy or St. Emilion of recent vintage produces exquisite results, as do the following one-to-three-year-olds: Italian Barolos, Caremas, and Spannas, and American Pinot Noirs, Gamay Beaujolais and Gamay/Napa Gamays.

For drinking, the varieties of wine seem almost limitless. There's no problem about making your choice if you can afford a vintage Lafite, Latour, Margaux, a Charmes Chambertin or a Musigny (from $70 to $200 or more the bottle). But there are many superb wines within a sane price range, and those are the ones that brighten our table. (Even if you're on a pinch-penny budget, do avoid jug wines except when you're making stock.) Which of them do we serve with what? Traditionally, we're supposed to have white wine with fish, and drier white wine with shellfish; light red wine with poultry and white meats; robust red wines with red meats. But we drink what our palates tell us go best with a specific dish, and that includes—heresy!—some red wines with fish.

Here's a baker's dozen of our favorite wines, and the kind of dishes with which they form a perfect blendship.

Barbara D'Asti, 1971 (Italian), red. Hamburgers, meat loaves, salads (fish, poultry and meat), my simpler chicken dishes, baked tuna with broccoli, cod fish cakes.

Borgogno Barolo, 1971 (Italian), red. For the more extravagant meat dishes.

Spanna, 1964 (Italian), red. Use it as you would a Barolo. It's a bit subtler, a bit more aristocratic.

Sterling Vineyards Cabernet Sauvignon, 1974 (American), red. The lighter meat dishes.

Sterling Vineyards Merlot, 1974 (American), red. Mellower than the cabernet sauvignon, and without that wine's spiciness, it's an admirable companion to the more sophisticated veal dishes, and to fish in spicy sauces.

Sterling Vineyards Pinot Noir, 1974 (American) and Souverain Pinot Noir, 1973 (American), both reds. For steak pizzaiola, and the lustier beef and pork dishes.

The wines of Bourg, Blaye and Fronsac, 1973 to 1975 (French), red. Lamb dishes and all my stews. Bluefish, swordfish, and fish chowder.

Ruffino Chianti Classico, Riserva, Gold Label, 1969 (Italian), red. Pasta, chicken cacciatore, shrimp Italian style, and so on. And for Russian shashlik.

Muscadet Sur Lie of recent vintage (French), white. Incomparable with any of my shrimp or heavier fish dishes.

Vouvray of recent vintage (French), white. A lighthearted wine that is a delight to be with when fish or poultry is on the table.

Pouilly Fumé, 1976, (French), white. For fish, poultry, roast fresh ham, sautéed medallions of veal and veal birds.

Meal Planning

It's a dollar-saving and time-hoarding idea to set up first a general plan for your weekly menus, then, at least 24 hours in advance, agree on each day's specific menus. Here's our general plan.

For dinner main courses: Meat twice a week, fish twice a week, chicken or turkey twice a week, pasta or vegetables on the remaining day. Rounding out the dinner are hors d'oeuvres, green salads, soups (occasionally), vegetables, desserts, and beverages which include wine.

For lunch: We eat my salads and luncheon dishes, and not infrequently fill sandwiches with leftovers which are, more often than not, gussied up. (That's why some of my recipes yield four portions and one leftover, or serve six.) Small portions of low-fat dessert cheeses and/or fresh and dried fruits are our sweets. Beverages include herb teas, Cafix, fruit juices, no-salt-added tomato juice, non-fat milk, and, of course, my Wish-I-Had-A Milkshake.

For breakfast: My breakfast dishes are supplemented by a variety of hot and cold breakfast cereals, no sugar, salt or coconut added. They range from childhood-favorite shredded wheat to sophisticated granolas. Jams and jellies made with honey as the sweetening agent are bright morning accompaniments to my oven-fresh bread and rolls. We drink herb teas and fruit juices.

I like a general plan because I can buy in larger quantities, and that always costs less in the long run, and I don't have to make as many treks to the market. I like planning my specific menus a day ahead because then I can make whatever preliminary preparations are necessary, like thawing out or marinating, and I'm well organized when I get down to the actual cooking. It adds up to extra hours of free time, and the right amount of unharried time to prepare meals with the tender loving care they deserve.

Money-Saving Hints

In practicing my new cuisine, the big savings come from using the more healthful and less expensive cuts of meat; limiting meat as a dinner main course to twice a week; making generous use of leftovers for luncheon dishes and hors d'oeuvres; relying in part on grain-based breakfasts and on salads for lunch; and setting up a general weekly menu pattern so you can plan ahead and buy in bulk. Here are some additional ways you can save money while eating better.

Since you're planning well ahead, stock up in large quantities on *specials* of ingredients you're going to need anyway. A windfall!

Don't be turned off by whole fish—they're less expensive by far than fish steaks or filets—just because you think you don't know what to do with them. You *do* know what to do with them. Just let my recipes for whole fish be your guide.

Remember that some of my more interesting recipes are for inexpensive fish, such as porgy, flounder, whiting, cod, scrod, bluefish, tilefish and haddock.

When you're shopping for chickens, keep in mind that fryers/broilers are consistently lower-priced than roasters, and are 10 percent less fatty. Cut chickens cost more, so cut them yourself with sharp utensils. Refer to my utensil list on Page 151.

Don't be turned off by overripe tomatoes and slightly bruised apples in your produce market. They make excellent tomato soups and applesauce respectively, and the price is *so* low.

Many of the recipes of my new cuisine call for parsley, dill and watercress. If they're not stored properly they'll rot, and you'll lose part or all of your investment. Here are the secrets of extending their storage life to 10 days:

Wash crisp green parsley well under cold running water. Store in covered jar, stems down, with just enough water to cover the stems. Refrigerate. Change water after four days. Treat watercress the same way. Green dill (don't buy it if there's even a suggestion of brown) should never be washed before storing. Place it in a covered jar and refrigerate.

Refrigerate your flours and grains in well-closured containers and they'll retain freshness for at least six months.

A surprisingly large portion of most households' food budgets slips away in wasted food. Here are some new cuisine ways to save food that you would otherwise discard:

Let's suppose you need a small quantity of stock. You remove a jar from a freezer, thaw, and extract what you need. It's too dangerous to refreeze the remaining stock, so you refrigerate, and if you don't use it in a few days, it's gone rancid. Instead, store some of your stock in miniature ice-cube trays and freeze. Each miniature ice cube equals about a tablespoon of stock. Use one or more as required—wastelessly.

Overripe berries can be redeemed by cooking them in a small amount of apple juice for two minutes, and serving as a cold dessert, a topping, or as a flavoring for my Wish-I-Had-A Milkshake. Thicken with arrowroot flour, and you have an instant jelly.

Instead of discarding cooking liquids, add them to stocks, or use them to boost the flavor of my soups and sauces.

A number of my recipes call for unsweetened pineapple juice, so save the juice from cans of unsweetened pineapples when my recipes call for the pineapples but not the juice.

After you've squeezed a lemon, grate the rind and freeze it. When one of my recipes demands grated lemon rind, you're ready.

And, finally, get used to the notion that there's no such thing as stale bread. My stale breads can always be used—converted into Melba toast (Page 107), cut into cubes for stuffing (Page 147), or blended into fine bread crumbs (Page 147).

Terms Used in This Book

Al dente. Firm-textured. Said of pasta.

Baste. To spoon liquid over food while roasting or braising.

Bouquet garni. A combination of aromatic herbs which are used in the preparation of soups, stews, sauces and braised dishes to add flavor. In my new cuisine, it's usually made with 3–4 sprigs of parsley wrapped around one bay leaf and tied into a small bundle with thread.

Braise. To cook with a small amount of liquid over low heat, after food has been browned.

Brush. To cover a surface of the

food lightly with liquid, usually using a pastry brush.

Coat. To roll food in flour, bread crumbs or other ingredients until coated.

Court bouillon. An aromatic broth of water, herbs, seasonings and sometimes wine.

Chopped. Cut into ½″ cubes (coarsely chopped) or ¼″ cubes (finely chopped).

Diced. Cut into ⅛″ cubes.

Flake. Refers to the flesh of cooked fish which comes loose in flakes when touched with a fork.

Fold in. A method to obtain an even combination of ingredients. Usually applied to egg whites (Page 128).

Garnish. To decorate food with tasteful artistry.

Grated. Extremely small pieces of food obtained by rubbing on a grater.

Marinate. To soak food in a flavorful liquid prior to cooking.

Minced. Cut into pieces smaller than ⅛″ cubes.

Parboil. To cook partially in water.

Peel, core and drain. Refers to fresh tomatoes. Skin pulls off easily after tomato has been immersed in boiling water for 30 seconds. Core is then cut away, and liquid is drained and reserved.

Poach. To cook in a broth just below the boiling point.

Preheat. To turn oven on at a specified temperature 15 minutes before using.

Purée. To put through a blender, food mill or food processor to obtain a smooth pulpy consistency.

Reduce. To continue cooking to concentrate liquid and, consequently, heighten flavor.

Rolling boil. Boiling at high heat so stream of bubbles circulate in a rolling motion.

Sauté. To cook in a small amount of oil over low or medium heat.

Score. To make shallow gashes, usually through the skin of fish.

Sift. To put through sieve or flour sifter.

Simmer. To cook just below boiling point over low heat.

Skewer. To fasten with skewers.

Skim. To clear floating substances such as scum and fat from a liquid. For rapid fat-skimming, let liquid sit until all fat has come to top, remove with large spoon, and finally blot gently with paper toweling. If liquid is to be used after day of cooking, refrigerate overnight, then remove caked layer of fat from surface.

Sliver. A long thin slice.

Steam. To cook with steam rather than with liquid.

Toss. To mix with fork and spoon, as for salads.

Trimmed. Unwanted parts removed.

Truss. To fasten body of fowl before cooking so that it holds its shape.

Whisk. To beat rapidly in a circular motion using a wire whisk.

The Utensils I Use

1. Large teflon or no-stick interior skillet (12″ in diameter).
2. Large cast-iron skillet (12″ in diameter).
3. Medium-sized skillet (10″ in diameter), either cast-iron or teflon interior).
4. Small teflon, or non-stick interior skillet, or electric non-stick skillet for making crepes or for reheating leftovers.
5. Kettle with cover for making soups and stocks.
6. Covered cast-iron casserole (or enamelware to go from stove to table) for making stews, with removable rack.
7. Rectangular aluminum, teflon, or enamelware shallow roasting pan with removable rack, for roasting

foods uncovered, permitting fats to drip.

8. Heavy-bottomed saucepan, for general heating and cooking and saucemaking.
9. Saucepans of varied sizes in which to cook rice, pasta, and vegetables.
10. Stainless steel pot or waterless cooker for making soups and stews; necessary to retain cooking juices.
11. Sharp straight-edged knives—2″–3″ for paring and mincing, and 10″–12″ for cutting and chopping.
12. Butcher's steel for sharpening knives.
13. Serrated knife for cutting bread, slicing tomatoes, and so on.
14. Heavy shears for cutting chicken bones through and cutting fins from fish.
15. Mallet for flattening meat and chicken breasts.
16. Long-pronged fork for lifting meats and testing for doneness.
17. Slotted spoons for removing meats, chicken, vegetables, or fish from liquid. Also large spoons for basting and stirring.
18. Various spatulas for turning meats and fish.
19. Wooden spoons for stirring foods while cooking, and beating batters of breads, cakes, and cookies.
20. Four-sided grater to grate vegetables, orange, lemon, and lime peels, cheese, and so on.
21. Covered oven-proof casseroles of varying sizes for baking rice, casseroles, and so on.
22. Various sized whisks for blending sauces, mayonnaise, and egg whites.
23. Measuring spoons and cups.
24. Loaf pans for breads and cakes (7⅜″ × 3⅝″ × 2¼″, and 8¼″ × 9″ × 2½″). Also jelly-roll pan, 11½″ × 15½″ × 1″, square 9″ baking pan, and aluminum pie pan 8″ or 10″ in diameter.
25. French bread baking pans (14″ long). I prefer double pans.
26. Stainless steel straight-sided bowl for bread risings.
27. Freeze-proof containers for freezing stocks and leftovers.
28. Colander for draining vegetables, rice, pasta, and so on.
29. Chinois with bowl for draining and pressing out juices in making stocks, stews, and so on.
30. Mortar and pestle for crushing dried herbs and seeds.
31. Poultry needle to sew up stuffed cavities of chicken, turkey, chops, and so on.
32. Blender. Indispensible for many recipes throughout this book.
33. Mixing machine for beating egg whites, cakes, and breads. Dough-hook attachment is helpful once you've learned how to make bread by hand.
34. Food mill for puréeing soups, apple sauce, prune whip and so on.
35. Grinder or food processer for grinding cooked and uncooked meats, fish, and vegetables, and for making dips and spreads.
36. Chopping board for all types of chopping, and for kneading bread.
37. Pastry brush for brushing meats, poultries and breads.
38. Fine sieve for preparation of smooth sauces.

Index of Recipes

BREADS

CHICKEN AND TURKEY

DESSERTS

FISH

HORS D'OEUVRES, BREAKFAST AND LUNCHEON DISHES, AND RELISHES

MEAT

SALADS

SOUPS

STOCKS

VEGETABLES, GRAINS, AND PASTA